THE DRESS DIARY

By the same author

Inside the Royal Wardrobe: A Dress History
of Queen Alexandra

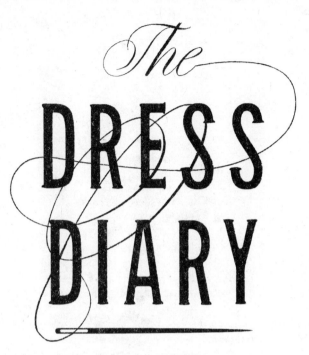

The DRESS DIARY

SECRETS FROM A
VICTORIAN WOMAN'S WARDROBE

—— // ——

KATE STRASDIN

PEGASUS BOOKS
NEW YORK LONDON

THE DRESS DIARY

Pegasus Books, Ltd.
148 West 37th Street, 13th Floor
New York, NY 10018

First Pegasus Books paperback edition June 2024
First Pegasus Books cloth edition June 2023

Paperback ISBN: 978-1-63936-691-0
Hardcover ISBN: 978-1-63936-421-3

10 9 8 7 6 5 4 3 2 1

Printed in the United States of America
Distributed by Simon & Schuster
www.pegasusbooks.com

For Stuart

Contents

Daywear in the late 1830s.

Preface – A Beautiful Mystery

In January of 2016 I was given an extraordinary gift. Wrapped in brown paper that had softened with age and moulded to the shape of the object within, I discovered a treasure almost two centuries old that was to reveal the life of one woman and her broader network of family and friends. Underneath the brown paper was a book, a ledger of sorts, that was covered in a bright-magenta silk, frayed along the edge of the album so that a glimpse of its marbled cover was just visible. The shape of the book had distorted, being narrower at the spine but expanding to accommodate the contents, reminding me of my mum's old recipe book, which had swelled over the years as newspaper cuttings and handwritten notes were added.

This book, measuring some twelve and a half inches long by eight and a half inches across, contained pale-blue blank pages, originally unlined and unmarked. As I carefully opened the front cover and looked at the first page, my breath caught: this was indeed a marvel. Carefully pasted in place were four pieces of fabric, three of them framed in a decorative waxed border – scraps of silk important enough to have been memorialised. Accompanying each piece of cloth was a small handwritten note inked in neat copperplate: names; a date: 1838.

As I turned more leaves, a kaleidoscope of colour and variety unfolded. There were small textile swatches – sometimes only two pieces at a time, and sometimes up to twelve – all cut into neat rectangles or octagons and pasted in rows that blossomed across each page. The notes were written above each snippet of fabric, sometimes curving around the shape of it, becoming part of the materiality of the volume. I knew from the very outset that this was something precious, an ephemeral piece of a life lived long ago. It was a beautiful mystery.

The elderly lady who gave me the book explained what she knew of its provenance, which was very little. While she was working in the London theatre world in the 1960s, a young man assisting her in the wardrobe department found this unusual curiosity on a market stall in Camden. He thought that the pages of the scrapbook, filled as they were with colourful textiles, might be of interest in the theatre wardrobes where she worked. The book remained in this lady's possession for fifty years until she passed it on to me.

There was no immediate indication of who might have created this amazing 'dress diary', as I called it; of who had spent so much time carefully arranging the pieces of wool, silk, cotton and lace into a chronological documenting of lives in cloth. Whilst there was much I was uncertain of, however, one thing I knew for sure from the careful handwriting that arched over each piece of cloth: this was the work of one woman. I just didn't know who she was.

In the months that followed I began to try and unravel some of the stories that might be contained in the album's pages. Rather than detail its contents digitally, I had a sense that, to be authentic, I needed to write everything down in longhand. I bought a leather-bound book of handmade paper and a black ink pen and started at the beginning, transcribing each tiny caption. I wrote down names, dates, fabrics, colours and patterns, trying to see who might emerge, looking out for clues about who the author could have been. I counted more than 2,000 pieces of fabric: some patterned, others plain; some large and others much smaller. There were pieces paired with longer captions, and others that bore simply a year or even nothing at all.

The book was full of names: Fanny Taylor, Hannah Wrigley, Mary Fletcher, Charlotte Dugdale, Bridgetanne Peacock, Maria Balestier. I recorded more than a hundred different names in the book, binding their wearers to clothes worn long ago – some appearing with great frequency across its pages and others only fleetingly, acquaintances made and lost amongst friendships of longer standing.

I found that only seventy fragments were associated with male garments, and only seventeen of the names recorded were those of men. It seemed that at a time when so much of literature and the arts was focused on the endeavours of men, this was a book dedicated to the world of women. I decided to try and piece together the lives of some of these women through the clues that were left behind, scant though they often were. Using what felt like a forensic approach in its detail, I focused on fragments of cloth to illuminate the world these women inhabited, enabling a wider context to emerge. What began to appear were the tales of an era, placing these lives into the industrial maelstrom of the nineteenth century with all its noise, colour and innovation.

The structure of the album, the names and the cloths themselves suggested that this was not a volume compiled in the rarefied spaces of the aristocracy, but something more quotidian: the creator being a woman of some means, but inhabiting the world of the well-to-do middle classes. This woman and others – women whose lives would otherwise go unrecorded, hidden in the shadows of history – found themselves unwittingly front and centre of this story.

The practice of making collections of one kind or another was a common activity in the nineteenth century. Taxonomies of the natural world, cataloguing flora and fauna, abounded. Plant-hunters were collecting seeds, entomologists were charting insect life and in the 1830s – the years in which this diary commenced – Charles Darwin was beginning to pose his theories outlining evolutionary changes in species that were to shake the very foundations of scientific understanding. The determination to bring order in a fast-shifting world reached into domestic spaces too, and households around the UK began to create albums of ephemera. Early photographers produced fantastical albums with prints and watercolours, and scrapbooks were filled with keepsakes, autographs, poems and drawings.

Women's creative pursuits were many and varied, but rarely were their efforts recognised as anything more than diversions. The decorative handicrafts of women have traditionally been read as acts of leisure: idling away the hours in the domestic spaces afforded to the middling and upper classes, and wasting time on inconsequential endeavours. Thankfully, more recent revisionist histories have begun to challenge these perceptions and to take more seriously the objects made by women, to view them as artistic practices rather than foolish accomplishments. Take the botanical collages created by Mary Delaney. At the age of seventy-two, Mary, whose colourful life up to that point had included friendships with Jonathan Swift, George Frideric Handel and the great social commentator of the day, William Hogarth, embarked on a project that would become her legacy. She watched one day as a geranium petal fell to the floor and felt compelled to replicate the fragile petal in paper, carefully cutting out its replica. She repeated the process until she had created a life-size collage of the plant, which she called a 'flower mosaick'. She then arranged the cutouts onto a piece of black paper and pasted them on. So lifelike was the result that her friend the Duchess of Portland proclaimed that she could not tell the real flower from the paper one.

Whereas the creator of the book I was examining used a pale-blue background for her own form of mosaic, Mary Delaney created the inkiest of black backdrops, by painting white paper in black watercolour until it was as dark as it could be. She practised her art form over the next decade, cutting thousands upon thousands of tiny slivers of paper in all the colours of the botanical rainbow to create hundreds more of her now-famous collages. 'I have invented a new way of imitating flowers,' she wrote in a letter in 1772. So detailed were her creations that botanists still refer to their accuracy, and they are studied with awe at their home in the British Museum.

A 'flower mosaik' by Mary Delaney, 1778.

The dress diary in my possession is rare, but is not the only one of its kind to remain. One famous surviving example was created by Miss Barbara Johnson, starting in the middle of the eighteenth century and continuing into the early nineteenth century. As a single woman whose finances had to be carefully managed, Barbara began to catalogue the textiles that she purchased for making up into clothing. She snipped pieces of precious cloth and pinned them into a large accounting ledger, including details of their type, cost per yard and the kind of garments that they would become, once sent to the dressmaker. She even pasted in small black-and-white engravings from early fashion publications to indicate the ambitions that she had for her new clothes. For more than seventy years she maintained her album, adding 121 samples to its pages. It served a practical purpose, helping her to balance her books and providing financial clarity. More than that, though, it was a colourful record of Barbara's journey through life and the central place that dress played in her day-to-day world. The album was saved by her extended family and eventually became part of the collections at the Victoria and Albert

Museum in London, one of their rare treasures. It is the only one of its kind in their collection.

In fact in the whole of the UK I failed to find another album like either Barbara Johnson's or the one that had fallen into my own hands. That is not to say they do not exist, or were not created in greater numbers in decades past. My mystery diarist could not have been the only one in the nineteenth century to choose to record an aspect of her life in this way, and the very tactility of cloth lends itself to this form of remembrance. There may well be volumes of fabric scraps languishing in trunks in attics, or wrapped in the bottom drawer of an elderly chest. There may even be examples that were once catalogued and then forgotten in an archive or a museum, their value yet to be identified.

A dress diary suffers from the double ignominy of being about largely female experiences and about dress – concerns that, in the nineteenth century at least, lent them little by way of artistic merit. The field of dress history has been an academic discipline that has had to fight for recognition amongst more traditionally respected scholarship, the study of clothing being perceived as an ephemeral concern. There have been many occasions during my own career when I have been introduced at an academic conference as a historian studying (cue a long pause and a raised eyebrow) 'fashion'. The slight bemusement that has so often accompanied such introductions reveals a deep-seated perception of dress as superficial and inconsequential – that to be interested in clothing is to lack seriousness. Yet here we all are dressed in clothes, making daily decisions about how we will face the world. We might use dress as our armour, a protective carapace to shield us from censure, or we might use it to express our place and space. Even if we have no interest in fashion, we still choose garments that are indicative in some way of the cultural landscape that shapes each one of us. The creator of my album shared these daily decisions, preferring this colour or that fabric in her own environs.

In America there are a handful of albums that share similarities with mine, volumes created by women describing, in material form, the decisions they made about the contents of their wardrobes. A few years ago, during a New York blizzard, I battled through snowy streets to visit the Brooklyn Museum on an entirely different research errand. I was the only visitor that day. The stewards were slightly bemused that anybody had ventured forth through the drifts on the pavements, but my visit to the US was of short duration and I was determined not to miss an opportunity. Having made notes on a number of documents in their collection, I noticed an intriguing facsimile volume on display in the reading room. It was a photocopy of a book that had little pieces of fabric attached to its pages, alongside annotation and photographs. I had never seen anything like it, as this was before the gift of my dress diary, but it proved to be a serendipitous discovery, unknowingly pre-empting the acquisition of my own album some years later. Thanks to the weather, I was the only person in the room, and the collections assistant asked if I would be interested in seeing the book itself. She brought it out for me to study and I spent a happy hour perusing its pages.

The album had been created by a woman named Ida Jackson, who was born in Cazenovia in New York in 1855, and her album was a personal journey charting her own life – from scraps of her childhood to her adult years. Unlike the album now in my possession, Ida attached the occasional photograph of herself, so that future viewers could bring to mind the wearer of the fabrics that she included, fastening cloth and the trimmings that went with it, alongside a description of the garment. Her chatty asides positioned her in a world of changing styles more clearly than the briefer notes appended to my own volume. Next to one blue-and-white striped cotton she wrote, 'Wore above draped black mohair skirt when overskirts began to come back into fashion.' She even recalled specific trips by means of the dress she had worn, including a beige-and-white striped silk worn in 1873, which she captioned, 'Worn on visit to

C——town for feet.' There are so many unanswered questions in *that* intriguing note.

Ida's was not the only example of a dress diary to emerge in the US. The Brooklyn Museum holds another album kept by Helen Ranney, dating to the late nineteenth century. Inside the cover of this book, Helen pasted a newspaper clipping that gave definitions of fabric names. Next to small squares of cloth she wrote briefly about their origins – 'Little Girl School' or 'Best Dress'. And she went even further, noting which ones she liked and which ones she didn't, a reminder that we are all prone to an impulse-buy that we later regret, then as now.

New Englander Ann Eliza Cunningham kept her 'sewing diary' in the mid-nineteenth century, attaching large swatches of cloth to the pages of a patented scrapbook that extended to 144 pages. She noted momentous occasions through dress and included the purchase of the cloth and the maker as well, uniting each stage of the garment, from store to body. Next to a boldly patterned printed-cotton rectangle she noted, 'Bought at Uncle Gideon's Store in May 1849, Rhoda cut it, wore to school the first morning I made my appearance at the Lunenburg Academy June 7th 1849.' Here are the owners of the drapery store, Rhoda Saville the dressmaker and Ann Cunningham herself stepping out in her new dress for her first day at school.

Another young woman, Mabel Lewis Patterson, continued to fill a scrapbook that was started by her mother Marcia in 1872, and recorded almost every item of clothing that she owned until the age of twenty-four, when she left home for college. Like Ann Cunningham, Mabel linked garments to special occasions, so that they became tied to that time and place. An embroidered white silk was described by Mabel as 'My graduation gown – Made by Miss Gano May 1893. Commencement the evening of June 12/93. Subject of my essay "A Lost Art".' These scraps serve to take the wearer back to a single point in time. There is something unutterably poignant about such scraps, and indeed about the clothing that was important to people in their lives. Dress curator Kay Staniland wrote of the public fascination with surviving royal dress that 'it offers an actual contact with its original owner, an outer skin which is still strongly permeated with the bodily characteristics of that personality'. For me, this extends beyond royal dress. Remnants of wardrobes are like the ghostly outlines of our ancestors. Perhaps that was how the maker of my album felt when she began to document her own life in clothes.

Where the diary in my keeping seems to differ from the few other surviving dress diaries is that it recorded lives beyond the maker's own, encompassing those in her orbit. This woman decided at some point to gather the contents not only of her own wardrobe, but of those of her family and friends, and to memorialise them in her bright-pink silk-covered album. The decision to refer to herself always in the third person made the identification of the author all the more challenging; and, unlike more intimate diaries, the captions establish a curious distance. Perhaps the point was to try and archive the fabrics objectively, rather than making this a personalised object. It is difficult to establish what her motives were. One caption alone hints at a strategy of collecting, inked above a woven silk picture of Queen Victoria and Prince Albert. The note reads: 'Mr McMicking's contribution to this book given to him by one of the Gentlemen of the French Embassy to China.' Her note suggests that she was actively sourcing textiles for her book, casting her net far and wide to find interesting additions to its pages. Over tea perhaps, making polite conversation, she may have shown Mr McMicking the book she was compiling and requested that he might add to its pages with a contribution of his choosing.

Finally my careful transcribing of each tiny caption paid off. Across a single square of floral printed cotton, on the top right-hand corner of one of the pages, came the breakthrough I had been hoping for. It was to be the revelation that cracked the code for the entire volume. In the same neat, fine script that populated the whole book were the words

'Anne Sykes May 1840. The first dress I wore . . .' She was revealed. The one and only time that she referred to herself in the first person, Anne Sykes identified herself as the keeper of the book; the creator of its 422 pages; the person who had pasted the 2,134 swatches of fabric into her album and recorded the names of those 104 different people and their clothes. I had found her.

Anne's identity radiated out in myriad hues and materials, connecting her to her world and allowing us to join her. Discovering that Anne Sykes was the hitherto-unknown creator of the book that I had been meticulously transcribing was at once both exciting and perplexing. I felt certain that she had to be a dressmaker, a woman whose role in life was to clothe her clients, taking a keen interest in shape and style, keeping the secrets of bodies. In that moment I could never have anticipated just how much I would be able to uncover.

Swatches in the album reveal that Anne attended parties and fancy balls, her book being full of the formal clothes that both she and her friends wore on these occasions. It is full, too, of the everyday. Of cotton and wool, of dressing gowns and slippers, bonnet ribbons, petticoats and cloaks. Cloth of all types was a valued commodity and its purchase was not undertaken on a whim. She recorded the purchases that she made from Miss Brennand's smallwares establishment and shopping trips that her friends made to Liverpool and Manchester. Individually the swatches give little away, but by piecing together clues, we can weave together the strands of Anne's life into a colourful patchwork of family and friends.

That Anne kept her dress diary more or less chronologically is evident from its structure and the dates recorded. The album starts at the very commencement of Queen Victoria's reign and maps those momentous decades of everything that came to be 'Victorian' – a parallel life synonymous with industry and Empire. Although the notes are brief, the writing changes. As the years pass, the notes become scarcer and the fine copperplate larger and not so neatly formed. All of life is revealed as the pages progress: mourning clothes to mark the loss of loved ones, dresses worn to christenings, gifts for birthdays and Christmas.

In a sense, Anne's album is a form of 'life writing', taking in ordinary folk; not the grandees of traditional written histories, but the bystanders, the participants in everyday life, their loves and losses, joys and sorrows. It is a fragmentary story of life experienced at home and abroad, a domestic world and an international one, of courage in unfamiliar lands and of building a community of friendship. Through small and seemingly inconsequential wisps of fabric, Anne Sykes's diary lays bare the whole of human experience in that most intimate of mediums: the clothes that we choose to wear.

Family

Friends in the 1840s.

CHAPTER I

My Charming Anne

Anne Burton & Adam Sykes

I wore a white satin gown with a very deep flounce of Honiton.

Queen Victoria's journal, 1840

The very first page of my book, now bulging with the fabrics of many lives, began with just two people: Anne and Adam Sykes and their wedding, which took place on 20 September 1838 in St George's Church, Tyldesley, an industrial town near Manchester. There are four pieces of material on the page, three of them framed with decorative paper borders, and the fourth, a length of lace, carefully pasted amongst them. The handwriting differs from the rest of the book – the only time that another hand made a contribution to its contents. The captions that are inscribed offer fond reminiscences of their wedding day. Above a rectangle of white checked muslin, Adam Sykes wrote, 'This is the dress my charming Anne was married in.' Alongside it is a sample of his own wedding outfit, the remnant of a cream satin with a woven floral tendril trailing across its surface, above which he wrote, 'And this is the vest I had on at the time. Adam Sykes.' The narrow trim of bobbin lace beneath is described, 'This is the lace that trimmed the dress that my charming Anne was married in'; and finally, occupying the width of the page below, a pale-oyster satin: 'This is the dress she wore after the wedding at Breakfast.' It is an orderly page, each piece of fabric a neat rectangle.

It was Adam who contrived to memorialise their day, and Adam who chose the pattern of display. It might seem obvious that the first page would reveal the most and that it was the natural place to start, but until I had discovered Anne's name as the keeper of the album, the first page actually made little sense. The nature of studying inanimate objects is that you have to try and hear the voices for yourself, and they are not always clear. Until the book was linked directly with the name of Anne Sykes, none of the other entries were fathomable. But now I had Anne, I had Adam and, thanks to a small swatch that mentioned the town of Preston, I had the county of Lancashire. I entered exactly that into an online search and was rewarded within seconds with a link to a digitised list of parish-register entries from the church of St George's in Tyldesley, recording their union. The sandstone church of St George's where they began their marriage still stands, the path to the church door running at right-angles to the solid golden blocks of the building – the path to Anne and Adam's union. A single document such as this acts like the first domino that sets all of the others falling. To find the marriage record is to find many others, from baptism to burial, and much of life in between.

Perhaps Adam bought the book for Anne as a wedding gift, visiting a smart stationer's establishment in the days preceding their marriage and deliberating over this book or that. Maybe a number of different volumes were laid out for his inspection, the marble-papered bindings each being unique in design. There is only a glimpse of the book's original cover visible beneath the frayed edge of the bright-pink silk, but it reveals a marbled design in shades of blue with a red-leather spine. Marbling was a technique that arrived in Europe from Japan in the seventeenth century and it had become hugely fashionable. Diderot's *Encyclopedia of Science, Arts and Industries*, published over a twenty-year period in the second half of the eighteenth century, depicts the art of the *marbreur de papier*; the marbler and the tools of his craft. In the late 1830s account-ing ledgers and all manner of other book bindings were decorated with marbled designs, curlicues of colour in gorgeous swirls and elaborately named – 'Shell', 'Peacock' and 'Bouquet'. Maybe Adam arranged this first page and then wrapped his gift after their wedding, presenting his charming Anne with this tender record of their special day. But what was the path to their union? Who were Anne and Adam?

Anne was born in Clitheroe, Lancashire on 27 December 1816, to James and Alice Burton. She was baptised in the Baptist Lower Chapel in Accrington. She was the fourth child that her mother, Alice, had borne and there would be another four sons to follow. Already, then, Anne arrived in a household whose nursery was busy with an older sister aged eight, a brother aged seven and another sister aged five. Anne would be twelve years old by the time her youngest brother Frederick was born in 1828, amounting to exactly two decades of the pressures of preg-nancy and the potential perils of birth for her mother Alice. According to records, only Elizabeth, Anne's older sister born in 1811, disappeared from sight before adulthood. It might be that her name has been mis-spelt somewhere in the transcribing of accounts. With so many names and variations, she may be there, but if so she is lost amongst the deluge of ancestral mnemonics. It might be that sadly she died, another notch on the list of countless infant deaths during this period before modern medicine was able to save children from any number of common but fatal illnesses – diseases such as typhoid fever, cholera, tuberculosis and dysentery.

Anne's father James was a prominent mill owner, so textiles were the foundation upon which Anne's life was built. Little is known of her life prior to her marriage in 1838. She was a daughter of industry, a consumer of the cloth, rather than a maker of the clothes. In 1828, ten years before Anne's marriage, James Burton moved with his family from Clitheroe to Tyldesley and, on entering into a partnership with the Jones brothers, his star as an industrialist steadily rose. He lived in Burton House on Factory Street, an unusual building at the very heart of Tyldesley's manufacturing district. For the next ten years James and Alice lived there with their eight children, surrounded by the evidence of James Burton's industrial successes and living a comfortable life as a result. The house is no longer standing, but an old and grainy photograph taken in the 1860s shows a building built at an angle, one face of it fronting onto Factory Street itself and the other onto a private garden. Two tall chimneys rise directly behind it, and beyond are the imposing mill buildings over which James Burton was the master spinner. By the date of Anne's wedding he had charge of New Mill in Tyldesley, and over the next decade he would go on to build a further four cotton-spinning mills of his own. James was 'new money' in the shifting social landscape of the period, a self-made man who would take a keen interest in his community.

Clothing required a long chain of transactions, beginning with the purchase of cloth, which was then handed to the dressmaker or tailor and made into a garment of the customer's choice. On 24 December 1798 Jane Austen wrote in one of her letters, 'I cannot determine what to do about my new gown; I wish such things were to be bought ready-made.' In the diary, notes that mention dresses – whether purchased or given – actually refer to the cloth required to make up the gowns, in the 1830s and 1840s especially. This is exactly the structure of the dress diary that was kept by Barbara Johnson, in which she pinned the snippets of cloth that she had purchased, as evidence of her financial expenditure each year. Next to a floral cotton, for example, she wrote, 'Seven yards and half of dark callicoe, ell-wide, 4s 3d a yard. Made at Bath.' The separate stages of the dress's creation were recorded, moving from draper to customer, from customer to dressmaker and, in its final incarnation, back to the customer. Women invested time and thought into these acquisitions, first choosing the type and pattern of fabric, assessing the amount required for the specific garment type and then discussing with their dressmaker the chosen style. It required a knowledge and vocabulary of dress and cloth on the part of both client and maker, which would be lost with the ready-to-wear revolution. At the turn of the nineteenth century clothing was made specifically to fit individual customers, and it was this manner of dressmaking – with scraps of leftover material retained for safekeeping – that facilitated the creation of a book such as Anne's.

Only a very few fragments in the album pre-date Anne's marriage, offering the merest glimpse of her life prior to her union with Adam. Across a single page she includes five pieces of printed cotton that connect her to some of the women in her life as a young unmarried woman. One cream-and-brown striped swatch with trailing florals is captioned, 'Maureen Mary and Anne Burton a Primrose Print'. The identity of Maureen Mary is, frustratingly, lost. Anne's sister was called Mary, but according to baptism records for the Lower Chapel in Accrington, this was her first and given name rather than a middle one, so the Maureen is a mystery. An especially bold design in a deep brown with green-and-yellow geometric motifs is annotated: 'Anne Sykes, Mrs Cruikshank and Mary had cloaks of this in 1836.' Anne did not marry Adam until 1838, but it is quite feasible that, post-dating these swatches as she added them to her album, she forgot to use her maiden name for the earlier swatch. Imagining this particular fragment as three generously proportioned cloaks takes a leap of the imagination, the colour and pattern being quite eye-watering, even with so small a piece as this.

Another brilliantly patterned piece bears the inscription, 'Maureen Mary and Anne Burton had dresses of this in 1834 – it was given to us by Mr Pope of Hurrick.' At the age of eighteen, Anne wore this colourful paisley patterned dress and Maureen Mary had one made from the same fabric. The clues are tantalising, but who is Maureen Mary and who is Mr Pope? It became clear, as the detective work continued, that not all of the people would be – could be – found. We might imagine them living a life that included a pink printed paisley dress and a wonderfully bold geometric cloak, even re-creating the silhouette of their clothed bodies to bring to mind the shape and colour of their chosen garments, but where that life began and the arc to its conclusion will for ever remain just out of reach. If Anne's mother, Alice, kept any of her childhood clothing, then Anne chose not to include it in the album. Possibly she recorded only those garments that she still possessed by the time she married: remnants of her old life that warranted brief inclusion, but merely that in a book dedicated to her future, not her past.

I often wonder how Anne and Adam first met. Was it a family connection forged through the power looms and printworks of Lancashire? Did one of Anne's brothers know Adam through his close connections to textile trading in Liverpool? It is impossible to know whether they liked each other immediately or whether it was a relationship that grew out of a longer-standing familial network. Was Adam romantically inclined, offering Anne a ring of his own choosing to mark their engagement, or was their union to be more pragmatic? I would like to imagine the former, since the very existence of the album was seemingly the gift of Adam himself. Perhaps it was a chance encounter that led to their courtship and eventual marriage, a now-unknown event that ended in the neatly written column in the parish register of St George's Church in Tyldesley. I hope theirs was a marriage based on a genuine fondness for each other. Whilst the album charts shared experiences over much of a lifetime, it cannot catch the emotions that went with them. Of the ups and downs, the tears and the tensions there is no evidence, but I like to think that laughter and warmth formed the foundation of their years, a joint endeavour that began on the day of their marriage in 1838.

When Adam Sykes carefully framed that square of cream figured-silk waistcoat next to a corresponding square of white checked muslin, he was uniting himself and Anne in cloth as in life, bound together on the very first page of the book that Anne would carry forward to document their lives through material remembrance. Without Adam, there would have been no album. He was a constant in Anne's world, historical records catching them at different moments in the course of their marriage; but in the glimpses of Adam offered by Anne in her dress diary we get to know him a little better, or at least have a sense of the character behind the silk waistcoats and the entries in mercantile records.

Adam was born on 12 July 1807 in the Lancashire parish of Accrington, the very town in which Anne herself would be baptised nine years later. His father, James, married Charlotte Dugdale in 1791. Charlotte's family warranted a page in *Burke's Peerage*, the directory of aristocracy and landed gentry first published in 1826, indicative of the minutely designated hierarchies of the period. On Anne and Adam's wedding certificate, James was described as a 'designer', probably a reference to a textile-related industry, designing patterns for printed cloth. Textiles were the foundation of Adam's family's life, as of Anne's. Whilst details of his childhood are absent, that he was an ambitious boy is a fair assumption, given that by the age of twenty-two he had formed a business partnership with a Robert Wise and was given the responsible charge of overseeing the company's trading affairs in the newly established settlement of Singapore. It was a bold step for a young man to take at the time, embarking into the unknown and tying himself to a part of the world that would have been unfamiliar in almost every conceivable way. Adam remained in Singapore for five years, returning in the mid-1830s to continue as a young merchant operating out of the Exchange building in Liverpool.

Sometime prior to 1838 Adam obviously considered that he had enough to offer as a husband and – time and place now unknown – began his courtship of Anne Burton. The merest hint of their relationship prior to marriage is given by Anne with the inclusion of a swatch of lustrous black silk brightened with a woven coloured spot, which Anne captioned, 'Mr Sykes' vest new one Sunday when he came to Tyldesley Aug 1838.' Only a month before their marriage, it is possible to imagine Adam buttoning his new black waistcoat and arranging his tie, before shrugging on his coat and making his way to Burton House to dine with Anne and her family, no doubt discussing the plans that were under way for their nuptials.

Compared with the ever-changing and chameleon-like nature of womenswear in the nineteenth century, which underwent frequent revisions in silhouette, fabric and pattern, menswear of the same period has often been dismissed as static, an aesthetic punctuated by sober colours and little innovation. The stereotype of the sombre Victorian gentleman even found its way into museum collections, accounting for the far higher ratio of surviving womenswear in collections around Europe and North America, early curators being less interested in the repetitious dark wool suits that were the accepted perceptions of nineteenth-century masculine attire.

By comparison with the peacock-like suits of the eighteenth century, which are often the sole survivals of a period that also saw buff-coloured jackets and plain wool breeches, nineteenth-century male clothing can sometimes be considered dull and sober. In portraiture and in the heavily embroidered and embossed surviving garments, the expensive menswear of the eighteenth century offered an entirely different view of how the well-dressed man might be expected to appear. The idea of the suit, the breeches being made to correspond with the jacket, was one that had first emerged in the seventeenth century, and in the eighteenth century the mass production of menswear began to gather pace to match the demands of both the British Navy and the redcoats of the Army. The woollen industry was a mainstay of the economy, and producers of hardy fabrics such as serge supported entire regions, from Devon to Scotland. Whilst embroidered coats may have fallen out of favour by the turn of the nineteenth century, exaggerated silhouettes were still evident in the cut of the male wardrobe, achieved through padding and tapering – and even, for the most committed dandies, the wearing of a corset-like girdle to create the greatest contrast between shoulder and hip. As an ambitious young merchant of the emerging industrial class, it is unlikely that Adam ever exhibited extremes of style in the 1830s that might have given rise to unfavourable comments amongst his peers, but the 1840s became the decade that witnessed the rejection of excess. The frock coat became the standard jacket, the top hat the new mainstay of headwear, and the white shirt with standing starched collar the ubiquitous uniform of the bourgeois man.

If Anne relied upon the speed and skill of her independent dressmaker, Adam might have had access to a greater spectrum of ready-made garments by the 1840s, although the tailor was still an important figure in garment production. Tailoring guilds had long fought the encroachment of mass production, in a bid to protect the custom trade that was their livelihood, and indeed the skill of tailoring in Britain had attained a reputation for quality by the 1840s. Adam would no doubt have been familiar with the high-end establishments that were opening on a small cobbled street in London. Running parallel with the bustle of Regent Street, a small avenue that had once been a part of the Burlington estate in the previous century had been named after the Earl of Burlington's wife, Lady Dorothy Savile.

Savile Row had been predominantly occupied by military families, but by the early 1800s an increasing number of trades relating to menswear began to take up premises there. By the 1840s it was beginning to gain renown for the high-quality tailors who were moving onto the street. The first was Henry Poole and Co., a business that had built up an impressive roll call of royal and aristocratic patrons from all over the world since it was first established in 1806. The bespoke service offered by Poole's saw business boom, its plate-glass-fronted showroom on Savile Row a temple of traditional masculinity. *The Tailor & Cutter* magazine described the richly appointed interior of Poole's in one of its 1880s issues: 'one large mahogany table of magnificent build was heaped with black cloths, on another was placed blues, on a third greys, on another fancies, the next containing half mourning goods; while away on one side was a magnificent show case, which had been prepared and fitted up by the firm with specimens of English tailoring'. Padded leather chairs and low tables invited the customer to sit at their leisure whilst they awaited a fitting – the atmosphere deliberately akin to a gentlemen's club, the preserve of the privileged male.

Whilst Adam would have been familiar with the reputations of the bespoke tailors of Savile Row, he would have acquired his own clothing closer to home. In the 1853 trade volume *Gore's Directory of Liverpool & Its Environs*, within which Adam himself is listed as a merchant trading from 16 Exchange Buildings in the city, there are more than 250 tailors recorded. It is likely that Adam would have patronised a number of different retailers – generic outfitters and drapers for his shirts, his undergarments, his cravats, shoes and hats – whilst potentially engaging a tailor for the narrow, tapered trousers and business-like frock coat that were part of the respectable gentleman's attire, both cut in a dark wool.

Anne left no evidence of Adam's suiting cloth in her diary. Given her propensity to record colour and pattern, it is likely that the plain, sombre colours of the merchant's wardrobe were of little interest to her and certainly did not match the aesthetics of the rest of the volume. What she does include instead are swatches of Adam's vests – the contemporary term for waistcoats. These preserved the last vestiges of the more colourful man of decades past, so that beneath the sober jacket were the resplendent vests ablaze with colour, like the plumage of a male bird puffing out its vibrant chest. From complex ikat weaves with their blurry warp-printed motifs to floral silks, shining stripes and soft velvet plaids, there is no lack of colour or design in these collared vests. A surviving example of a plush plaid vest in the Los Angeles County Museum of Art is near-identical to a swatch in the album, demonstrating how fashionable these young merchants were. They may not have shopped on Savile Row, but they were fluent in the vocabulary of masculine trends.

~

Particular scraps of cloth in Anne's dress diary are awarded special significance – a handful of pale fragments that are each framed carefully in a white waxed lace-like paper border. As the pages turn, they stand out as they are encountered, signalling a garment apart, a dress that was not of the everyday and therefore was to be protected and preserved from association with the hoi polloi of the ordinary. These elevated samples are all associated with weddings.

In 1838 Anne's white muslin dress that she wore for the ceremony would have consisted of a bodice arranged in soft pleats, forming a V from shoulder to waist and falling into a relatively full skirt. The sleeves were still generously proportioned, although they had lost the extreme size exhibited by the gigot sleeve that was fashionable earlier in the decade. Adam's vest, or waistcoat, appears to be similarly fashionable, based on the cream silk fragment remaining. Men's wedding attire could still be splendid. The V&A in London have in their collections a figured-silk waistcoat worn by the merchant John Montefiore for his wedding in 1845. Like Adam's, it is a cream silk featuring a trailing pattern, fastened with a row of self-covered buttons and a neat shawl collar. As a prosperous young merchant, Adam could afford to make a fashionable show on his big day in his splash of gleaming ivory.

On the second page of the book is a pale-lilac silk captioned, 'Jane's wedding dress October 10th 1833' pasted amongst seven other scraps on this one page, all associated with her. Jane Sykes was Anne's sister-in-law, marrying Adam's brother William five years before Anne and Adam's own union. William was Adam's older brother and worked as a calico printer for the firm of Messrs Hargreaves & Dugdale. The Broad Oak printworks were part of the Hargreaves & Dugdale enterprise, so William was well placed to acquire and gift fashionable fabrics to his young bride.

Five years before Anne and Adam's wedding, and outlined in a very different silhouette, Jane Sykes's dress of palest lilac silk would have ballooned at the arm with the fullest of sleeves, popularly described as the 'leg of mutton'. The ceremony at which this dress was worn took place in St James's Chapel in Accrington, and the bride was twenty-three and the groom was thirty-nine. More than any other woman in the album, Jane's presence features prominently amongst Anne's friends and family, a figure central to Anne's life and one of the most consistent presences in the album across its more than 400 pages. More than fifty samples of Jane's wardrobe from the 1830s to the 1860s appear, indicating an enduring friendship between the two sisters-in-law. On the 1851 census, Jane is listed amongst visitors staying with Anne and Adam in their home. In 1836 Jane and William's first and only child Charlotte Dugdale Sykes was born and, like her mother, Charlotte featured regularly throughout the book, from her earliest childhood into youthfulness and beyond, to her own marriage in 1862. Jane's dress – in keeping with all the other wedding dresses represented in the book – is, if not white, then certainly very pale. By the early eighteenth century white and silver had become firmly associated with wedding attire for those who could afford it. Jane's shade of lilac was both fashionable and wearable, so that it might be worn again as an evening dress, the large gigot sleeves and bell-shaped skirt gracing both chapel and assembly room.

Part of the mythologising that has grown up around nineteenth-century womenswear is that the white wedding dress originated from the most prominent woman of the century, Queen Victoria, whose marriage took place on 10 February 1840. Certainly it was the most famous wedding of its era, but Anne's own white wedding of 1838, captured so poignantly by Adam, reveals that this is a popular misconception. The Queen's wedding did, however, popularise white. It became aspirational as a bridal aesthetic for more women, as the accounts of preparations and the ceremony itself dominated the daily news. Entries in Queen Victoria's journal reveal that she gave a great deal of thought to how she, as Queen, ought to appear at her wedding. She consulted Lord Melbourne and records of precedents past before deciding that she would not wear her crimson robes of state, but would simply adopt the role of bride, rather than Queen. Two years earlier Melbourne, her then Prime Minister, had informed the young Queen that there were some rumblings in the press concerning her patronage of Parisian dressmakers and so, for the important occasion of her wedding, Victoria ensured that her bridal clothes were entirely British in their manufacture. Although there was no public record of the maker of the dress itself, it is likely that it was created by Victoria's favourite dressmaker, Mrs Bettans of Jermyn Street. On the morning of the ceremony the young Queen wrote in her journal, 'Dressed . . . I wore a white satin gown with a very deep flounce of Honiton, imitation of old. I wore my Turkish diamond necklace and earrings and Albert's beautiful sapphire brooch.'

The dress was safely and conventionally fashionable in a style that had already been in vogue for some time. Perhaps the contribution that was most popularised as a result of her wedding was the prominence of lace and, in lieu of a crown, the simple wreath of wax orange blossom that she wore on her head. The commission of Queen Victoria's wedding lace had been awarded to the lacemakers of East Devon, creators of the finest British bobbin laces. Although nominally described as Honiton lace, it was in fact made in many towns and villages around East Devon, Victoria's lace being supervised by a Miss Jane Bidney and made by lacemakers in the coastal village of Beer. Individually, they wove small sprigs of floral motifs on their domed pillows, the bobbins all a-click as they moved back and forth, each sprig being pieced to another and another until the great flounce of wedding lace was finished and applied to the white satin of the gown. The lace that decorated Anne Sykes's wedding ensemble was a handmade lace of more modest proportions, a neat Bedfordshire trim, a nod to the popularity of a technique that was still much in vogue but could be expensive.

We can't tell if Anne or Jane wore wreaths of wax orange blossom in their hair, but it is likely, given that this had become a ubiquitous addition to the mid-century wedding aesthetic. Orange blossom, aside from its delicate fragrance, was associated with virtue and fertility, and throughout the nineteenth century brides wore silk and wax blossoms in their hair or attached to their dress. The artificial materials from which these were created – the wax, the curls of paper leaves and stiffened wire – mean that many of these small keepsakes have survived where the fresh floral bouquets have not, fragile little remnants often encased in yellowed tissue paper. Any such mementoes of Anne's or Jane's are absent, but the ghosts of their dresses remain.

Whilst lace does appear fairly frequently in Anne's pages of fabrics, only the narrow trim on the first page is linked to a wedding and there is no reference to the wearing of a veil. Photographs from the 1860s reveal that wedding veils had become a fashionable addition to the bridal aesthetic, but in the 1830s and 1840s bonnets were often chosen instead, in spite of Queen Victoria's extravagant example. A bonnet was a useful accessory since it could be re-trimmed after the ceremony. Bonnet ribbons appear throughout Anne's album in a rainbow of shades, differing degrees of width and a whole range of patterns. It is easy to forget that the bonnet was universally worn by women young and old, the covering of the head being both a practical and a respectable necessity. Re-trimming a bonnet allowed for a frequent and relatively inexpensive change of mood, as Jane Austen often recorded in letters to her sister Cassandra. In December 1798 she wrote, 'I have changed my mind and changed the trimmings on my cap this morning, they are now much as you suggested . . .' Certainly a bonnet was the choice of Anna Coubrough, whose wedding Anne recorded as having taken place on 10 December 1840. Against a cream silk moiré ribbon, Anne wrote, 'Anna's wedding bonnet'. The bonnet might have included a spray of orange blossom and a short veil, but not the froth of expansive lace that would become more common later in the century.

Preparations for weddings started from a different perspective to the twenty-first-century experience. Middle- and upper-class brides would be leaving their family home for the first time when they got married and needed to equip themselves accordingly. Young women would accrue items for their trousseau: the colloquial 'bottom drawer', so called for the storage of garments that would be needed, they hoped, for their future. The trousseau varied depending on the wealth of a family, but its purpose was universal – to be as sartorially prepared as possible for life in a new home. The mid-nineteenth-century publication of *The Ladies' Book of Etiquette, and Manual of Politeness* written by Florence Hartley advised, 'In preparing a bridal outfit, it is best to furnish the wardrobe for at least two years, in underclothes, and one year in dresses, though the bonnet and cloak, suitable for the coming season, are all that is necessary, as the fashions in these articles change so rapidly.' Appropriate quantities of garments for a trousseau were clearly a source of anxiety, based on correspondence in some of the weekly periodicals. Responding to a letter sent to *The Englishwoman's Domestic Magazine* in 1862, the reply advised, 'Marion. By reducing the number of articles in the Trousseau, and having six instead of twelve of different things, you will arrive at something suitable for your income.' Canny retailers recognised that weddings might offer a source of reliable income and, by the 1860s, establishments like Mrs Addley Bourne's, a popular draper in Piccadilly who specialised in underclothes, was selling a complete trousseau. In 1866 she was advertising a £20 trousseau that included a variety of chemises, drawers, corsets, crinolines and vests, numbering some eighty-six items altogether.

For many women, the undergarments and other linens for the new home would be made by the bride and her female relatives, but gowns might need to be ordered elsewhere. Charlotte Brontë wrote of her own, rather hurried preparations for the purchase of her trousseau in a letter to her friend Ellen Nussey in April 1854: 'I suppose I shall have to go to Leeds. My purchases cannot be either expensive or extensive – You must just revolve in your head the bonnets and dresses something that can be turned to decent use and be worn after the wedding day will be best – I think.' She described purchasing a soft fawn silk and a drab barège with a green spot in addition to her wedding dress: modest additions to her wardrobe. For Jane Sykes, the prospective bride of a prosperous textile manufacturer, her trousseau may have been more extensive than Charlotte Brontë's and is likely to have included snowy white hand-stitched undergarments, gowns and accessories to be carried into her marital home. Whilst trousseaux are not mentioned directly in Anne's album, there are three samples that she captioned to indicate a new wardrobe fitted out to accompany a bride into her new life. Above a burgundy silk, a plain bronze silk and a pale-pink silk, Anne wrote, 'One of Anna's dresses when she was married.' Each of these belonged to a gown whose fabric had been chosen, the pattern cut and fitted to young Anna, made up by the dressmaker, collected and packed into a trunk to be transported to the home she would share with her husband – no longer dependent daughter, but married woman.

If preparations for married life were considered and quite extensive in the 1830s, those for the wedding day itself were much less so, in stark contrast to the wedding industry that was to emerge in the twentieth century. Many weddings were small affairs, the ceremony itself taking place in the parish church of the bride before retiring for the wedding breakfast, usually in her parental home. Although small compared to the large parties in attendance at contemporary wedding receptions, the table at the wedding breakfast would be lavishly decorated with myrtle and varieties of white flowers. There might have been a cake, which, by the end of the eighteenth century, could have been fashionably decorated in sugar paste to form the centrepiece of the setting around which the select guests would seat themselves.

Thanks to Adam's meticulous recording of the garments for their wedding, we know that Anne wore a different dress for her wedding breakfast: a white muslin check, a modest choice of fabric that Charlotte Brontë also chose for her wedding, describing it in a letter to Elizabeth Gaskell, '. . . white I had to buy and did buy to my own amazement – but I took care to get it in cheap material – there were some insinuations about silk, tulle and I don't know what – but I stuck convulsively to muslin – plain book muslin with a tuck or two'. Anne allowed herself a touch of luxury for the dress that she wore to the wedding breakfast after the marriage had taken place: a champagne silk satin that probably consisted of a plain, softly domed skirt with a skilfully pleated bodice, the pale shade of satin glinting in the peaks and troughs of the gathers. If Jane Sykes changed into another dress on her wedding day, then the evidence is missing from Anne's album. Perhaps the choice of her palest lilac silk carried her seamlessly from ceremony to breakfast without a desire to change.

An important female role associated with wedding practices, and acknowledged in Anne's album, was the bridesmaid. According to a caption above a cream figured-silk swatch, Anne had two bridesmaids for her 1838 wedding. 'Anna and Mary's dresses when they were my bridesmaids,' she wrote above the floral fragment. Photographs of later nineteenth-century weddings often show a disarming similarity between the dress of the bride and that of the sometimes numerous adult bridesmaids. Their bride-like attire and bouquets of flowers make it difficult to discern the figure of the woman getting married – a curious sartorial choice to the modern eye, but one whose traditional roots stretch as far back as the Roman period. Attendants would dress in clothing that was similar to the bride to act as a distraction, to protect the bride from evil spirits by obscuring her with a phalanx of female protection. In a nineteenth-century context there is something poignant about this shared experience, this united appearance, that speaks of the connections between women who were about to enter a new phase. As the young woman married, so she might move away, become geographically distanced from her confidantes, see less of the network of friends who would have been central to her existence prior to marriage. On this day, which was both the last of one life and the first of another, the uniformity of their appearance might bind them together in one final unmarried performance of sisterhood.

There are records of fourteen weddings in Anne's book. Most of them offer scant information relating to the day, and capture only the name above the wisp of fabric that featured so prominently in a life. A white muslin is 'Mrs Scrimshire's wedding dress'. A pale-gold satin is 'Mrs Garstang's wedding dress'. Although these occasions are lost to us, each of these pieces of cloth represents a significant moment in the lives of fourteen different women, each of whom had kept their wedding dresses and were willing to share a part of it with Anne Sykes. Although separated by pages in the album and by time and place, each of those gowns is united by a preference for pale colours. This is, in part, a marker of status. For most women in the working classes, a wedding dress would have to be wearable after the day itself and so a coloured dress would be favoured as a practical and economical choice. Some women might wear the smartest dress that they already owned, a new dress for the occasion being beyond their financial capabilities. That each of the women of Anne's acquaintance could afford a dress in a shade that placed it out of the everyday signalled their relative comfort.

There are two dresses that hint at a thriftier approach. On page 224 of the album, placing it well into the 1860s, there is a swatch of royal-blue damask that Anne has described thus, 'Wedding dress dyed. Mrs Gregg.' As dye technologies advanced from the 1850s, so might a silk dress of bright white be transformed into a shade that could take it into more varied social settings. A silk dress was still a costly garment, but Mrs Gregg was apparently practical in her reuse of the dress, putting the expanse of an 1860s crinoline dress to extended use. This is not the only example in the album of dyeing garments associated with a wedding. Eight years after her own wedding in 1833, Jane Sykes attended the wedding of Mary Fletcher, and above a plain mulberry-coloured swatch Anne wrote, 'Jane's drab satin which she wore at Mary's wedding as it <u>appeared</u> after it was <u>dyed</u>.'

Jane's dyed dress is not the only reference to the garments worn by wedding guests, as distinct from the bride herself, in Anne's book.

Although weddings were traditionally small, those guests who were invited to attend a wedding would dress with care for the ceremony and breakfast afterwards. A white figured silk bears the caption 'Mrs Martin's dress at Mr McEwan's [*sic*] wedding', and to go with a grey-blue ribbed moiré silk the description reads, 'Anne 1851 worn at Alice's wedding.' More than perhaps other garments, these dresses carried memories of a specific point in time. A day that could be called to mind as distinct from others, and the dress that went with that day, was comfortingly familiar. Where later brides and guests could recall a day through photographs, this silken ephemera was a material reminder of a special moment in time.

Jane Sykes's married life, which began in her shining pale-lilac silk in October 1833, was sadly to be short-lived. On 7 February 1837, a little over three years after their marriage, William Sykes died. He was forty-two years old. Jane was widowed, aged twenty-seven, with a seven-month-old daughter. She never remarried, but lived as a widow until her death in 1883. In the pages of the album, however, we are offered the merest glimpse of her life as represented through the garment snippets that she donated to her sister-in-law. We see her move from black satin-clad widow in the late 1830s to brighter shades. Through the 1840s, the 1850s and 1860s we see flashes of her gowns across the pale-blue pages and they speak not of a widow's weeds, but of white embroidered muslins, of blue-and-white striped silk, purple-checked cotton and gold damask. Jane is colourful and fashionable. What her life became after the untimely death of her husband, we do not know. We *can* say that she did not retire into everlasting mourning for William.

Anne's own marriage was of longer standing, being married to Adam until his death in 1888 – a half-century of life shared together. Along the church path of St George's we might imagine the ghostly outlines of Anne in light white muslin holding onto the arm of her Adam, resplendent in his ivory waistcoat, moving forward together into a life as yet unknown.

CHAPTER 2

Spinning into Gold

The Burtons

I believe I've seen Hell and it's white. It's snow white.

Elizabeth Gaskell, *North and South*, 1854

There is a thread that runs through the entirety of Anne's life and the part of it that she captured in her diary, and it is made from cotton. Hundreds of the fragments she saved and pasted into her album are woven from the cotton yarn that was the staple of the Lancashire industries around which she had grown up, providing the very foundations of her own family's prosperity. The patriarchs of the cotton mills scarcely feature in her album, but her father James Burton and her brothers John, James, Frederick, Edward and Oliver built their careers and a prosperous living from the textile that clothed a nation. The imperative to meet consumer demands drove those technological advances in industrial practices that subsequent generations of schoolchildren encountered in history classes. I remember learning as a child the names of the mysterious-sounding machines that heralded the revolution of industrial practices – John Kay's flying shuttle, James Hargreave's spinning jenny, Richard Arkwright's water frame and Samuel Crompton's mule: inventions that heralded the mechanisation of a process that had traditionally taken place within the four walls of the cottage industry. In countless homes the work of the floor-loom fed the family, its creaks and clacks the soundtrack to lives in a pre-industrial textile industry that had operated along the lines of piece work and outsourced labour for centuries.

The story of cotton is that of globalisation. It was a raw material that could only be produced in certain parts of the world, but came to be in universal demand. During his travels to Asia in the 1320s the English traveller Sir John Mandeville described an unusual-looking tree. In India he saw a 'wonderful tree which bore tiny lambs on the end of its branches'. The balls of raw cotton fibre were unlike anything he or any of his acquaintances had ever encountered before.

By the beginning of the fourteenth century India had developed different regional processes and fabric styles that involved the cultivation, treatment and weaving of cotton into desirable products whose market began to stretch beyond national borders. Other countries on other continents started to develop a cotton-growing industry as well, and the fibres of the cotton plant are spun across numerous countries, with too many different stories to tell here. As well as a raw material that represents global trade enterprise, however, the fibre also lies at the heart of great wealth – and, consequently, great inequality. It is not possible to weave the story of cotton into the context of Anne Sykes's life without acknowledging that her comfort came at a terrible human cost.

By the time Anne moved with her family to Burton House in Tyldesley, the juggernaut of the cotton industry was already unstoppable. Whilst cotton had first been imported to Britain in the seventeenth century, it was the results of mechanical innovation in cotton manufacture in the eighteenth century that would change the face of the industrial world. Laborious processes – such as the carding of the tangled cotton, the drawing or smoothing of the fibre and the spinning of the untangled filament into a long continuous yarn – had all previously been undertaken on small hand-reliant tools. The eighteenth-century imperative to speed up these processes in the face of increasing demand meant that those inventors whose names now form the liturgy of revolutionary machines gave rise to mass production.

Sometimes names become so synonymous with a process that we forget to really consider what that process was, and why it mattered. Those men linked directly to the changing manufacture of textiles were at the heart of tremendous change, which would go on to impact lives immeasurably, and technology for centuries to come. They themselves were witnesses to the limitations of the cottage industry as the desire for large quantities of cloth grew, with existing technologies unable to meet the demands of mass production. In 1733 Lancashire-born John Kay patented his invention for what he termed his 'wheeled shuttle'. Having been apprenticed at a young age to a hand-loom reed-maker, Kay knew that to speed up the hand-weave process would considerably improve output in terms of fabric production. Traditionally, even with a small floor-loom, two workers were needed to weave the cloth: one to throw the shuttle and operate the loom, and the other to catch the shuttle as it passed through the warp threads as they were lifted and shifted by the weaver. The wheeled shuttle – or 'flying shuttle' as it became more popularly known – greatly accelerated the speed of weaving a broader piece of cloth and dispensed with the need for a second person to catch the shuttle. Through such innovations whole industries were changed.

Less than thirty years later another development enhanced the manu-facture of cloth. James Hargreaves, another Lancashire lad, was described by Edward Baines in his 1835 *History of the Cotton Manufacture in Great Brit-ain* as the 'stout, broadest man of about five-foot ten or rather more'. A weaver himself, he knew first-hand what challenges the industry faced in terms of production speed. As a talented carpenter, he came up with a solution to one of the central processes of textile manufacture – the spinning of the yarn. For centuries, both wool and cotton were spun into a weavable yarn using a traditional single-drop spindle. An early form of mechanisation, the spinning wheel improved on the process, being capable of drawing fleece into one long, strong thread. As with so many innovators, Hargreaves came up with his idea after a happy accident, supposedly noting that when a spinning wheel fell over, both the wheel and the spindle continued to revolve. He conceived that several spindles might be turned simultaneously, generating more consistent threads in one go, and so the 'spinning jenny' was born.

James Hargreaves' spinning jenny.

This pioneering technology was further improved by Richard Arkwright's water frame, a spinning frame that was powered by a water wheel and produced a stronger and more reliable yarn than the jenny had achieved. The final extension of this work was the 'spinning mule', invented by the fourth Lancashire son to have such a huge impact on the landscape of the industrial world. Having lost his father at a young age, Samuel Crompton contributed to the family income by spinning yarn on a jenny machine of Hargreaves's invention. He was all too aware of its shortcomings, however, and over a period of six years revealed his own ideas for a mule-jenny in 1779. Taking parts of those earlier inventions and combining them with his own engineering, he created what would ultimately become the spinning 'mule' that would dominate the huge mills of Lancashire until the turn of the twentieth century. The carriage of the mule could carry more than 1,300 spindles, requiring only the labour of a minder and two boys to act as piecers, should one of the threads break. Progressing from single-thread, single-operator spinning wheels to the 150-foot-long mule in fewer than twenty years ensured that Britain was at the centre of the mechanised world; and by the middle of the nineteenth century British industrialists like James Burton contributed to more than 30 per cent of the world's cotton production.

~

To be growing up amongst the belching chimneys of Lancashire's factories was to be at the heart of a maelstrom in the mid-nineteenth century. Anne Burton was born into this eye of the cotton storm, her family one of those at the centre of innovation and growth that would change the face of the United Kingdom for ever. At the height of his career, James Burton was a prominent mill owner, presiding over five large mills in and around the town of Tyldesley in Lancashire. He was born in Clitheroe in 1784 and by his mid-thirties was already invested in the burgeoning textile industries, exploring new calico-printing ventures and going into partnership in 1828 with two brothers, John and Richard Jones. Their interests lay in developments within the silk industry and the partnership was dissolved sometime in the mid-1830s, leaving James to follow his instincts and open cotton mills instead. By 1838, settled in Tyldesley with his young family, James was running New Mill in the town and lived in Burton House on Factory Street, a house that faced both street and garden, seemingly torn between town and country – the new urban industrialist with an eye on his rural upbringing.

The new industrial landscape of cotton.

Much like John Thornton, the master of Marlborough Mill in Elizabeth Gaskell's 1854 social novel *North and South*, set against the backdrop of the cotton mills, Burton chose not to relocate to the suburbs, but lived amongst the factory buildings over which he presided. In 1839 James built his own premises, Atherton Mill, followed by Lodge Mill, Field Mill and Westfield Mill, making him one of the largest employers in the area. By 1860 he had created a cotton empire, overseen not only by himself, but by his sons, each of whom would be involved in the family business at one of the mills. How he related to his daughters it is impossible to guess. On the 1861 census he is counted as a visitor to Anne and Adam's home, but none of the swatches in Anne's diary are attributed to her father. Like all children who are indifferent to their parents' wardrobes, it is possible that Anne was simply not interested in acquiring his clothing, especially given her affinity with vibrant modern textiles.

Anne was surrounded by men and boys while growing up, but of her five brothers only Edward was awarded the honour of finding himself recorded in her album, one of the pages being devoted to pieces from his wardrobe. Having made his fortune in cotton, Edward had converted his riches into silk and wool: three of the swatches are shades of smooth grey silk punctuated with bright points of colour, and the other two are black wool fragments, lifted with a contrasting stripe. Was Edward perhaps the snappiest dresser amongst Anne's male siblings, and so the only one of them to warrant a place in her diary? These five pieces are the only reference to any of the male members of her family.

Whilst cotton would become king in Anne's world, providing her with a comfortable childhood and optimistic prospects for the future, the working conditions found within the imposing walls of the new factory system – and the journey that the raw material itself made from the southern states of America, having been picked by the hands of the enslaved – add a grim origin to the miles of cotton that were being churned from the looms of the North of England. Before the outbreak of the American Civil War, raw cotton accounted for 61 per cent of the value of US exports. The country had the land and the labour to produce such quantities, but it was a terrible forced labour. Of the 3.2 million enslaved people in the United States by 1850, 1.8 million found themselves on the cotton plantations of the south, engaged in the human tragedy that would define the nation. The raw material was shipped from the US, with more than 90 per cent of the cotton produced there being exported to Lancashire, amounting to almost two million bales a year. It arrived in Liverpool, where cotton brokers acted as middlemen, selling it on to the mills. Bales of cotton were unloaded into the warehouses of the factories, ready for the work to begin and the factory system to roar into action. It was a system that, by the end of the nineteenth century, employed more than half a million hands, becoming the largest cotton-producing industry in the world.

There were three important processes that had to be undertaken. First, the bale of raw cotton had to be opened and machines called scutchers would remove impurities from the newly unpacked cotton. Next, large carding engines with steam-powered revolving drums would smooth out the filaments of the cotton into a thin wad of unspun cotton, before it was sent to the upper two floors of the mill to be spun. Boilers and beam engines, steam and spindles all developed at the beginning of the nineteenth century, and the huge mills to house them sprang up around the Lancashire hills. With such development in the creation of the yarn, it was the turn of the loom next. From the practice of outsourcing weaving to the cottages of the workers whose relentless back and forth produced limited-width cloth, the power loom replaced the single hand. First invented by Edmund Cartwright in the late eighteenth century, it was improved upon by Richard Roberts in 1820, the wooden machine being replaced by one of cast iron, whose robustness vastly increased the speed of the weave. But it came at a cost. Having earned twenty-three shillings a week on their hand-looms, weavers now found that they were worth less than half that amount. Protests erupted and, in 1826, when Anne was nine years old, rioting took place in Accrington, the town of her baptism. The march of technology was inevitable, however. By the late 1820s increasing numbers of spinning mills were incorporating weaving sheds into their operation, and the entire process of turning raw bales of cotton into woven cloth could be undertaken at a single establishment. The centralisation of these processes meant the centralisation of labour, and countless workers found themselves populating the new urban sprawl.

The Burton brothers continued to run the four family mills, employing hundreds of local families in the endless cycle of spinning and weaving, with the vast power looms requiring constant feeding. The timing of their venture meant that the brothers lived as prosperous men. Did they ever feel a twinge of conscience towards the source of their wealth? It is likely that they did not, although there was a growing public consciousness that cotton from America was a fabric that bore the stain of slavery. Much like the fast-fashion practices of the twenty-first century, which support atrocious working and living conditions in countries far from our uneasy eyes, many people felt there was no alternative, and that the

The power loom being worked.

cheapness of the cloth and the lack of a viable alternative forced them to be complicit. Then as now, it was easy to consume, when the affected lives were out of sight on distant shores.

Cotton was an ever-present fibre in the wardrobes of the masses in the mid-nineteenth century. Anne and her peers – the wives and daughters of mill owners – purchased cotton dresses, undergarments and household linen in abundance. It was the fabric of the people, a natural fibre that could be easily dyed, printed, sewn and laundered and was available at different price points for many different purses. But from the early 1700s onwards, cotton was at the heart of economic, social and political upheaval, the very fibres of the cloth being infused with protest, law-making and law-breaking. The cotton industry would force humanity to confront its own terrible legacy in the trade of enslaved men, women and children whose destinies had become entwined with the harvesting and exporting of raw cotton.

During the seventeenth century a particular type of dyed cotton known as chintz had been imported into Britain from India, the colour and design of the bright fabrics finding favour with customers who delighted in their far-flung origins. In 1700 Parliament forbade the import of calico from India, following widespread protests by those British workers whose livelihoods depended on the domestic textile industries. Female consumers of imported cotton were lambasted in pamphlets, reproached for their fashionable treachery. British wool was the cloth to which women, both aristocratic and working-class, should aspire, rather than the flimsy ephemerality of Indian cotton. It was to be yet another means by which women were criticised for their vanity and another excuse to link women to fashion, and fashion to general profligacy and a lack of seriousness. Popular songs pursued this narrative – songs such as 'The Spittle-Fields Ballad' published in 1721, which cried:

None shall be thought
A more scandalous Slut
To appear like a Callico Madam.

In 1721 the Calico Act was passed, banning the sale of almost all cotton textiles. According to its own wording, the aim of the act was to 'Preserve and Encourage the Woollen and Silk Manufactures of this Kingdom and for more Effectual Employing the Poor by Prohibiting the Use and Wear of all Printed, Painted, Stained or Dyed Callicoes in Apparel, Household Stuff, Furniture or otherwise'. The only raw cotton that was permitted to be imported was that used in the domestic production of fustian, a heavy cotton most popularly required for menswear. These protectionist policies brought cloth to the heart of colonial destruction. The Bengalese muslin industry, which had thrived via exports to Britain, was now almost completely shut down. In an additional act of devastating irony, the raw cotton that did find its way to British manufactories was often exported back to Bengal, further destabilising an already decimated industry. Such was the legacy of Empire for so much traditional commerce. It was to prove the trigger for wider British production, however, and in 1774, with the new technologies of Hargreaves, Arkwright and Compton offering novel models of production, the Calico Act was repealed. Far from sabotaging the domestic industries, the potential of cotton might now prove to be their saviour.

The desire for cotton goods, from across the social spectrum, was not unproblematic. The reality of the raw material, however, was one of exploitation and the labour of the enslaved. It was not until the 1860s that the British cotton industry would be free of the awful reality of its supply chain. The Slavery Abolition Act passed by the British Parliament in 1833 freed more than 800,000 enslaved men, women and children under the jurisdiction of the British colonies. The cotton that was imported into Britain long after abolition, however, came predominantly from across the Atlantic and from the southern states of America. There the abolition of slavery was not ratified in Congress until December 1865, with the ratification of the 13th Amendment to the US Constitution, which stated that 'Neither slavery nor involuntary servitude, except as a punishment for crime whereof the party shall have been duly convicted, shall exist within the United States, or any place subject to their jurisdiction.' In reality, the implementation of the 13th Amendment was patchy. In some states it was not ratified for years and in others control was exerted in different ways, ensuring that hundreds of thousands of the formerly enslaved were exploited for generations to come.

For almost twenty years British manufacturers clung on to an industrial network of cotton threads, trading in a raw material produced through the labour of tens of thousands of enslaved plantation workers. There was evidence of growing dissent at this state of affairs. In 1859 Mr George Hadfield made a lengthy statement during a public meeting in Sheffield, during which he advocated exploring the market in Indian cotton once again, emphasising that 'The people of Manchester have issued a statement showing that we are paying for the slave-grown cotton of America 10,000,000 a year more than its fair marketable value.' It was hardly a compassionate angle, appealing to the commercial rather than the ethical merits of change, but it was one voice amongst a growing number. The same year the Congregational Union of England and Wales met and debated the issue. The American Rev. Theodore Bourne was invited to address the meeting and appealed to British manufacturers to rethink their options, pointing out that 'as long as the people of this country paid 25,000,0000 a year to the slave states of America for cotton, so long would slavery be upheld there'. Lord Brougham regularly lobbied Parliament to explore different commercial options, but British markets felt overwhelmed by the growth in the industry. *The Times* reported in 1860 that the importation of cotton since the import duty had been abolished had grown sixteen-fold: 'It tells of sixteen times as many mills, sixteen times as many English families living by working these mills, sixteen times as much profit derived from sixteen times as much capital . . .' It was a monstrous industry that needed constant feeding.

Increasingly there were other options, although for many years these were few and far between. Dissenting voices from within Nonconformist religious communities tried to precipitate change. The free-labour cotton movement was an initiative driven by both British and American Quaker families, but it required a determined effort since there was so little raw material that could meet that criteria. Free-labour stores opened sporadically in America, selling a variety of produce including cotton. Quaker Lydia White opened her premises in 1830, but wrote to a friend in 1831 to say that she was sorry she did not have 'a full supply and a better assortment of domestic cotton goods'. Cotton was one of the topics discussed at the World Anti-Slavery Convention held in London in June 1840, but this meeting itself was riven with division since many of the male abolitionists resented the presence of women amongst their number. However, free-labour produce was a movement that was driven principally by women, the chief consumers of cotton within the domestic sphere. The female call to arms had been accelerated in no small part thanks to Harriet Beecher Stowe's publication of the anti-slavery novel *Uncle Tom's Cabin* in 1852. It was to become one of the bestselling novels of the century, and its largely female readership motivated the abolitionist movement and initiatives such as free-labour produce.

In the small village of Street in Somerset one woman set about making her own small contribution to the cause. Eleanor Clark was a Quaker, married to James Clark, whose family ran the successful footwear company Clarks Shoes. The family's philanthropy was well known, and they had made great changes to the lives of the inhabitants of the surrounding area who worked for the firm and lived in the environs. Historian Anna Vaughan Kett, one of the few scholars to research the realities of the trade in free-labour cotton, has uncovered much that was unknown about the work of Eleanor Clark. In May 1853 she set up her Free Labour Cotton Depot in the village – a rather imposing name for what was a series of trestle tables and shelves that she opened each week in the Temperance Hall of Street village. Here she sold all manner of cotton fabrics that she purchased from another Quaker, Josias Browne, in Manchester. Browne was one of the only merchants trading in free-labour cotton in the UK, purchasing from farms in America that had rejected the labour of the enslaved. Eleanor charged a fair price for her cotton, proving cheaper than some of the larger drapery stores of the period. She sold to friends, family and other local women in her community for a period of five years.

Eleanor Clark's and other free-labour produce depots represented a tiny fraction of the overall cotton consumption. Some abolitionists felt that it was a fruitless mission, with one Samuel May writing to a friend that trying to sell free-labour cotton was 'very like bailing out the Atlantic with a spoon'; but it was the public profile of the act, rather than the quantity, that those promoting free-labour cotton hoped to raise. Some larger manufacturers who might have experimented with the notion of free-labour cotton knew that the mixing of the raw material that was required to get the best fibre risked contaminating the end product. Machines would have to be cleaned of existing thread and fibre in order not to pollute the free-labour cotton, and this was felt to be not financially viable for most mill owners. The quantities simply did not exist.

There were other labour issues that began to permeate the realities of the factory system. During Anne's childhood the factories grew brick by brick, but so too did concerns about the working conditions of those men, women and children required to work inside their walls. The Factory Act of 1833 aimed to curb some of the worst practices, instructing that no children under the age of nine might work at all; that children between the ages of nine and thirteen must work reduced shifts; and that children must receive two hours of schooling a day. Ten years later these laws were reviewed once again and limits were placed on the number of hours that women could work, reducing them to twelve at most. By 1847 all women and children under the age of eighteen were forbidden to work more than ten hours a day. Legislation was one thing, but the enforcement of those laws quite another. Factory inspectors were appointed in the 1830s and their reports made for grim reading. Workers were asked to describe the conditions of their employment, their hours and their duties. The resulting reports were instrumental in drawing attention to the plight of the workers. Friedrich Engels wrote his now-famous book *The Condition of the Working Class in England* in 1844, prompted by his observations of the privations under which the inhabitants of Manchester lived, many of whom worked in the cotton industries. Manchester itself had become known as 'Cottonopolis', such was its dominance of the industry and the region.

Not all factories were built on the same model of exploitation that came to characterise the world depicted in Elizabeth Gaskell's *North and South*, where so many of the masters of the mill in her fictional town of Milton were tyrants. Milton stood in for Manchester, the Cottonopolis itself, where Gaskell had lived for a time and witnessed first-hand the deprivations of the mill hands. There were other models, however. On the banks of the Falls of Clyde in Scotland, New Lanark stood as a model of good practice in its day. New Lanark Mills were founded by Glasgow banker David Dale and his then business partner, Richard Arkwright, inventor of the revolutionary spinning frame that partially mechanised the spinning of cotton thread into a usable yarn. In 1785 Dale opened the mill at New Lanark, a site of remarkable size and industry. Although the hours were gruelling (certainly by today's workplace standards), Dale was seen as a progressive man, providing his workers with decent food, clean and well-maintained accommodation and education for children. It was under the management of Dale's son-in-law, Robert Owen, that New Lanark became famous. Having worked as a manager at Bank Top Mill in Manchester, Owen knew the logistics of cotton manufacture, from the purchase of the raw material through each process to the finished product. What he was most interested in were the conditions of the workforce. His innovations were impressive, in the context of his time and place in the world. He reduced the working day significantly, to ten and a half hours. He created what is believed to be the world's first nursery to support working mothers. He employed a village doctor and encouraged the election of spokespeople to sit on the village council. Residents had access to allotments, education, woodland walks and a co-operative grocery store, in moves that would have left other mill owners incredulous.

So where does Anne's father, James Burton, sit within this litany of human exploitation? His determination to live close at hand to both his mills and his workers might be read as displaying a desire to remain true to his roots, and that to remove himself to the prosperous suburbs would be a traitorous act. It might also, however, be the actions of an ambitious man who did not want to distance himself from the source of his wealth and kept a beady eye on his empire. Politically he was a Liberal, so it is possible that his was a more benevolent hand than those of some of the crueller masters amongst his peers. He certainly adopted the trappings of a philanthropist, and he represented his town of Tyldesley on the Board of Guardians for the Leigh Poor Law Union. I would like to think of him as an entrepreneurial young man whose ambitions and vision made him a wealthy older man. Was he a sympathetic employer? Was he a stern and overbearing father? When he visited Anne and Adam in 1861, were they happy to receive him or did they both draw a sigh of relief when he left? James survived his wife by almost thirty years and never remarried. He shared his home with various sons as their circumstances changed, but in 1868, at the grand old age of eighty-four, James Burton died. He was buried in the churchyard of St George's, Tyldesley, in the parish where so much of his professional and personal life had been conducted, and where Anne and Adam had themselves married exactly thirty years earlier.

The cotton empire that Burton had founded in the 1830s continued to thrive for the rest of the century, notwithstanding a devastating fire at one of the mills in 1883, which caused more than £15,000 of damage. According to records, in 1901 the Burton mills comprised 157,196 spindles and 570 looms, operated by hundreds of hands and controlling the lives and livelihoods of hundreds of families. However, in the early years of the twentieth century, long after Anne's own death, the industry was beginning to suffer. By 1926 Burtons was an empire no more. The machines were stripped and the mills demolished. For more than seventy years the Burton cotton mills had thrived, but by the 1960s British textile manufacture was in dire straits. In a sense it was to be the architect of its own demise, for having once been at the cutting edge of mass-production technology, those processes were latterly established in developing countries where labour was cheap and retailers need not look too closely at factory practices. By the 1990s most textile manufacture in the UK had been offshored, representing a loss of skill and the dereliction of those industrial premises that had powered the North of England for decades.

Anne Sykes had witnessed the fruits of her father's ambition, clothed in the lightweight cotton that his workers had brought to life on their looms. Her entire family – the marriages that were forged, the careers that blossomed and the wider networks of friendships that emerged – was driven by the powerhouse of the cotton industry. Whilst fragments of her garments and those of her friends and family are present in her dress diary, their thoughts are not. Did they ever stop to ponder the origins of their prosperity or were they too in thrall to its success to question the labour that supported it? As an extended family, they were socially aware to a degree and extended their largesse in appropriately philanthropic acts; but we will never know what they really thought. We might learn much from Anne's beautiful scrapbook of cloth, but never that.

Whilst so many of the mills no longer exist, some of the imposing architecture that formed the backdrop to Anne's childhood remains. Gentrified now, often converted into apartments, artisanal retail experiences or heritage centres, it contains only whispers of the industry and noise that once filled it. Of the countless thousands whose livelihoods depended on the turn of the beam engines and the insistent back and forth of the mules and power looms, we hear little beyond the verbatim reports of the factory inspectors, and see little beyond occasional photographs that attempted to capture the life of the mill hands. The evidence of their labour exists in museum stores, surviving garments, old sheets, nightgowns and tablecloths. It survives in the static swatches pasted by Anne Sykes into her album, frozen in a colourful moment – a small, silent memorial to the hands that picked, smoothed, spun, wove, dyed and printed the cotton that came into her life.

CHAPTER 3

A Lady's Laundry List

Alice Burton & Mary Fletcher

Many a penny can a careful housewife save if she will but
spare a few moments to the occupation of simple dyeing.

Beeton's Housewife's Treasury of Domestic Information, 1865

Early in her endeavours to record the clothing of those around her,
Anne pasted in a slightly jagged fragment, the scissored edges not as
clean as some of the other more precisely snipped fragments. It is a dull
black floral figured silk, above which Anne wrote, 'Mary Fletcher. Old
Burnous – after it was dyed also like a dress of mine long ago.' With this
description, she captured two important elements in her world. One
was an infrequent reference to the care and maintenance of clothes that
women in all walks of life would have learned from a young age, and the
other was the centrality of female relationships in her life. Mary Fletcher
was Anne's eldest sister, her only surviving sister amongst a jumble of
brothers.

Further into the album, and somewhat curiously placed amongst
clothing that dated to a much later period, is another significant familial fragment. It is a piece that is much larger than most of the other
swatches in the volume, taking up most of a single page: a colourful

printed cotton that is all a-swirl with the then-fashionable paisley motifs. Anne simply wrote above it, 'Mamma's dress 1829'. It is the only reference in the diary to her mother, Alice Burton. Alice was in her forties when she died, making the single sample of fabric attributed to her even more poignant – the only material connection with her mother that Anne included in the book. So here are the two earliest and closest female relatives who shaped Anne's world and provided the blueprint for her domestic and sartorial life.

Caring for clothing was an important part of a woman's domestic routine, whether she was in the privileged position of directing somebody else to do it or undertook the work herself. As cloth was valued, so were the processes of cleaning, repairing and maintaining it invested with consequence. But how did women in the nineteenth century clean their clothes? Garments that are so wildly unfamiliar to us now, trapped in an era that pre-dates such mod-cons as washing machines and modern detergents, appear almost impossible to maintain – but this is the kind of knowledge that Alice would have passed on to her firstborn daughter, Mary, and then to her younger daughter, Anne. Laundering, spot-cleaning, repairing and refashioning textiles were vital to their longevity, and the resourcefulness of those women responsible for their care is an often-overlooked part of their daily labour. Yet were it not for Anne's decision at some point to care about clothes, she might never have created her remarkable diary.

Alice Burton would have been responsible for the smooth running of her house on Factory Street in Tyldesley when she moved there in the late 1820s, the colourful dress preserved by Anne being a part of her wardrobe as she left her former marital home in Clitheroe and moved to the distinctively shaped house that overlooked her husband's mill. Mary was their firstborn child, born in May 1808, less than a year after James and Alice married in July 1807. Anne was Alice's third daughter, born more than eight years later. By the time her baby sister Anne arrived, Mary would already have learned something of dress and the everyday routines associated with it. As the wife of a newly prominent mill owner, Alice would not have had to tackle the more labour-intensive tasks required of certain laundry practices, but would have overseen the smooth running of the process as a whole and would have instructed her daughters in the arts of domesticity as they grew older. The laundering and repair of clothing divided into a number of different areas in the first half of the nineteenth century. The most onerous task was the laundering of the household's linen. Next came the more delicate cleaning requirements of garments that were not suitable for the washtub, followed by the cleaning of sundry items such as shoes and accessories. There were running repairs to keep on top of, and finally there was the refashioning of garments as they wore out or no longer fitted the original wearer. This cycle of cleaning and repairing required planning and an investment of time to ensure that garments were wearable.

Layers of cotton and linen undergarments served a specific purpose in the eighteenth and nineteenth centuries. They were the first line of defence in protecting outerwear from the skin, ensuring that the delicate and more difficult-to-wash garments were protected from soiling. The chemise or shift was a ubiquitous T-shaped piece of underwear that had been worn in one form or another for centuries. Its relative simplicity meant that whilst shielding the body from the clothing, it was also a garment that could be more readily washed at higher temperatures. The notion that women in the nineteenth century did not wash their clothes as frequently as we do today is a myth that has gathered traction in popular imaginings of past lives. In fact men and women alike changed this bottom-most layer of clothing frequently, filling the houses of the thousands of independent laundresses with their linen.

The heavy-duty laundry followed a process that began on Monday morning. Mrs Beeton gave detailed instructions for the laundry maid to follow, the first task being 'a careful examination of the articles committed to her care and enter them into the washing book'. The various fabrics had to be sorted and written up, before each mark, stain and grease spot was assessed. The larger, more robust linens and cottons were then placed into the first tub, which should contain only lukewarm water, within which a little soda had been dissolved. Soap would be bought in large chunks, usually measured by the stone, and would then be cut into smaller cakes using a wire cutter. Paraffin was sometimes used as an alternative on more stubborn marks for both soaking and boiling as a solvent for grease, mixed in with the soap. Textiles that required deeper cleaning underwent a more forceful approach, being placed into a separate tub, 'in a liquor composed of ½ lb of unslaked lime to every six quarts of water'. The late-nineteenth-century advice manual *Enquire Within Upon Everything* offered its own recipe for whitening household linens: 'To make a good washing preparation, put one pound of saltpetre into a gallon of water, and keep it in a corked jug; two tablespoons for a pint of soap. Soap, wash and boil as usual. This bleaches the clothes beautifully, without injuring the fabric.' This kind of household advice and homespun recipe was popular in the pages of the expanding range of periodicals available to women from the mid-nineteenth century. Tips ranged from a solution of borax in a pail of water, to rubbing the linens with par-boiled potatoes to soften and whiten them. Woollen items had to be washed at speed to avoid shrinkage, with a solution of ammonia in cooler water.

After the first washing, the linen would be put into a second tub with water 'as hot as the hand can bear', where it would be both scrubbed and inspected for any lingering marks. In the absence of a technological solution, the most popular tool for the manipulation of linen in the tub was a washing dolly. This wooden contraption resembled a kind of four-legged stool and had a long pole that ran up from the centre, and a handle at the top for pounding the fabric, once submerged in the hot water. Once the cloth had been sufficiently scrubbed, it would then be rinsed and wrung. The mangle became the most necessary object for squeezing as much water as possible from the heavy linens and undergarments. In *The Rainbow*, first published in 1915, D. H. Lawrence described Tilly's reaction to the gift of a mangle that could attach to the side of the washtub: 'My word, that's a natty little thing! That'll save you lugging your inside out.' Mangles came in a variety of shapes and sizes, depending on the size of household and the budget that went with it. The Harrods catalogue of 1895 included small tabletop mangles such as 'The Superior', which could be purchased for £14, and large cast-iron floor-standing mangles with a many-toothed cog to turn the wooden handle with twin rollers, costing a more princely £41.

Once the clothes were wrung, their drying was the next, most long-winded part of the process. Drying outside was considered the most effective. In rural areas, drying would take place on the grass, but in larger households and in cities a clothes line was used. Of course given the propensity for rain in a northern European climate, sometimes the only alternative was the rickety wooden clothes horse. Flora Thompson, author of *Lark Rise to Candleford*, recalled the unpleasantness of indoor drying days: 'no-one who has not experienced it can imagine the misery of living for several days with a firmament of drying clothes on lines overhead'. Alice Burton and her family would have been spared such misery – the drying of their clothes taking place in the home of their laundress or on the premises of the larger professional laundry, or else in that part of their house where they need not venture, it being left to the ministrations of their own laundry maid.

Once dry, the final processes might be undertaken: that of starching and ironing the sheets, caps, aprons, shifts, collars, nightgowns, napkins and handkerchiefs that made up the regular contents of the wash. Mrs Beeton advocated a half-pint of cold water and a quart of boiling water to every two tablespoons of starch, boiling the solution before straining it into a clean basin, then covering it to prevent a skin forming on the top. The dry garment 'should be dipped into the hot starch made as directed, squeezed out of it and then just dipped into cold water and immediately squeezed dry'. At last then – after the inspecting, boiling, scrubbing, rinsing, wringing, drying and starching – the bright clean cottons, muslins and linens could be ironed. This was no less onerous a task, revolving the flat irons on a hot stove to ensure consistent temperatures. Whilst a clean table was suitable as a base on which to iron the larger, flatter items, other solutions were required for more delicate objects. A skirt board was recommended for complicated muslin skirts, whilst the folds and frills that might be found on a nightgown or a cap could be revived using a special 'goffering' iron. These long, hollow cigar-shaped contraptions, resting on a stand, would be heated with a central rod, the cloth wrapped around to shape smaller sections of the decorative cap or petticoat.

By the middle of the nineteenth century the up-and-coming middle classes had begun to purchase linen in greater quantities, so that they might dispense with the weekly wash and instead commit to one only every few weeks. It became a sign of prosperity in late-nineteenth-century rural society, as indicated by postmistress Dorcas Lane in *Lark Rise to Candleford*. She had grown up with the social anxiety that it would have been 'poor-looking' to have to wash weekly or fortnightly. Laundresses would also undertake the washing of whole garments, and not just the household linen. Mrs Beeton advocated that these items of coloured cottons, muslins and linens should be washed with a lighter touch to avoid deterioration of the dye: 'When ready for washing, if not too dirty, they should be put into cold water and washed very speedily, using the common yellow soap, which should be rinsed off immediately.'

The logistics of laundry, and how it could be successfully managed, were a concern to all. At the same time as Anne and her peers would have been overseeing arrangements for their own household laundry, similar issues were proving a challenge to Queen Victoria's husband. The complications presented by such quantities as were produced by the various royal households were a cause of some concern to the Prince Consort, who was dismayed at the poorly organised regimen that Queen Victoria had inherited. He devised a scheme to ensure that the laundering of the royal linens was achieved both discreetly and smoothly. In 1846 he oversaw the construction of a dedicated royal laundry situated on Kew Foot Road. Every day a miniature train brought the one and a half tons of royal linen from Windsor, London and Osborne House to Richmond Station and on to the laundry, where it would be cleaned, ironed and sorted prior to being returned to its respective residence. The mixing of household linen gave rise to that most important identifier, the laundry mark. For Queen Victoria, this took the shape of a hand-embroidered cipher, but for most people it would involve the stitching of initials in a contrasting colour – red-threaded identifications or hand-inked names tucked away in a waistband, so that the overworked laundress could reunite linen and household.

Whilst the bulky laundry would be undertaken outside the home, there were still many clothes-cleaning practices that took place indoors under the jurisdiction of the women, part of their daily duties in maintaining domestic harmony. Everyday accessories that were a part of a woman's wardrobe might be attended to using a variety of ingredients. Gloves were worn with far greater frequency then than now, and their cleanliness reflected on the good domestic practices of the wearer. *The Ladies' Treasury* of 1857 stressed that 'a soiled glove, or one with a hole or a palpable repair, is quite inadmissible where you are paying a call or frequenting a public place'. Strategies for cleaning leather gloves varied from cream of tartar to benzene – potions and chemicals that could be purchased readily in the nineteenth century. Stale bread and flour was a popular solution for cleaning suede. Oats, bran, Vaseline and kerosene were all advocated in the cleaning and care of shoes, whilst borax was a chemical treatment that appeared frequently in all manner of advice manuals, cleaning everything from linen to leather boots.

At the same time as Anne and Mary were managing their own

households in the 1840s, new developments in the cleaning of clothes were making headlines across the Channel. In 1849 a Parisian tailor named Jolly-Bellin knocked over an unlit lamp onto his wife's treasured tablecloth. Fearing retribution, he hid the cloth away, intending to try and clean it undetected. To his surprise, however, when he unrolled the cloth sometime later, he discovered that those areas of spilt turpentine were brighter and cleaner than the rest, and the possibilities of cleaning fabric by spirits were revealed. After some experimenting, Jolly-Bellin began to advertise his *nettoyage à sec* cleaning services. It was not until the mid-1860s that the first British firm began to advertise a postal dry-cleaning service as an alternative to the labour-intensive cleaning of more delicate garments. It was a costly process. It worked on the same principle as dyers of the period, requiring the piece of clothing to be unpicked and its constituent parts laid in the cleaning solution, before being re-sewn and returned. It was a time-consuming act, but one intended to prolong the life of a still-useful object.

Many shops offered a dyeing department for their customers. Perhaps Mary sent her 'Old Burnous' to a local establishment or to her favoured dressmaker to have it dyed – a burnous being a type of cloak popular in the mid-nineteenth century. Often when garments had faded or were no longer in the first flush of fashion, they would be dyed to refresh the cloth for an existing or new wearer. That Mary dyed her burnous black suggests that it was worn as a mourning cloak, changing its identity from the everyday to the occasional. Its placement in the diary, near the beginning of the album between Anne's marriage in 1838 and her own in 1841, might position it against the sad loss of their mother. Alice Burton died in 1840, not living long enough to see her eldest child married.

For the larger items of outerwear – dresses, suits and cloaks – the most important strategy was spot-cleaning. There were many recipes available to try and eradicate the inevitable grease spots and food stains that were a part of daily life. *Cassell's Household Guide* gave the ingredients for balls used especially for removing grease. Fuller's earth was moistened with lime juice and pearl-ash, and the resultant mixture was rolled into balls that were then dried and applied to spots as and when required. Candle wax was a frequent cause of staining in the nineteenth century and this could be removed with turpentine. Long skirts that were prone to catching grass stains or muddy spots might be dealt with by vigorous brushing, a solution of bicarbonate of soda or a good scrub with half a potato. One of the hazards of a fitted silk bodice in an era that pre-dated effective anti-perspirants was, of course, the semicircle of sweat that might stain the wearer's garments. Whilst there was no chemical solution to this in the nineteenth century, there was a material one. The January 1864 edition of *Godey's Lady's Book*, an American periodical, included a pattern for a dress shield: an oval of reinforced or waxed cloth that would be sewn into the underarm of the dress to protect the outer layer from perspiration stains. By the 1880s dress shields were produced commercially, often made from a rubberised material that was thought to be more effective. They might be sewn into and removed from garments on a daily basis if necessary, although they were mainly reserved for more formal dresses. The concentrated attention paid to these remedies, and the regular inspection of garments, meant that outer garments were maintained more frequently perhaps than popular myth has allowed.

~

When Mary married Thomas Fletcher, a Manchester merchant, on 22 April 1841, Anne received a snippet of Mary's ivory damask dress to add to her book by way of a memento. Mary's presence ebbs and flows in her sister's album – perhaps both life and circumstance preventing regular contributions. From the 1850s, however, Mary's name appears with greater regularity, her swatches perhaps signalling a renewed closeness between the siblings. They reveal a woman interested in the changing vagaries of fashion, from the printed cottons of her younger years to the heavier silks of the 1860s. As a woman of older middle age, Mary would wear garments that were at the cutting edge of new trends – black silks studded with bright rose motifs and brightly patterned ombré gauze gowns. Were they alike, these sisters? Did they share similarities in style or was their taste wildly different? Judging from the scraps of fabric alone, and in the absence of any other evidence, it seems that Mary was perhaps the more colourful of the two. By the 1850s and 1860s her swatches were more vivid, where Anne's were perhaps a little more muted. Did Anne secretly tut over her sister's love of the new, or did Mary think Anne a little dull in her choice of dress?

It is likely that both sisters would have continued to manage and care for their clothing as they matured, being adept with a needle and skilled in the art of repair. In their respective drawing rooms, Anne and Mary would most likely have owned a workbox of some kind, a repository of needle and thread, pins and tapes, buttons and braids. It is likely that there would have been a wooden darning mushroom – a small domed wooden article over which the toes of a holed stocking would be pressed, in order to work the fine criss-cross of stitching that might invisibly affect a repair. These were the kinds of skills passed from mother to daughter: from Alice to Mary and Anne. Darning samplers were sometimes undertaken by young girls, objects that to us appear as beautifully embroidered squares of fine linen, but which in fact served a much more practical purpose, the coloured threads acting as markers for the newly instructed child as she learned the art of mending. Holes did not mean the end of a garment's life, but they did require an act of rescue – ideally an invisible solution that required the finest of stitches, the neatest of patches.

We can only imagine the degree of closeness between the two sisters. As her closest living relative and as an older sister, perhaps Mary stood in for the mother they had lost when they were both young women. A shared upbringing in the heart of the Lancashire textile industry may have given them that appreciation for cloth and its variations that was to compel Anne to capture at least a part of that world in her diary.

Caring for clothes in so laborious a manner is at odds with the pace of twenty-first-century life. Most of our clothing can be washed and dried in a matter of hours. Socks with holes in the toe are discarded, new ones easily acquired. The knowledge handed down through the generations, advising on effective clothes maintenance, lessened with each passing modern convenience and each turn of the fast-fashion wheel. But we would do well to look back and listen to some of those nuggets of advice that Mrs Beeton shared, or that Alice Burton passed on to her two daughters. Impossibly time-consuming though most of the nineteenth-century practices were, when it came to the act of laundering clothes, the imperative that lay behind it was one of value: to value the textiles, the processes and the time required to care for those garments with which we choose to clothe our bodies. As twenty-first-century dress practices are revealed as being increasingly unsustainable, so might we learn much from Alice Burton, Mary Fletcher and Anne Sykes. There are signs of change. There are small businesses embracing the art of mending and rediscovering the finely wrought skill of darning, making the repair a visible and beautiful part of the garment's biography. We can slow down, buy less, repair more and learn once again to cherish the clothing we own. I think Anne and her generation would approve.

CHAPTER 4

Cobwebs of Fashion

Anne Sykes and I

This fabric, like those of porcelain, stained glass and others essentially artistic, has, from its first origins, been an object of interest to all classes.

Mrs Bury Palliser, *A History of Lace*, 1865

Were it not for lace, the secrets bound within the covers of Anne's book might never have been uncovered. All of the lives and stories it holds would have remained forever untold, a curious scrapbook lying at the bottom of a trunk hidden from view. In the end, the act of lacemaking would reveal the identities of the women and men within.

I began to make lace in the late 1990s. As a newly wed young woman living in Devon whose husband worked away from home during the week, I was in search of a distraction from long evenings on my own and signed up for an evening class in making Honiton lace. I was the youngest member of the class by some decades, but lacemaking had long fascinated me. I used to watch my aunt and my cousin – their domed pillows a mystery of pins and bobbins, their hands moving back and forth across the cloth to produce ephemeral snowy-white motifs. Handmade bobbin lace is an act of slowness. There is no instant gratification here.

The pattern emerges thread by thread, hour by hour, requiring concentration and patience, so that only after many hours of weaving the small wooden bobbins along their path, and eventually removing the hundreds of slim steel pins, are the fruits of all the labour revealed in a piece of lace only a few inches square.

Adult-education classes in the provinces were gradually phased out, and eventually I joined a group of women once a month in an independent meeting of like-minded spirits. In between the chaos of parenting two small boys and developing a career, it was an oasis of calm, and the fifty or so women who met each month provided a different network from the everyday cares of the world. That group was itself a place of fragmented stories. Once a month our lives intersected for a few hours. We shared little pieces of our worlds. I would share tales of parenthood, and the women around me would nod knowingly, having been through their own experiences of child-rearing and emerged on the other side. Over coffee and biscuits, bobbins clicking across pillows, I was able to be my best self for a short while.

It was here that I met the elderly lady who owned Anne's book, her gift of it to me somehow a continuance of the female friendships that I was to discover in Anne's world almost 200 years earlier. We will never know how Anne's bright silk album progressed through the world and made its way to London in the 1960s, to Camden Town and a market stall of bric-a-brac – the flotsam and jetsam of lives lived long ago – to be acquired by a curious young man; but here it now was, shared through a connected interest in a textile art, 198 miles from that market stall in a rural town in Devon. Ironically, there are not many lace samples in the book, relative to the number of fragments it contains. Out of the 2,134 pieces, only eighteen are lace, varying in size from the smallest scrap of a handkerchief trim to the decorative flounce that once edged the silk of an evening dress. This catches the boundless possibilities of lace as a textile whose varieties, by the middle of the nineteenth century, permitted ownership across a broad spectrum of social strata. A narrow lace edging might trim the edge of a relatively cheap chemise, whilst a broad cobweb of bobbin lace, costing huge sums, might be applied to more costly garments.

In the twenty-first century, lace is not the cloth it once was. The mass production that began in the early nineteenth century has superseded the cottage industry of hand-makers who once characterised an industry. Where once skilled artisans produced a highly prized commodity woven in their homes to be worn by royalty, now lacemaking is a relatively rare hobby. As the art of handmade lace is practised by fewer and fewer people today, it is important to tell the tale of nineteenth-century ingenuity, of female textile artists who were often under-appreciated, and of an industry that represents a significant part of British textile heritage.

Lace could be a chameleon-like fabric in a woman's wardrobe. Most of the scraps in the album belong to Anne herself, and they range from the ephemeral trim along the edge of a white handkerchief, to the broader, more dramatic flounce of lace trimming an evening dress. As small as the fragments are, it is still possible to distinguish those that are machine-made, in all their uniformity, from the handmade lace, where the uniqueness of the human hand weaving the bobbins or passing the needle back and forth created its own fingerprint of sorts. Of the eighteen samples Anne included, eight of them are handmade and ten produced by machine. Four samples on a single page belonged to the edging of Anne's white handkerchiefs – those necessary scraps that we have all but dispensed with in the twenty-first century, but which were an essential component of daily life for so long. Many of the lace fragments in Anne's book were gifts. She described the origins of each snowy trim as 'Lace given to me by Mrs Butler' or 'Lace given me by Mrs Panting'. It was a convenient choice of gift, particularly if it was being sent via letter. It could tuck easily into an envelope, with little additional bulkiness. It could be purchased to suit most budgets, dependent on quality, and it was always useful. It is likely that Anne would have reused a length of lace, removing a trim from one handkerchief to add to another, or carefully unstitching a flounce from an evening dress to roll safely into storage, ready to add to a future garment.

~

The art of lacemaking has a long tradition in different European contexts. From the sixteenth century expensive needle laces were depicted in the finery of portraiture, the pointed edges of Italian reticella lace stiffened into the familiar collars of aristocratic dress. Bobbin laces found their individual forms in different geographical spaces – the weaving of the thread conducted on different-shaped pillows with distinctly turned wooden bobbins, depending on the variety practised in that region. Today the different lace types are baffling to the uninitiated, with those in the know being able to distinguish styles from a twist of the thread here or a turn of the bobbin there. Colourful names describe their variations – Binche, Mechlin, Point d'Angleterre, Brussels, Valenciennes – which are rooted in their places of origin, with each producing a distinctive style.

Bobbin lacemaking in Britain was attached to the migrations of Protestant refugees fleeing persecution from parts of Europe in the fifteenth and sixteenth centuries, bringing their artistry with them. Flemish lacemakers settled in Bedfordshire and Buckinghamshire, giving rise to the regional laces that still exist there. Lacemakers from Flanders, skilled in the art of Brussels bobbin lace, travelled to the south-western counties of Devon and Dorset. The similarities between Brussels lace and Honiton lace capture the shared DNA that was indicative of the migrant population bringing their skills to the area. The first reference to Honiton lace in a historical document appears in 1620 in T. Westcot's *View of Devon*, in which the author wrote, 'bone lace much in request, being made at Honiton and Bradnich'. Bone lace was the earliest term given to the technique and indicated that at this time the bobbins were often carved from bone rather than wood.

The skills involved in lacemaking, and the beautifully crafted end results, made lace an increasingly desirable and costly textile. The seventeenth-century diarist Samuel Pepys enjoyed the decadence of lace, writing on 8 October 1662 of his delight at his new lace 'scallop', a fine collar with scalloped edges. On another occasion he recalled an encounter with one of the King's mistresses in the White Hall Gardens: '. . . in the Privy Garden, saw the finest smocks and linen petticoats of my Lady Castlemaine's laced with rich lace at the bottom, that ever I saw, and it did me good to look at them.' The most prolific of royal spenders at the end of the seventeenth century was Mary, daughter of King James II, whose bill for her lace orders in 1694 amounted to £2,000 – a staggering £239,000 today. Lace remained a popular decorative addition to dress throughout the eighteenth century, with paintings often capturing the lavishness of flowing cuffs, cravats and caps. The colour itself was a signifier of wealth: to maintain whiteness in an age when laundering cloth presented certain challenges indicated resources at one's disposal.

Lacemaking in Devon was especially fine. Mostly made by women, it grew into a valuable industry in the rural county, with the men engaged in the fishing industry whilst their wives sat at their pillows. Honiton lace pillows are round and domed, sitting either in a simple wooden frame or resting on the lap, angled against a table to ensure that the bobbins hang at an angle to create tension in the thread. The slim wooden bobbins would be carved by the men of the household in the evenings or on days when it was not possible to take out the boats. Patterns were often incised into the wood, as were dates and the names of loved ones, sometimes with crude colours pressed into them, so that each bobbin became a unique little object in the collection of the maker. Others were made as love tokens or as remembrances of family members passed away. Not being willingly disposed of, bobbins that had lost their rounded top might have a red ball of sealing wax melted on. A popular method of decoration was to stain the bobbin with aqua fortis, the historical name for nitric acid, which gave the wood a uniquely mottled surface.

Honiton lacemaking operated via a system of piece work. The individual pieces or sprigs of lace woven in the cottages would be sent to a central bleaching house to ensure that they were all the same shade of pure white, before they were sewn together to take whatever form was required – a dress flounce, a collar, a pair of cuffs. The women were paid by the sprig, so they would often work long hours in order to produce as many sprigs as possible. Those dealers with a reputation for particular stringency would go so far as to weigh the fine cotton threads doled out to each worker and then weigh the completed sprigs at the end, to ensure that scraps of cotton were not being retained to be made into additional pieces that might be sold on the side. It was low-paid, highly skilled work, and those pieces that survive today are a testament to the women artists who created them.

In the early years of the nineteenth century, whilst handmade lace was still highly prized, there was change afoot in manufacture. There had been an interest expressed by emerging industrialists in the late eighteenth century in producing a machine-made lace. This was eventually realised by John Heathcoat of Derby. Heathcoat was born in 1763 and by the age of sixteen had decided that the greatest wish of his professional life was to invent a lace-making machine. He described his early researches, watching lacemakers at work: 'I set to work to inform myself in what peculiarity in the texture of pillow lace consisted and for this purpose obtained a sight of the process of making it. A pretty heap of chaotic material I found it! Like peas in a frying pan dancing about.' He set about unpicking a piece of lace in order to understand its construction, making sense of the mysterious dancing threads. The eventual result was a frame upon which he could add multiple threads, and in 1808 he took out a patent for the bobbin-net machine. He began to make his hexagonal twisted net, which could be woven as a plain cloth or with embroidered motifs in a tamboured chain stitch. The business thrived, and garments of machine net became all the rage. Ironically, the early machine-made garments were expensive, reflecting the nature of the innovative technology. This was a techno-textile that commanded a high price.

As Heathcoat's business thrived, so he fell victim to the Luddites. Textile workers, whose way of life and labour practices were being threatened by industrialisation, broke the machines that they held responsible for the change. In 1816 John Heathcoat's mills in Loughborough were attacked and fifty-five of his lace frames were smashed. He decided to relocate to a part of the country that was less notorious for such activity, moving to the mid-Devon town of Tiverton, where he opened a large factory. It brought him to the same part of the world as the Honiton lacemakers whose livelihoods his invention had begun to impact.

By the 1830s handmade lace had begun to fall from favour. The machine-made alternatives were becoming more affordable and it was becoming impossible for lacemakers to compete. An 1841 newspaper report from the region described 'destitute lace makers', and in the Report on the Employment of Children that was published in 1843 a local lace dealer from the town of Exmouth said that 'the nominal value of the hand-made lace had fallen off at least 60 or 70 per cent'. A recent find in the small Devon village of Woodbury highlighted the plight of the lacemakers, and also the source of their resurgence. Upon a handkerchief of eau-de-nil satin, a message written in lace rib read: 'To her most Gracious Majesty, Queen Victoria, with humble gratitude from the poor lace makers of Woodbury Salterton.' Upon another piece that was covered with small samples of different lace trimmings were woven the words: 'To her most Gracious Majesty with the humble hope of future orders'. Here then was to be the salvation of the Honiton lace industry, in the shape of the young Queen, who did indeed support the handmade bobbin-lace industry with one of its most significant commissions.

Miss Jane Bidney was appointed as 'Lace Manufacturer in Ordinary to Her Majesty' on 14 August 1837, and by 1839 she was engaged with the creation of her most ambitious work – the Honiton lace veil and flounces for the Queen's wedding dress. The lace was made from a thread so fine that it is no longer manufactured. The yards of lace were the product of hundreds of hours by many hands. On 15 February 1840, after the ceremony had taken place, *Woolmer's Exeter and Plymouth Gazette* reported, 'At Beer in the afternoon about 150 of the lacemakers who had the honour of working on Her Majesty's Bridal Dress drank tea at the New Inn, her Majesty so well pleased with the dress that Miss Jane Bidney, who superintended its execution, sent down Ten Pounds for the purpose.' In order to preserve its uniqueness, Miss Bidney destroyed the designs for the wedding lace after it was made, so that it could never be copied. The lace was to remain one of Queen Victoria's most treasured possessions. Throughout her life, and long after the death of Prince Albert, she wore the flounce from her dress and her veil to a variety of ceremonial occasions. She even allowed it to be worn at subsequent weddings – her daughter Princess Beatrice being photographed wearing the lace on her own wedding day in 1885.

This important contribution to the Honiton lace industry saw a great surge in popularity, and designers in the area were sought-after for their artistry. One of the prominent makers and dealers was John Tucker, whose daughter Mary designed the wedding lace for the family's fashionable shop in London and was responsible for the design of another royal bride's lace in 1863, when Princess Alexandra of Denmark married Edward, Prince of Wales. Her cousin who ran their shop, located at 1 Percy Street in London, wrote to Mary on 28 February 1863, just ten days before the wedding, 'I have yours of the 27th instant & the Box with Royal Lace is to hand & I think looks most beautiful and I hope will give satisfaction, indeed I do not see how it can be otherwise.' Thanks to these high-profile commissions, handmade lace became, in the second half of the nineteenth century, a prized possession once more.

The growing availability of both hand and machine lace democratised the cloth, so that by the middle of the century it was available to more people, who could acquire it to suit their budget. The incomplete scraps that Anne carefully fixed into her diary vary in type and quality. Some of the larger pieces graced evening dresses that Anne and her friends wore to parties, decorating the colourful silk beneath with an extra layer of embellishment. Above one such piece Anne wrote, 'Blond worn by Anne, Fanny and Emma Taylor at their first ball.' Blond lace originated in France, and rather than being woven from cotton, it was a pale-cream silk thread that lent the resulting cloth an elegant sheen that was perfectly captured in candlelight, icing their evening gowns. Narrow lace trims were much cheaper and might be bought at a draper's or haberdashery counter by the yard to apply to underwear or to edge a handkerchief.

Ephemeral though it may seem, lace did also serve a practical purpose in terms of dress. One of the lacy frills that Anne has captured on her pages is labelled, 'Part of a cuff bought in Liverpool July 1840.' Lace collars and cuffs were a popular decorative feature in the middle of the nineteenth century, with an additional function. The complexity attached to the laundering of clothes meant that any means of protecting garments from dirt or wear was welcomed. Collars and cuffs were designed to be detachable, not belonging to any one garment, but tacked on at the neck and wrists. They could be removed at the end of the day and laundered. They could be whitened and pressed, ready for wear again on another day and another dress, protecting the garment itself from soiling.

Lace is where Anne's story and my own became entwined. Were it not for that desire to learn a traditional textile technique as a young woman, I would never have joined the lace group amongst whose members was the custodian of Anne's diary. In the years since, and along the path of discovering Anne's life, I realise that whilst our experiences of the world inevitably differ, there is that which connects us: female friendship and an appreciation for the threads of textiles woven into our lives.

CHAPTER 5

The Chemistry of Calico

Charlotte Dugdale Sykes

There are few industries which require the same amount
of skill and practical ability, combined with so much
science and art, as this wonderful manufacture.

Antonio Sansone, *The Printing of Cotton Fabrics*, 1887

Jane Sykes entered Anne's album with her wedding dress, her plain lilac
silk worn in 1833. On that same page of new beginnings, and the very first
page that Anne herself wrote in the book after Adam's entry on the first
leaf, sits evidence of Jane's daughter Charlotte's own entrance into the
world. A printed wool challis was, according to the caption, the dress that
Jane Sykes wore for the occasion of her daughter's christening in 1836,
and beneath this were the first printed cotton samples worn by Jane's new
daughter – Anne Sykes's niece – Charlotte Dugdale Sykes: the Dugdale
being a tribute to Adam and William's mother, Charlotte Dugdale. The
cottons bear the hallmarks of a child's dress, the tiny floral repeats suited
to the small body within. There are two little samples dating to 1846 that
are both labelled with Charlotte's name: a pink floral cotton and a colourful wool, worn by Charlotte when she was ten years old. An entire page
is devoted to Charlotte a little further on. Anne inscribed the year 1848

in the centre of the page, the eight swatches of cotton and wool radiating outwards – the twelve-year-old Charlotte being decked out in white cottons printed with a variety of coloured repeats, or wrapped more warmly against the Lancashire winds in turquoise wool.

Charlotte's father died before she reached her first birthday and so her world revolved around her mother, Jane. At the age of twelve, the first snippet of silk appears in her wardrobe, a sign of her growing maturity, shedding the cotton of her youth and, for special occasions only, donning the sophistication of navy-blue-and-white striped silk. It was the bright spectrum of printed cotton, however, that was oh-so-briefly at the centre of her family's world – her father William earning his livelihood from the fabric designs that he created until his untimely death, before his baby daughter ever had a chance to know him. If silk was the indicator of wealth, then printed cotton was the mark of the innovator, a wearer who held herself up as an arbiter of new technologies and new processes.

Charlotte's life weaves in and out of the pages, appearing sporadically but consistently, the changing contents of her wardrobe capturing a life in flux, from childhood to that of a young woman; from her mother's only child and companion to her marriage and life as the wife of a prosperous cotton broker in Liverpool. Textiles sit at the heart of Charlotte's existence, central to the employment of both her father and her husband. Casting our eyes back towards her, as with the myriad other lives in Anne's book, our image of Charlotte is constructed through the snippets of textiles that she left behind. Many of these, in Charlotte's case, are brilliantly coloured printed cottons: testaments both to the career of her father William Sykes, a junior partner and designer in the Broad Oak calico printworks in Accrington, and to her husband John, whose brokering of the cotton on arrival into the port of Liverpool determined access to the raw material of the manufacturers around Lancashire.

Her printed cottons represented the cutting-edge technologies of textile design that were emerging from the mills and printworks of

Lancashire in the 1830s and 1840s, producing designs of a complexity and variety never before seen, drenching garments in colours and patterns that can only really be appreciated from the cloth itself. Mid-nineteenth-century design has found itself marginalised, the undervalued filling between the Regency and Romantic periods and the drama of the crinoline, aniline dyes and bustle that was to follow. Yet even a cursory glance at those captured cloths in Anne's album, and in the trade pattern books of the period, reveals an explosion of colour and content in contemporary design practices.

Anne's book is full of fashionable cotton. During the first half of the eighteenth century, when Indian chintzes had become all the rage in fashionable circles and cotton became king, colourful prints found their way into households around Western Europe and North America. For decades the traditional methods of printing cotton were applied. Beautifully carved wooden blocks in hundreds of patterns were the skilled printer's tool, with an eye for the placement of each block on the length of cotton to ensure the smooth repeats. It was a trade that found its way to Britain along with the raw material itself. Godfrey Smith's 1756 edition of *The Laboratory; or, School of Arts*, published in London, described the complexity of the calico printer's art, which began with the block: 'In this the artificer exerts his skill, not only to keep the pattern he has before him drawn upon a block but by his judgement to improve and finish the design to greater perfection.' Smith continued that not all cutters were the same and might 'mangle' the pattern drawn on the block, so that no matter how good the original design, it would never appear at its best, with inferior cutting. He described the time-consuming processes of applying colours and mordants to fix the chosen shades, applying the woodblocks and knocking the pattern onto the fabric with mallets. The lengths of cotton moved from one table to the next, a process that would be repeated if a 'second colour is to be grounded in'. In the eighteenth century most of the British calico printers operated in areas along the banks of the River Thames, but as the industrial production of cotton gathered pace in the North of England in the early decades of the nineteenth century, so the processes associated with its finishing moved there too. Calico printworks sprang up in towns around Lancashire that were also dominated by the larger spinning mills, these subsidiary practices waiting to collect the snowy products of the relentless power looms.

A calico printer at work.

Two of these printworks are mentioned by name in Anne's album: the Broad Oak printworks in Accrington, and the Primrose Printworks situated in Clitheroe, the town in which Anne was born. From amongst the many hundreds of printed cottons in the book, only six acknowledge the origin of the cloth, but these six draw Anne into that world of textiles. Near the start of her book, underneath the pretty printed cottons that belonged to the infant Charlotte, Anne pasted in a beautifully intricate patterned cotton above which she wrote, 'Jane's dress an

Oak print given her by William in old times.' It is a poignant entry, the 'old times' referring to the brief period of Jane's marriage to Adam's brother, William, before his untimely death in 1837. It captures the art of the printer in a six-inch-square fragment: broad stripes of trailing floral repeats interspersed with the then-fashionable motif in the paisley tradition. Soft pinks and greens mix with darker shades against the cream background. William had been employed as a designer, so it is tempting to imagine that this gift to his young wife was a pattern of his own creation, brought to colourful life in yard upon yard of brilliant cloth.

The technologies associated with printing are revealed in records that the Lightfoot family, the owners of Broad Oak, left behind. Broad Oak was the most important calico printworks in Accrington, and John Lightfoot was its chief chemist, tasked with the complexities of dye recipes. Twenty-eight notebooks were created by Lightfoot, who filled the pages with dated entries – describing problems that could arise and outlining experiments in different dyes and chemicals to produce new colours, different patterns. These are diaries of an entirely different kind to Anne's album, detailing the day-to-day problem-solving and innovative thinking that characterised textile production in the middle of the nineteenth century. The Broad Oak works were still operating in the early years of the twentieth century, and photographs exist of the long wooden tables in the printing sheds, with the printers standing in rolled-up shirt sleeves. Woodblocks in hand, they go through the same motions as their forebears a century earlier – plain white cotton in front of them and the fruits of their labour hanging like ceremonial banners around them as they work.

James Thomson was born in 1779 and, after graduating from Glasgow University, was engaged as a chemist at the printworks owned by Messrs Peel of Church Bank, Accrington. In 1811 he left to establish his own printworks in Clitheroe and one of his first partners was Mr James Burton, Anne's father. An 1869 memoir described this working relationship: 'the chief cause or attraction of intimacy between Mr Thomson and him consisted in Mr Burton's natural genius and leanings towards mechanism, having a large cellar arranged and fitted up with turning lathes and other conveniences and facilities for his favourite pursuit'. The men would meet at Burton's house to experiment with the new mechanical possibilities of textile manufacture, an environment of innovation and exploration under Anne's own roof, her connection with the Primrose Printworks stretching back to her childhood. It is no surprise that James Thomson was drawn to the new mechanical adventures that were beginning to emerge in the manufacturing world – namely, the slim, engraved copper rollers that were revolutionising textile printing. Primrose and Broad Oak, those establishments mentioned by Anne in the album, were two of many dozens of calico printworks operating in the North of England at this time, the evidence of which can still be found in collections around the UK.

In the late eighteenth century, engraved copper plates measuring usually around thirty-six inches square were used in many instances instead of woodblocks to create a more sharply realised pattern on the cloth. By the 1820s these flat copper plates were being made in the round – the resultant cylinders meaning that cloth could be printed continuously as the rollers turned and the cloth ran beneath. James Thomson was especially keen to embrace this evolution in print manufacture and went to great lengths to ensure the quality of his men and materials. 'Mr Thomson resolved to have the engraving performed upon his own establishment, and not only so, but his resolution pushed still further. He would have the workmen for this artistic department, manufactured, so to speak, on his premises too.' Thomson hired a master under whose instruction he placed a number of apprentices to learn the trade of the engraver and thus keep all of his design processes in-house. The results of his visionary endeavours find themselves in Anne's album. Early in the volume there is a striking cream-and-brown striped cotton interspersed with pale zigzags and florals that reads, 'Maureen Mary & Anne Burton a Primrose Print.' Here is Anne Burton, still a young unmarried woman in her father's home, wearing the cutting-edge cottons of his business partner at Primrose. Thomson's own expertise in the arts of chemistry and how that could relate to dye technologies, coupled with his insistence on the good design of his engraved cylindrical patterns, created some dazzling outcomes. On page 20 of the album a cotton dress fragment belonging to Mercy Taylor is described as being 'printed at Primrose'. It is a shaded ombré – the process of colours graduating into one another – fading from the brightest magenta through to a paler shade and cut through at intervals with a wavy stripe in emerald green. If the four inches of fabric still sing from the page today, what impact must an entire dress have made?

The subsidiary industries that were part of the manufacturing processes that brought these textiles to life exist in the shadows of other narratives about the history of cotton production and finishing. The engravers were skilled artisans in their own right, and only a few calico printers had their own in-house professionals. Most printers in Lancashire sent their designs out to one of more than a dozen engraving workshops. Painted designs were drawn up and these were etched onto the copper. Some designs required up to four rollers to complete one pattern, each of the cylinders adding another layer of pattern and colour to enrich the cloth. Engraving was charged per roller, and the price varied depending on the complexity of the design. Only a fraction of the engraver's art is visible on each of the swatches that Anne saved in her book, but they are enough to appreciate the vision of the designer, the skill of the engraver and the precision of the printer, brought to bear at each stage of the fabric's creation before it ever found its way to a dressmaker to be made into a garment.

The designs themselves were subject to variations in taste and fashion. Anne brought together a huge variety of colours and styles that were the products of these designers at work, following contemporary trends. Some of the cottons feature coral motifs that mirrored the mid-nineteenth-century fascination with the natural world and the desire to discover and delineate species of flora and fauna. Some of the 1830s samples are sharply geometric, in patterns that might appear more suited to the Art Deco design that was fashionable a century later, whilst other patterns experiment with shading techniques that are almost three-dimensional at first glance. That Anne labelled a handful of these patterns with the printworks of their origin attests to the centrality of fabric in her world – a world of colour and pattern that was reaching the peak of its innovation during her lifetime.

Pattern books were essential records in the industry. They were created not as collections of a company's history, but purely for business purposes, either to show customers the range of available patterns or as records of design trends that had evolved. Each company kept their swatches in books that were not dissimilar to Anne's own album, although their motives were very different. Nonetheless, they capture the same sense of vivid colour that is absent from popular imaginings of the early Victorians. When the British textile industry began its sad decline in the middle of the twentieth century the thousands of pattern books that spoke of the heritage of an industry in glorious technicolour were mostly destroyed. Their value went unrecognised and they found themselves on the bonfires that accompanied the destruction of the mills, or in the very rivers that had powered the machinery that once brought the designs to life. Luckily some were saved, so there are sporadic pattern records for some businesses across some of the years that they were active. There is a possibility that, with a forensic analysis, patterns that have been preserved by Anne might meet their twin in these trade books, a cotton thread connecting maker with wearer, and that some of the other mills that populate Anne's album might be identified. For now, however, these connections can only be guessed at, with pattern books scattered in institutions around the UK.

When confronted with the photographic portraits of men, women and children from the mid-nineteenth century it is all too tempting to believe what we see before our eyes. The unsmiling faces and the sepia tones drain their lives of colour and emotion. This has become a part of the popular chronicling of the nineteenth century, and yet to turn the pages of Anne's album is to be let into a well-kept secret. These were not colourless people, but ones who lived in an age of technical innovation and fast-paced change. Charlotte and Anne wore techno-textiles that were every bit as advanced then as smart fabrics might be in the twenty-first century. They clothed themselves in the brightest of colours and the busiest of patterns – patterns designed in a world of sartorial invention and experimentation that relied on creativity and craftsmanship. These skills still survive in certain parts of the world. India has an artisanal woodblock-printing tradition that has transcended the centuries, maintaining practices that William Sykes and James Thomson would still recognise. So much of Lancashire's cotton-printing heritage, however, is found now only in the precious swatches left behind. In the pattern books and in Anne's album we see the ghosts of an industry that was once a kaleidoscope of colour.

Anne's appreciation for this industry went beyond the purely aesthetic. The very motive for her collection – that desire to memorialise her life and her acquaintances through the clothes they wore – adds a poignant element to the fabric that has survived. And it was a swatch of printed cotton that was the key to unlocking the contents of the entire album. Anne chose to wear a sprigged floral printed cotton for the greatest adventure of her life and recorded this fact for posterity. When she wrote that caption, the single acknowledgement of her identity as the keeper of the diary's contents – 'Anne Sykes May 1840. The first dress I wore in Singapore, Nov 1840' – she unwittingly allowed us into her world.

It was a moment of breathtaking revelation for me. After transcribing so many of the tiny captions and wondering over and over again who might have been the person behind the meticulous handwriting and carefully scissored scraps, here she was. Questions began to tumble around in my head, but briefly I just sat and marvelled over that little floral cotton fragment and its wondrous annotation. It was a momentary lapse in Anne's otherwise disciplined description of her swatches. She never again acknowledged herself or captioned anything else in the first person. The journey she had embarked upon had perhaps been such a momentous occasion in her own life that the desire to own it was overwhelming. I shall be ever grateful that she did, for without it her album would have remained stubbornly anonymous – a lovely curiosity, but one that was adrift from its roots. This was the code-breaker, and now all I had to do was follow the clues that it unlocked.

~

Almost exactly two years after her marriage, Anne stood on the deck of the sailing boat that had been her home for almost four months. She was standing alongside Adam and surveyed the harbour of Singapore, a world away from the industrial landscape of her native Lancashire; the other side of the world, in fact. She would miss the early years of her little niece's childhood, growing up far away in the North of England. Charlotte was four years old when they left, and she would be a much older girl before she saw her aunt and uncle again.

As they approached their journey's end, Anne must have unfolded the floral printed cotton dress from the trunk in their cabin, smoothing its familiar pattern and recalling home. It was her dress of choice for this auspicious moment and so, bonnet secured by a bright ribbon tied under her chin and a shawl about her shoulders, she faced the unknown. In a garment woven and printed by the machines of her home and her family, she arrived in this colonial outpost, friendless but for Adam, recording, 'The first dress I wore . . .'

Abroad

The many layers of the 1850s.

This is the Dress my charming Anne
was married in —

And this is the Vest I had
on at the time of Styles

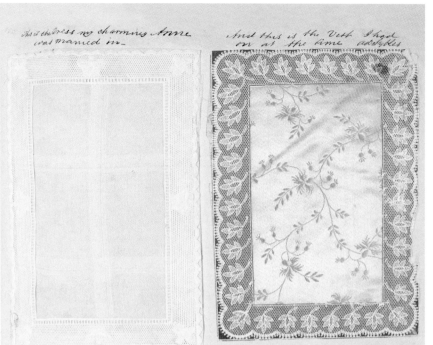

This is the Lace, That trimmed the Vest
That my charming Anne was married in —

This is the Dress she wore after the Wedding
— At Breakfast —

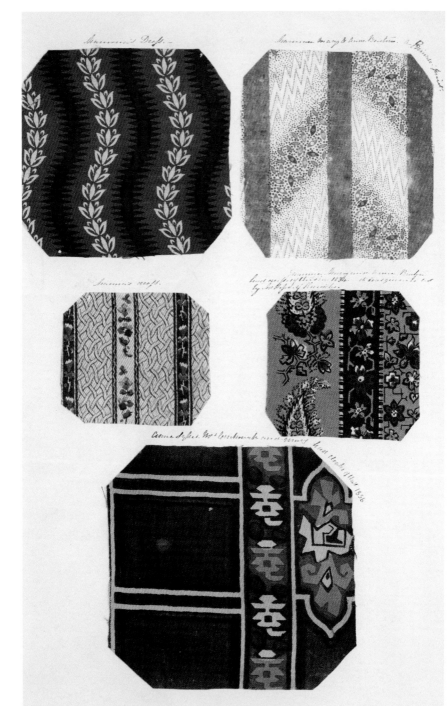

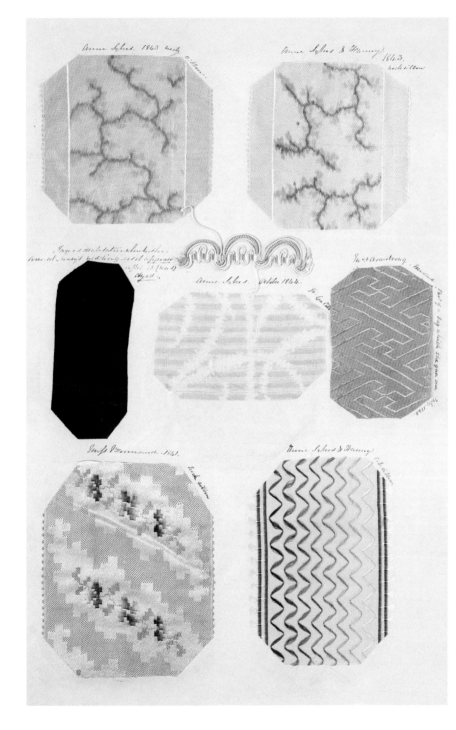

Anne Sykes. Malta. Feby 1840.

Anne Sykes May 1840. The first dress I wore in Singapore Nov. 1840.

Anne Sykes. Malta. Feby 1840.

Anne Sykes. Malta. Feby 1840.

Drawing-room damask. Singapore. May 1841.

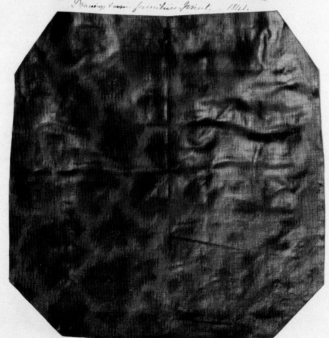

Drawing-room furniture print. 1841.

Mrs Balestier

Mrs Balestier

Mrs Balestier

Part of the "Pirate's Flag).
Taken in Borneo. by the Admiral.
1845.

(Mrs. Sykes & Kenny).

April 1845.

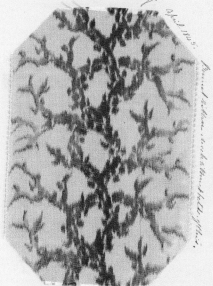

Gp. Sykes birthday slippers
July 12th 1846.

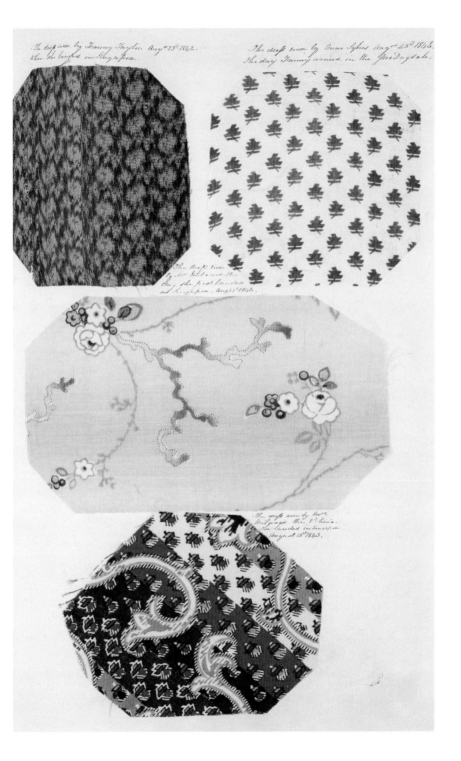

Anne & Fanny. a cush. sent overland. (by Miss Bowman)

June 1846

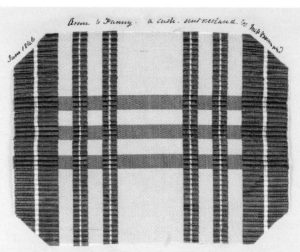

Mrs Willie's Wedding Dress. 1840.

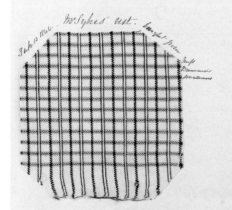

Mr Sykes' vest.

July 13 1846.

Fanny's sash, given John
by Mrs Sykes.
Sash. White & scarlet. Sleeves.

Mrs Unsworth 1846.

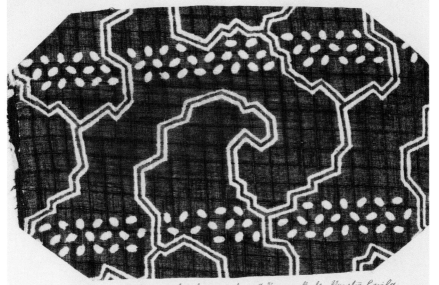

Emma Taylor's sash. at Searcy Bale Preston Guild
Sept 1842.

Mandarin Satin

Anne & Mess. & Fanny Taylor's

Mary's

The Dresses worn at Miss Wrigley's dance. January. 1845.

Hannah Wrigley's dress. with two deep black lace flounces.

Harriet Ashton's dress. trimmed with
two deep white lace flounces.

Sarah Simmons's Dress
with 2 deep white lace flounces.

Harriet Ashton & Jane's dress a mandarin satin

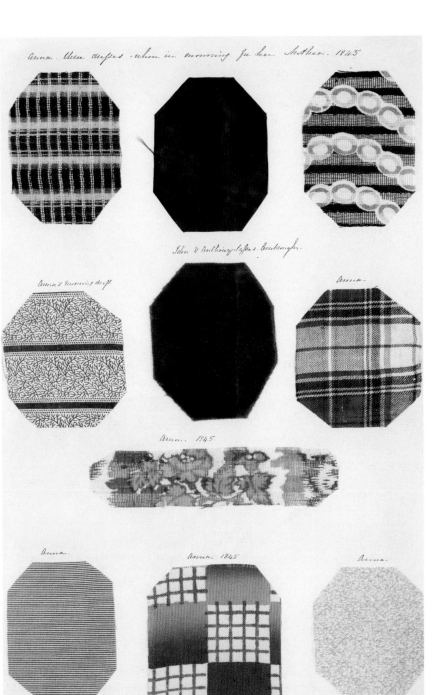

Anna. Anna dresses when in mourning for her Mother. 1843

John & Anthony Sister's Exchange.

Anna's mourning dress

Anna.

Anna. 1845

Anna.

Anna. 1845

Anna.

Hannah Wrigley's Fancy Ball dress, for the character of
"Dolly Varden".

Hannah Wrigley.

Hannah Wrigley.

Hannah Wrigley's wrapping dress, worn with 2
white lace flounces.

Margaret Ellen & Catherine from Preston 1862

Mrs Cavene

Margaret & Ellen

Margaret & Ellen

Ellen's wedding dress & 2 Bridesmaids

Ellen Charnock

Margaret Charnock

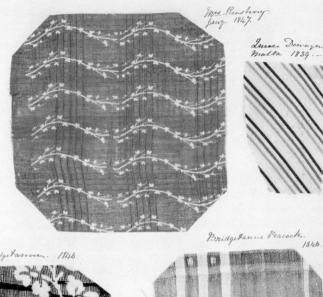

Mrs. Rewsbery
Jany 1847.

Queen Dowager dress
Malta 1839.—

Bridget Anne. 1846

Bridget Anne Peacock.
1846

Bridget Anne.

Bridget Anne. 1839.

CHAPTER 6

The First Dress I Wore . . .

Anne & Adam Sykes

'Singapore ahoy!' exclaimed the man at the mast head as
the white houses and shipping rose above the horizon
while we were abreast of the large red cliffs.

J. T. Thomson, *Some Glimpses into Life in the Far East*, 1865

The white cotton of the dress that Anne wore as she disembarked and
set foot on Singaporean soil is finely woven, printed first with a delicate
blue fleck and then overprinted with trailing sepia tendrils, small flowers
picked out in pink and green. It was an important garment for Anne, to
be marked as the first that she wore in this small settlement on the other
side of the world, far from home.

Her destiny was tied, inevitably for a middle-class woman in the mid-
nineteenth century, to her husband, and it was Adam's fortunes that
directed the path of Anne's life in such an unlikely direction. In 1833 Adam
had started to work for the merchant firm of Robert Wise, whose trade
with the Far East would shape his professional career. Having already
headed up commercial operations in Singapore for those five years prior
to his marriage, opportunities arose once again. As his professional star
continued to rise, Adam found himself faced once more with the offer of

work in the emerging Singaporean merchant world. This time he had a twenty-three-year-old bride who would accompany him on his journey.

The briefest of entries in the 'Shipping Intelligence' column of the *Singapore Free Press and Mercantile Advertiser* captures Anne's arrival in Singapore on 31 October 1840: 'By the *Friends* Mrs Sykes. Adam Sykes.' That is all. Nothing more to convey the hardship of months at sea or the uncertainties of a new life and a culture unknown. The ship *Friends* was a 400-ton copper-fastened packet sailing ship, one of the many vessels that plied its trade around the world transporting mail, trade-cargo and passengers on regular routes. An early advertisement includes a lithograph of the *Friends* at full sail, an optimistic illustration, pennant flying from the mast as it forges its path across the waves. Passengers were assured of its 'superior furnished accommodation', with the added bonus of a cow on board to supply them with fresh milk.

On 12 July 1840 *Friends* set sail from Liverpool under the command of Captain Arnold, taking Adam and Anne on their long voyage to a new life. We are allowed the briefest of glimpses of this momentous occasion: a small fragment of white lace, above which Anne writes, 'Part of a cuff bought in Liverpool July 1840.' Passengers were advised to ensure that their luggage arrived in advance to be loaded onto the ship – trunks that contained the barest of essentials for an as-yet-unknown future, objects that had been carefully considered, pored over in advance, packed and repacked. New clothes were ordered, printed cotton dresses folded and laid amongst undergarments, shawls, shoes and stockings. And tucked into one of these trunks was Anne's album, her pink silk-covered book with its thin pale-blue pages mostly blank, like any diary awaiting the promise of experiences yet to come.

How many garments did Adam feel were necessary when he was packing his trunks for life in Singapore with his new bride Anne? He was already familiar with both the mercantile community and the climate of the settlement when they departed from England in July 1840. Over the course of the next seven years Anne would include seventeen vests that belonged to Adam during their time abroad. Unlike the majority of the other garments recorded in the diary, she was likely to offer details of their origins. Against a cream-and-brown floral silk, Anne wrote, 'Adam's favourite vest new in 1841 p. "Friends"', referring to the now-familiar boat by which the new vest arrived. Two years later another vest, this time a cream-coloured garment with a thick raised velvet pile, had arrived via the same route: 'Adam's vest new on his birthday July 12th 1843 p "Friends".' Many of the vests that Anne included were gifts to Adam, either from her or from other family members and friends. Anne's brother Edward sent Adam a rich black velvet vest in 1846, and above a bright silk tartan in squares of green, red, blue and black Anne wrote, 'Mr Sykes' vest given to him by Mr Campbell and worn on his birthday July 12th 1844'. Another colourful plaid, this time in a soft wool, was described as 'Adam's vest given to him by Mr Harvey'. Since both Mr Campbell and Mr Harvey appear as merchants participating in the same professional sphere as Adam, these gifts indicate the ties that bound the European community in Singapore during these tumultuous years.

Anne's first impressions of Singapore must have been overwhelming. The sights and sounds of a world that was so culturally different from her own, in a pre-digital age, are almost impossible to imagine now. Any ideas that she must have had of the tropical archipelago before their departure would have been gleaned from written accounts or perhaps some drawings. No doubt she would have hung on Adam's every description of his own life there prior to their marriage, but her knowledge would have been based on these linguistic observations alone. Visualising such difference was another matter entirely. It is similarly difficult for us to imagine the realities of mid-nineteenth-century Singapore, since so little of it remains today.

Thanks to John Turnbull Thomson, an amateur artist who was appointed as Government Surveyor for the Straits Settlements in 1841, there are watercolours that show us Singapore as Anne would have known it. In one, titled *The Esplanade*, he captures the social scenes of that waterside area, which was popular for promenading amongst the European residents of Singapore. An open carriage bowls along, with a lady and gentleman clad in top hat and bonnet – markers of their cultural status that made no concession to climate or local aesthetics. Another lady sits side-saddle in a black riding habit on a white horse, whilst other members of their community walk in tandem.

View of the town and roads of Singapore from the government hill,
by Robert James Elliot, published 1828.

The local Malay residents feature, clad in their entirely more suitable garments: loose white cottons and colourful Chinese ensembles. In the background the evidence of commerce is writ large in bricks and mortar, sturdy white buildings at odds with the traditional Malay architecture, and the spire of the Anglican church piercing the bright sky. In another composition, captured at the top of Government Hill and looking out over the harbour, the colonial expansion of what was so recently a small settlement is all too obvious. Rows of newly built residences crowd the banks of the river and you can almost hear the tumult arising from the numerous ships at anchor in the harbour, the pace of trade relentless.

Thomson evoked much of life as he saw it. He painted Malay men and women in their homes, seated on mats and clad in traditional garments. He drew soldiers stationed in the region mingling with the merchants and their wives, and he captured the landscape, the architecture, the flora and the fauna, all of which Anne would have been confronted with in a colourful assault on the senses as she stepped ashore. As she familiarised herself with the immediate locale, she would have seen gambier, the vine-like plant used in dye processes, and pepper plantations, Chinese lanterns and many sailed junks at anchor. She would have heard the unfamiliar cries of the market traders and the array of languages that punctuated life in a trading community.

~

Adam Sykes was a prominent figure amongst the European traders. He was one of the early committee members of the Singapore Chamber of Commerce, contributing to the frequent dialogue that flew back and forth between the governing bodies and official representatives of Crown and country. Untangling the business interests and partnerships of Adam during his professional career revealed a dizzying network of connections. Records were scarce, but tantalising. His name appeared in contemporary newspaper reports. He was mentioned on a handful of occasions in early published histories of Singapore. He was acknowledged on subscription committees for charitable works. But each time it was his name alone that placed him in these activities. Of the colour of his world, his feelings, his personality, there was nothing. It was an oddly frustrating endeavour. Each time my eyes locked onto the name Sykes in the myriad digital archives in which I found myself buried, my heart flipped at the possibility of some other detail that might fill in the blanks of their lives. It was strange to have whispers of intimacy, owning a scrap of his dressing gown or favourite velvet vest – and yet of the man himself, nothing.

Yet each titbit of information did, somehow, begin to shape at least the outline of a life, once it was reconciled with all of the other clues. When Wise's closed down in 1838 Adam joined the trading company of Boustead, Schwabe and Co. and seemingly became great friends with Edward Boustead, a merchant of long standing in the settlement, having founded his initial venture in 1830. Mr Boustead appears on several occasions in Anne's diary, both as gift-giver, in the shape of two dresses received by Anne, and as gift recipient. Anne recorded against a patterned silk that it was 'From Miss Brennand Mr Boustead's vest Aug 1846 which we sent him'. A letter written by another merchant's wife in 1834 described Mr Boustead thus: 'He has a fine gentlemanly appearance and is the most active merchant here.'

The merchants in Singapore were the funnel through which trade between East and West was possible. They were the go-betweens, earning between 0.5 and 1 per cent commission on the goods that they arranged to pass through their hands, from Chinese bazaar to British port. One of the first merchants, Alexander Guthrie, described the reciprocal nature of his business endeavours in an issue of *The Straits Times* in the 1840s. His job was to 'ship out the spices, nutmegs and pepper of the East and bring in the knives of Sheffield, the cotton goods of Lancashire and the other substantial exports of Victorian England'. Whilst they lived in residences amongst the gambier plantations, the merchants worked within the bustle of the harbour, able to coordinate the consignments arriving in the port. Edward Boustead traded from a property known, somewhat grandly, as the 'Seven-and-Twenty Pillar House' and it was from here that Adam undertook his daily responsibilities.

Adam may already have been in partnership with one Gustav Schwabe, who joined Boustead's and became a partner in 1834. Boustead, Schwabe and Co. worked with Butler, Sykes and Co. as well as Sykes, Schwabe and Co., the various interests overlapping with the frequent forging and dissolving of connections. Newspaper reports detailed these complexities in 1838, announcing, 'Notice is hereby given that the Partnership heretofore subsisting between us the under-signed, Adam Sykes, Edward Little, Edward Boustead, Gustav Christian Schwabe and Benjamin Butler is this day dissolved.' An almost identical announcement appeared in 1854 between most of the same parties. It was a financially strategic back and forth that had nothing to do with relationships and everything to do with commercial strategies, as the partners navigated the fickle and fast-paced world of trade in the Straits Settlement, a place where long-term investment was not possible, given the often volatile political situations in the region. Trade was fast and unpredictable, with mercurial dealings that required quick thinking and moveable expectations.

During his time in Singapore, Adam was an active member of the various organisations that were established to further the interests of the European community, including being a member of the Chamber of Commerce and one of the jury members of the Grand Jury, the system via which merchants tried to regulate both commercial concerns and criminal ones. It was not a successful institution, although in lieu of an official police and legal infrastructure, it was sometimes the only means by which grievances might be settled. As well as offering advice to the governors of the settlement, the Grand Jury also dealt with more serious matters. In 1835 Adam sat on the jury for the murder trial of one Nasing Row, who was accused of killing Lalloo Sing. The Grand Jury found 'a true bill' against the prisoner, who was immediately arraigned for the murder. It was an important case, since Nasing Row was the son of a minor rajah and so was treated with great deference by his subjects, whilst the victim was a convict overseer. Such were the life-changing decisions that Adam Sykes was concerned with, as he shaped his career in the settlement.

In 1844 the body petitioned for a public meeting to discuss the founding of a Pauper Hospital, Adam Sykes being listed as one of the petitioners.

As befitted a man of his standing in the community and the expectations of a benevolent, respectable businessman, Adam accepted that he would undertake such duties outside his mercantile interests with an appropriately philanthropic ambition. He sat as Foreman to the Grand Jury in the mid-1840s, his status cemented by the conferring of the title and all that it might bring, and he contributed to various funds aimed at broadening the facilities of the settlement.

Some of these compatriots, competitors and colleagues of Adam feature in the pages of Anne's diary. They are infrequent guests, but a few swatches are present. A white cotton with a blue floral repeat belonged to Mr Wise in 1844 – Adam's first employer captured in a colourful square; a brown, black and cream silk plush belonged to the merchant John Connolly; and a multicoloured wool tartan was worn by Mr Duff. Mr Bergeest showed a predilection for the then-fashionable coral motifs for his waistcoats, whilst Mr DeWinde owned a wide variety of figured cotton, wool and silk examples. There is also the inclusion of a single cravat, a silk gauze swatch in blue and white that is described as Manila silk. Adam combined the soberness of the industrialist with these brighter accessories, influenced perhaps by the colour of the world around him in Singapore.

Adam appears in the local newspapers as an active member of society, his name listed as one of the first subscribers for the theatre that opened in 1842. Anne, along with all the other merchant wives who were making a life in such an unfamiliar setting, appears not at all in the formal records of the settlement, but she exists in the shadows. Where Adam subscribes to the theatre, Anne is surely there alongside him in the audience. When the merchants are accounted for as attendees at a ball, their wives are there on their arms. When history is written by and about the men whose fortunes built the libraries, churches and courthouses of Singapore, the women were no less present, their lives no less colourful.

But what of Anne whilst Adam was making his presence felt both as trader and as philanthropist? Where was she when Adam was striking deals in the godown warehouses around the harbour, or taking account of the goods leaving on the next ship home? Most of her concerns would have been social and domestic, charged as she would have been with the creation of a comfortable home and a network of friendships. One of the most aesthetically dramatic fragments offers a small glimpse of this early domestic experience of Singapore, and of Anne's decisions as a home-maker as she embarked on her new life. Page 54 of the album is dominated by two striking swatches. The first is a bright cerise fig-ured damask labelled 'Drawing room damask Singapore May 1841', and beneath it is a dark waxed cotton in a leopard print that bears the cap-tion 'Drawing room furniture print 1841'. Anne and Adam had arrived in Singapore at the end of October the previous year and, six months later, Anne was beginning to decorate her new home.

Trying to locate their exact residence is not easy. Adam was recorded as having built two prominent houses, Bonnygrass and Annanbank, adjoining each other on River Valley Road. In 1844 he had purchased the whole area around Institution Hill, along with Dr Mungo Johnston Martin. Martin lived in Annanbank from 1843 to 1846, and his partner Dr Robert Little occupied Bonnygrass for almost forty years, but whether and when Adam and Anne lived in either of these properties is difficult to unpick. Contemporary newspaper records state that having built these houses, Adam '. . . lived close by with his wife'. The building work car-ried out in Singapore in the 1830s and 1840s followed European tastes, constructed in the classical style, with two-storey Palladian villas spring-ing up along the newly built roads of the settlement. They replaced the timber houses and godowns that had previously populated the town, with the rapid expansion changing the face of the swampy land that was flanked by nutmeg and gambier plantations. Most of the residences conformed to these formal styles and included the customary verandah -- an important feature of colonial life that could be used as an additional sitting room, with the added benefits of cooler air if the venetian blinds were kept drawn until the afternoon.

The all-important drawing room was usually situated on the first floor of the house, and this is where Anne would have placed her leopard-print upholstered furniture, shaded in part by the bright damask curtains. Leopard print feels like a curiously modern trend, a fad that leapt into vogue from the 1950s onwards, but it has in fact been fashionable for far longer. This form of animal print had become especially popular in eighteenth-century France, with Louis Bosse's flirtatious engraving *La Matinée* depicting a woman dressed in a loose robe decorated with a deep flounce of leopard print around the hem. A surviving gown from the mid-eighteenth century is woven from a brocade that is patterned with a looping leopard-print ribbon design, and a rare piece of daywear from the 1840s features a leopard-print motif across the entire surface of the dress. This was to be a recurring theme throughout the eighteenth century and into the nineteenth, particularly as travel and expanding imperial ambitions took more people further afield. For Anne, leopard spots may have been her interpretation of the 'other' that she was to experience in this emerging settlement on the far side of the world from industrial Lancashire.

Contemporary views of the expatriate drawing room in Singapore are rare, but those that do survive show large spaces that include upright upholstered chairs, chaises longues and settees, all arranged in groups around the room. A piano might sit in one corner, while round tables covered in photographs, books and plants were evenly spaced. A picture rail accommodated the frames that formed part of the merchant family's identity – views of home and family perhaps. The windows were shaded with venetian or French louvred blinds, and often an opening led on to the verandah, which overlooked the lush gardens of the residence. As Adam was one of the prominent merchants in Singapore and somebody who was clearly keen to acquire land and build properties, it is likely that his own house would have conformed to those that were proving so popular all over town.

Anne's duties would have included all of the minutiae of daily house-keeping that fell to the woman of the house. An existing resident in the settlement, Maria Balestier, was forced to interrupt one of her letters to her sister in 1839, 'I hear a foot on the stairs, it is the cook coming for his orders so for the present he must be attended to . . . you would laugh at the immeasurable things that fill my time.' The Balestiers employed fourteen servants in total, all of them male – a fact that Maria found iso-lating, after moving to a sugar plantation beyond the other residences in the colony. She described the configuration of her new house: 'The floors of our sitting room are covered with new Bengal mats. They are very neat and cool and with the white paint and pictures give the house a much better appearance than you would expect.'

The climate dictated both the use of the house and the times of day that chores might be achieved. Anne's furnishing of her new house in this distant outpost must have seemed both exciting and daunting to a young woman so recently arrived from Northern Hemisphere temperatures. The leopard-print waxed cotton and the splash of cerise damask are the only tantalising glimpses we have of her Singaporean home. No doubt she became increasingly accustomed to acquiring the fixtures and fittings for her home in a different space, and to entertaining in her boldly deco-rated drawing room as cooler air from the verandah circulated.

Anne would undoubtedly have learned new ways of attending to garments and accessories in Singapore, a climate that presented very dif-ferent challenges compared to the wet and cold of home. The servants that she employed would have brought their own strategies with them. The naturalist George Bennett noted in his 1834 memoir of life in the settlement that the indigenous Malay population used the hibiscus plant 'for cleansing shoes by rubbing them with the petals of the flower, which contain a quantity of purplish black astringent juice. After rubbing them over the shoes, they polish the latter by aid of a brush; it certainly prevents the white dresses usually worn in Eastern climates being sullied by the shoes which often happens when blacking has been used.' As a result, the Europeans dubbed the hibiscus plant the 'shoe flower', and it is possible that Anne herself came to apply the 'shoe flower' to her own and her husband's footwear. The everyday of her life is largely hidden from view, however, the mundanity of chores not being considered worthy of recording, so we can only imagine the shape of her day reconstructed from other records, from snippets of biography and contemporary memoirs, and from the colours that she herself preserved in her book.

The only hints of domestic intimacy come in fleeting references to those items of clothing that were designed to be worn indoors, away from formal visitors. These glimpses offer a different view of Anne and Adam, one that was about privacy and their time away from the world of merchant life and daily interactions with others. It was not just waistcoats from Adam's wardrobe that found their way into Anne's record. There are two dressing gowns, one a surprisingly familiar navy-blue-and-red striped design that would not look out of place in a menswear department today; the other a fine wool twill in a brown-and-green paisley design. A bright-blue velvet fragment bears the label 'Mr Sykes's birthday slippers July 12 1846', meaning that we might imagine Adam in all the informality of home, relaxing in dressing gown and slippers, as well as being the man of business, the respected merchant in respectable suit and patterned vest. Similarly Anne marked her own garment in which to relax. A white diamond-patterned cotton fragment is described as 'dressing gown, Anne Sykes, 1844'. Here are Anne and Adam at home and behind closed doors, breathing in the cool morning air on the verandah, wrapped in a white cotton robe and padding across the unseen bedroom in blue velvet slippers. These are the spaces far from the drawing room, the ballroom, the promenading on the Esplanade. These were the objects that marked their early married life in Singapore, when the ambitions of the merchant world might be forgotten for a moment. Here were two young people enjoying their own space amongst a landscape that was so very different from the hills and mills of Lancashire, working out their married life against a backdrop of palms and pepper plantations.

Anne had travelled thousands of miles by sea to embark upon a life that would have been unimaginable only a few years earlier. She had emerged into a world of heat and colour and noise. She had created a home from the fittings and fabrics around her, and she had intermittently recorded her sartorial life in the pages of her material diary. Now it was time to try and forge a life in this bustling community of the unknown.

CHAPTER 7

An American Abroad

Maria Balestier

The society of Singapore is constantly changing, we are
nearly the oldest persons in the settlement, not only in
years but as residents . . .

Maria Balestier, letter to her sister, 1844

Captured across several pages of Anne's book, sixteen dress swatches
simply bear the name 'Mrs Balestier'. Their static paralysis in the album
belies the life that inhabited them. These dresses once floated in a climate
far from the mill towns of Lancashire – lightweight cottons being the
perfect fabric to tolerate the ever-present heat of the Far East. The dress
fragments belonged to Maria, wife of the first American Consul in Singapore and long-time resident of the settlement, a prominent member
of colonial society whose acquaintance Anne made during her time in
the region. Where Anne's thoughts and feelings are absent, Maria Balestier's have survived. Born in Boston, Massachusetts, on 14 July 1785,
Maria Revere was the daughter of the American silversmith and industrialist Paul Revere, who was immortalised in the poem 'Paul Revere's
Ride' by Henry Wadsworth Longfellow. Published in 1860, this was a lyri-
cal account of Revere's 1775 midnight ride to warn his fellow American

patriots of an imminent British attack. Maria married Joseph Balestier in 1823 and eleven years later they left American soil to embark on a new life in Singapore.

The extent of Maria's and Anne's relationship is unknown. There is no surviving correspondence between them, and no indication of a friendship other than a single line in a letter that sixty-one-year-old Maria wrote to her husband Joseph in January 1847. Recuperating from illness in Penang, Maria wrote frequently to Joseph, her letters full of the minutiae of her days, and in one of these missives she asks a favour of her husband: 'I also neglected to ask you to send Mrs Sykes $1.50 for the "Garters" she sent me.' That they liked each other might perhaps be intimated by the inclusion of a small piece of cream silk figured ribbon that Anne placed in her book with the caption 'The ribbon of the cap Mrs Balestier gave me Sept 1846'. The thinnest thread of their connection with each other is there. What does survive, in the letters that Maria sent home to her sister, is an account of life's hardships in this emerging community, one that was being forged at the narrow intersection of jungle and ocean. Singapore was a melee of different cultures, a diverse population trying to carve out an existence that was at odds with the surrounding landscape. Anne's experiences must, in part, have mirrored those described by Maria and by others who recorded life in the settlement.

The mercantile community in Singapore was booming. In 1818 the British statesman Sir Stamford Raffles was appointed Lieutenant Governor of Bencoolen (a possession of the East India Company stretching along the south-west coast of Sumatra), and his greatest ambition was to free the archipelago from the trading monopoly of the Netherlands. Raffles acted as an arbiter for Empire, recognising that the port of Singapore would make an ideal base from which the British merchant fleet could operate. A canny negotiator, he worked alongside local Malay leaders to resolve indigenous disputes in exchange for the rights to establish a British trading post. It was a delicate and complex intervention that resulted ultimately in the dismantling of the Dutch stronghold. The Anglo-Dutch dispute lasted until 1824 when Singapore was formally declared a British colony, and merchants flocked there to establish branches of their business. European businesses were keen to capitalise on the well-placed peninsula's potential. Acting as an intermediary point, Singapore saw goods from China and India pass through en route to ports in Europe and America. Silk, cotton, spices and tea filled the merchant warehouses, destined to be haggled over and reloaded onto one of the dozens of vessels that passed in and out of the harbour. Government Surveyor John Turnbull Thomson described his first impression of the harbour at Singapore as his ship dropped anchor: 'In the foreground, busy canoes, sampans and tongkangs bore their noisy and laughing crews about the harbour. Hundreds of Chinese junks and Malay prows lay further in shore. Behind these stretched a sandy beach, glistening in the sun and overhung by the graceful palm trees, the glory of Singapore planters.' A similar experience was described by Maria in one of her first letters home to Boston, writing to her sister in 1834 of their arrival, '. . . in a very short time boats with natives of different parts of India in all their variety of dress, colour and language surrounded us'.

Like Adam Sykes, Joseph Balestier was first and foremost a merchant, with ambitions to build a trading base of clients from the ships that arrived with cargo for sale. Maria's early months in the colony were based around the harbour, residing above one of the large warehouses on the waterfront, with the world passing before her window. She entertained officers and sea captains, desperate for news of home carried forth on American ships, ever hopeful for a packet of letters and a box of trifles from her distant family. Communication was rare and therefore precious, with letters arriving on average four or perhaps five times a year – the news of family and friends eagerly awaited and pored over, followed by the hurry to write back and find a sea captain willing to take letters on their voyage home. The days were long, and Maria articulated her frustration in one of her letters at the enforced lack of industry that she and women in her position had to endure: 'There is nothing here that a lady can do for a living. Her needle is of small use where labour is so cheap and men do all that kind of work, for schools there are already sufficient and I do not see anything that I can do to aid the exertions of my husband.'

Acceptable society for expatriates was limited, but the community of European inhabitants was fast establishing entertainments and cultural diversions. Balls were held to celebrate all manner of different national festivals. Horseraces took place every New Year, and daily promenades along the Esplanade allowed men and women alike to gander and gossip. Unfamiliar spectacles injected excitement into their lives, festivals of Chinese and Indian traditions being described in minute detail to far-away relatives, who no doubt marvelled at the sights and sounds enshrined in ink.

However, the reality of life in Singapore during the 1840s extended beyond promenading and parties. Maria Balestier and Anne Sykes were on a frontier of sorts, pioneers in a harsh landscape that had built a veneer of European comforts, but harboured a maelstrom of challenges beneath. Tiger attacks were violently frequent, with local plantation workers and others living on the edge of the settlement being particularly vulnerable. As the development of residences encroached onto the jungle, so the big cats ventured onto the new roads that snaked into it. Deaths were recorded in growing numbers in each issue of the local newspaper, often within a mile of the settlement's environs, and in 1844 the Tiger Club issued cash rewards for each capture of a tiger, in a bid to reduce fatalities. House robberies were a frequent occurrence, with gangs of armed men breaking into residences with little fear of recriminations from a barely formed police force. Large fires ravaged homes and warehouses, and throughout the 1840s there were calls for the establishment of a local fire brigade. Piracy was so common that the British

Navy sent ships to the region to try and curb these violent incidents, which often strayed into the very harbour of Singapore itself. It was into this turbulent and unpredictable landscape that Anne Sykes and Maria Balestier were catapulted, following in the wake of their husband's life choices, trying to build their own lives.

~

In a climate such as Singapore's, clothing acquired a different level of significance, both in terms of practicality and scarcity. In spite of the luxurious fabrics that were passing through the warehouses of Singapore, cloth was scarce for the American and European women living there. They relied on the infrequent gifts from home, morsels of valuable fabric and trimmings that they could adapt for their wardrobe. Maria often spoke gratefully of such supplies, writing to her sister in July 1841, 'the needles and pins are a great comfort to me, and the cap ribbons, a present that has not fallen to my lot for a long time for you cannot procure a yard of ribbon of any description or thread, lace and for some time I have not been able to get any spool cotton for every day use'. Sometimes garments that she herself had not found useful were sent back to Boston to be reused by her relatives there, a mark of the value that cloth held. In 1844 she wrote to her sister Harriet of a silk gown, 'It is a very soft plum colour and worn under your black velvet spencer could hide the waist. I hope you may find it useful. It has been worn only a very few times.'

This exchange and flow of small objects and hand-worked garments was also a means of maintaining a material contact with beloved family members so far away. As the memory of faces faded, the objects became imbued with greater significance, the hands working the objects that, in turn, would be held by other hands across the ocean. Making became an act of love and of connection – a reminder of presence. In September 1844 Maria wrote to ask if the rumour of a female relative's pregnancy was true: 'If I was certain of it I would send by Captain Webb some little caps of Lydia's work and a cap belonging to our mother's little wardrobe and which was worn by all her children . . .' Small dress sundries made interesting souvenirs to send home. The exotic 'otherness' of somewhere like Singapore could be shared through such trifles, and Maria regularly posted boxes of local items to Boston. In 1845 she sent her sister 'a pair of fine cloth handkerchiefs for yourself and another pair for your good minister Mr Waterston in whom I feel a great interest and I thought it might be pleasant to you to offer such a trifle as it comes from such a distance'. Chinese fans and slippers found their way across the world, to be marvelled over. The cultural exchange worked both ways, as European garments were a puzzle to locals and Maria wrote of her thrill in sharing garments with one of her servants: 'When he went to China to see his wife he asked me to give him a suit of my old clothes that his wife might see how a Europe lady was dressed so I gave him an entire one – corset, chemise, stockings and all to his great delight.'

From the outset, Maria had made some adaptations to her appearance and she braided her hair around the back of her head, rather than trying to maintain the ringlets that were then fashionable amongst Europeans. She was delighted when other women of her acquaintance began to copy her style.

All but two of the sixteen fabric samples from Maria Balestier that are included in Anne's book are printed cottons. Their bold prints differ in aesthetics from European designs, with hers hailing from printworks in America. The lightweight cloth was well suited to the tropical climate, the patterns varying in complexity: colourful garments in an unfamiliar world. She describes in her letters that they lived a relatively quiet life, choosing not to socialise as much as perhaps some of the other women in the settlement. Strict etiquette was observed around visiting – a European habit that Maria found frustrating, since her husband was reluctant to make the required first call to other merchants, without which she herself could not invite ladies to tea. During the course of her time in Singapore, Maria distanced herself from the petty hierarchies of social standing, writing to her sister, 'You must live among the English and see the little murmurs of rank and the constant struggles for its distinction among persons of small pretensions to feel its little value.' This accounts for the contents of her wardrobe: cotton dresses suitable for daywear, but only two silk fragments, remnants of dresses for more formal occasions.

Of the Bachelor Ball of 1838, given by the single men of the outpost for the ladies, Maria wrote that it was a 'dull affair'. She did not dance and therefore observed the entertainment from the fringes. A party that she did enjoy was one that she and her husband Joseph hosted on Friday 15 May 1840 to celebrate the twenty-first birthday of their beloved son and only child, Revere. She declared, 'Our party was very numerous and splendidly attired for so many uniforms made it so with their lace and embroidery; about twenty ladies and over a hundred gentlemen.' Revere had travelled with his parents to Singapore in 1834, then just a boy of fifteen. He tried valiantly to build a life for himself there. Without access to formal education, he undertook a programme of engineering projects and spent days working at the Counting House with his father. Maria's letters are full of his plans and ambitions, although Revere was often laid low with fever.

In spite of his elevated status as American Consul in Singapore, Joseph Balestier's fortunes never matched his title and the family struggled financially for the entirety of their life there. In a bid to revive their income, the Balestiers moved from their residence in the town to a sugar plantation, an enterprise that Joseph was determined would succeed. For Maria, it only compounded her loneliness, placing her at an even greater distance from what little society she found amongst the residents of the settlement. In one of his rare missives home, Revere himself described the pattern of their days to his aunt: 'We jog on very quietly at the Plantation and our lives are as little varied as possible. I have no time to go out and with the exception of an occasional dinner engagement, we are a humdrum sort of people as you can imagine.' Maria too described the shape of her day, with her husband visiting the plantation early in the morning before leaving for the Counting House, returning at 5 p.m. for an early dinner and then visiting the plantation again until 8 p.m. Worn out, he would return home to go to bed with his books, leaving Maria to read in their small parlour. She notes that sometimes she would go for days without seeing another face, other than her household servants.

In 1844 tragedy struck their small family. Revere had sickened with another fever, which this time would prove fatal. He died in his room early in March, leaving Maria heartbroken. Her letters home recount her terrible loss and the reality that she would never see his dear face again: 'It would be a great pleasure to me if we had a portrait of him.' Items of his clothing were to be the only lasting connection with her lost child. In the absence of an image, they at least bore the imprint of his life, and she kept his room just as it was when he died – 'his cap, whip and spurs hang in his dressing room as if ready to put on'. These items were all kept as a means of material remembrance to be touched, and to recall happier times, and Maria writes, 'one of his riding caps gives him to me in his gayest spirits and good health, it is a Chinese cap such as is worn by their learned men and he generally wore it of an evening when he drove me out in the phaeton . . . that evening drive was always a gay one'.

Those bold printed cotton dresses and the colour that infused them became redundant in Maria's wardrobe, and none of her garments appear in Anne's album after Revere's death. Maria never wore coloured garments again for the rest of her life. Thanking her sister for a parcel in November 1846, more than two years after Revere's death, she wrote, 'Your light materials for dress was very acceptable to me and I have promised Mr Balestier to resume a white dress as soon as I feel able to attend to their preparation but I made it a point that he should not require me to wear colours and a white ribbon keeps us clean and fresh in this climate as any other would do.' It had been twelve years since she had last seen her family and friends. She recorded the number of letters that she wrote – ninety in one year – such correspondence being the only connection with her old life as she strove to maintain relationships at such a distance.

Although Maria continued to entertain occasionally and take part in some of the social events put on, her interest in life waned. She became increasingly fragile, the climate taking its toll on her constitution. As early as 1841 she told her sister, 'I find from experience that the human frame requires great care to withstand the effect of the climate when you cannot change it for a long time. I am nearly as thick as I am long yet I eat but little and take a great deal of exercise for a tropical climate.' From 1845 she would begin to suffer from bouts of ill health, with items sent from home providing longed-for solace: 'I find the shawl you sent me just as much covering as is required in our evening dinner; I have been feeble for some time past and take it with me and find it light and comfortable; I wear black ribbons on white; strange it is my dear sister that our feelings are so influenced – I like to see others in colours but I own that I am sure that I should feel very much troubled to have to put on colours.'

By the end of 1846 her spirits and her health would fail still further. Joseph would wake Maria early each morning to drive her in their small carriage for an hour in the cooler air before the heat became insufferable. In January 1847 she travelled with Sir William and Lady Norris to the cooler climes of Malacca in a bid to restore her to health, their hillside residence being a tranquil respite. She still took an interest in the flow of small objects and souvenirs, asking her sister to send her two feather fans and thanking friends for the gift of a pair of black mittens. Her sister regularly implored Maria to come home, to take ship at the earliest opportunity, forget their ambitions in Singapore and return to Boston and the embrace of family. It is the only time that the correspondence between them becomes discordant, tensions that took months to share and resolve, as Maria outlined the impossibility of such a move, both financially and physically. She would never see her sister's face again. On 22 August 1847 Maria's body could take no more, and she passed away in her bedroom at the plantation house, united in the Singaporean soil with her beloved Revere.

In spite of her well-documented life, her famous father and her contributions to the early settlement of Singapore, there is no surviving likeness of Maria. We are lucky that through her letters we hear her voice so articulately describing the realities of her world, but through those colourful cottons we might imagine her more clearly, a flutter of fabric in the shimmering humidity.

CHAPTER 8

Pirates!

Admiral Sir Thomas Cochrane

> . . . an enterprising tribe of pirates, of whose daring
> adventures I had heard much.
>
> Admiral Henry Keppel, *The Expedition to Borneo of*
> HMS Dido *for the Suppression of Piracy*, 1846

One of the most intriguing fabric samples in Anne's album is, at first glance, one of the most unremarkable. Cut into her customary elongated octagon is a plain piece of red wool, with a dimple of moth damage crimping the upper edge. Below it are two swatches whose captions attest to the humdrum of daily family life. The first is a cream-and-purple silk ribbon worn by Anne and Fanny Taylor (see Chapter 10), below which sits the fragment of soft bright-blue silk velvet described as 'Mr Sykes's birthday slippers July 12 1846'. The caption written above the red wool, however – inked in a larger-than-usual curling cursive script – speaks of drama on the high seas that is at odds with the homely comfort of Adam's velvet house-slippers: 'Part of the "Pirates" flag. Taken in Borneo by the Admiral. 1845.'

This is such an unexpected addition. On my first encounter with it, I stopped short, gazing at the incongruous coupling of fuzzed red wool with so dramatic a description. Which pirates? Admiral who? Knowing nothing about Anne at this point, I could make no connection between her collection of domestic dress textiles and this exciting anomaly, placed so nonchalantly above a cap ribbon and house-slippers. Preliminary research was surprisingly revealing, and within an hour I had made two important discoveries. The British Navy was, indeed, patrolling the seas around Borneo in 1845 on anti-piracy missions; and on board HMS *Agincourt*, taking charge of the Borneo station, was one Admiral Sir Thomas Cochrane. How the Lancashire-based merchant's wife Anne Sykes had acquired the scrap of a pirate flag was, for the time being, a mystery, and it was not until the revelation that Anne herself was a resident of the same tropical archipelago, and would have borne witness to the ravages of piracy amongst the population of Singapore, that its inclusion made any sense.

There are revelatory moments in historical research that, in a moment, open up whole new worlds. Side-by-side lay the evidence of a young Englishwoman living in the bustle of emerging Singapore and a celebrated British admiral. That they should share any connection is a marker of the extraordinary society they both inhabited at this time, one that was far removed from the conventions of home. It was a curiosity that the traveller J. T. Thomson remarked upon in his memoir *Some Glimpses into Life in the Far East* when he described the diversity of the 30,000-strong population of Singapore: 'Subjects of nations at war are friendly here, they are bound hand and foot by the absorbing interests of commerce.' Witnessing members of the Jewish faith mixing with Hindus, Chinese traders and Arabian merchants socialising together at sporting events and banquets, he wondered, 'How was this conglomeration of divers tongues, creeds and nations held together?'

Thomas Cochrane's journey started far from Singapore, having been born the son of Admiral Sir Alexander Cochrane, who had made his naval career as a commander during the Napoleonic Wars. At the tender age of seven, the young Thomas Cochrane was recruited as a volunteer on board his father's ship HMS *Thetis* on the North American station, commencing his naval education before he had even reached double figures. It is difficult to imagine such an experience today. Doubtless his position as son of the ship's commander would have afforded Thomas greater privilege than other boys in a similar position, but the privations on board ship in the late eighteenth century were universal. Popular the Cochranes were not, it seems. John Jervis, the first Earl of St Vincent, wrote that 'The Cochranes are not to be trusted. They are all mad, romantic, money-getting and not truth-telling.' Certainly it was an act of gross nepotism on the part of Sir Alexander to secure a position for his very young son on board his own ship – a springboard for his future naval endeavours. Aged only eleven, Thomas transferred to the Channel Squadron as midshipman, and on board HMS *Ajax* saw action in support of French royalist exiles. His naval star continued to rise, thanks to his connections, with the patronage of his father often operating in the shadows of his swift promotion. By the age of twenty-four Thomas Cochrane had returned to the North American station, only this time he was in command of his own ship, HMS *Surprise*. In 1813 HMS *Surprise* captured the American ship *Decatur* during the conflict between America and the UK. Already he had travelled widely and had had his fair share of adventure on the high seas.

Having spent twenty-six years at sea, many of them in and around the North American station, Cochrane was handed an entirely different role. In 1825 he became the first resident Governor of Newfoundland. For more than a century the colony had been governed by the Admiralty at a distance, but here was a naval commander leaving the deck of his ship for a new life ashore. Cochrane was fond of the good life that was afforded him in his new position, with all its pomp and ceremony. One officer of the Army, Sir Richard Bonnycastle, who was stationed in northern Canada at the same time, recalled that Cochrane 'displayed a magnificence in his vice-regal function before unknown'. He arrived in the notoriously poor colony with enough household trappings to 'fill a palace' and immediately undertook the construction of a new Governor's residence. The original estimate for its completion was £8,778, but Cochrane's frequent changes to the floorplan saw the final cost reach £31,000. So embarrassing was the over-spend that a court of inquiry was instigated. In all, Cochrane spent nine years as Governor, a chequered experience that witnessed frequent squabbles with other local dignitaries, as well as endeavours to achieve some reform on the island and to improve the living conditions of the population. He remained largely unpopular, and on his removal from office in 1834 Cochrane departed the colony with his daughter, pelted with missiles on the journey down to the wharf. Seven years later, at the age of fifty-two, he had returned to his seafaring life and was appointed second-in-command of the East India and China station, amidst the conflict that had erupted around the British supply of opium to China.

When Anne and Adam stepped on board their ship bound for Singapore in July 1840, they did so in the knowledge that Britain was at war with China and that the entire region was disrupted by conflict. As a relatively experienced merchant by this date, Adam was presumably prepared to take on the challenges that the interruption to Chinese trade routes were creating, but for Anne it was a leap into the unknown. They surely would have read the reports of 'the China expedition' – the fleet of British ships that had sailed into Singapore harbour between April and June 1840, a mere month before their own departure. The flotilla used Singapore as a base from which to launch their offensive against China, and so the settlement found itself at the very centre of international affairs. Anne and Adam would perhaps have followed the debates taking place in Parliament in April on the British response, while packing their belongings for their impending departure.

The roots of the conflict, popularly known as the First Opium War, actually originated not in a Chinese addiction to the potent mix of opium and tobacco, but in the British passion for tea. China was the only country to export tea to Britain in the eighteenth and early nineteenth centuries. It was not until the 1850s that an Indian trade in this most prized of commodities was founded. The Chinese government was uninterested in harnessing the potential of an export market and so only accepted solid silver by way of payment for the much sought-after tea chests. Depleted of silver and desperate to find a solution, the British government struck upon a solution. They would illegally import opium to China and trade it for tea, via this illicit route. As the trade monopolies held by the East India Company diminished, so there was a free-for-all on traded goods, and British merchants began to flood the Chinese market with opium from India. From 1,000 chests of opium in 1767, trade had increased massively so that by 1838, 40,000 chests of the drug were illegally entering the country, to the increasing anger of the Chinese rulers.

Historians have estimated that by 1840 as much as 3 per cent of the Chinese population was addicted to smoking opium. The wider availability and falling prices saw the drug move inland and along the coast, creeping into ever larger sectors of the population and the working poor of China. Some figures suggest that as many as twelve million people in China were now opium addicts, and the ruling Qing dynasty decided to take a stand. Officials began to seize the imports of opium and destroy them, forbidding British vessels to enter Chinese ports. The conflict escalated, and more and more ships were sent to the region. Singapore was a convenient harbour, with its Western population and sympathetic officials, and whilst hostilities did not encroach directly on Singapore, the relative proximity of the turmoil and the occasional stopover of both troops and ships brought this unimaginable event directly into the path of the young Anne and Adam Sykes on arrival in their new home. Mrs Balestier recorded, 'Ship after ship assembled in the roads and tents sprang up all over the Esplanade and other available places.' Mercantile interests were threatened by the instability in the region, and Adam Sykes's name appears frequently as one of many signatories in letters appealing for clarity on changing tariffs and transports.

However, as the conflict resolved, following the British capture of Nanking and the subsequent peace treaty in 1842, it was to be a war of a different sort that brought the old admiral and the young merchant's wife into the same orbit. It was as Rear Admiral that Cochrane was eventually to command the station at Borneo, as part of the Navy's forces committed to tackling the scourge of piracy that terrorised and disrupted the populations around Singapore in 1845. His presence in the settlement, and therefore his opportunity to have encountered Anne Sykes, is recorded in a contemporary newspaper account: 'The Races were held in March, on two days in the afternoon . . . Rear Admiral Sir Thomas Cochrane was here, in his flagship the *Agincourt* and there was a large party from his vessel at the races.'

The horseracing events in Singapore were a highlight in the social calendar for the varied population of the town. Merchants and their wives enjoyed the thrill of an entertainment that differed from the everyday, with a ball to anticipate in the evening. A Rear Admiral in full dress was an impressive sight. Cochrane was well known as a stickler for correct attire, a less-than-complimentary account of his appearance featuring in the *Singapore Free Press* in 1845: 'The Admiral . . . is at times disagreeable about dress and very pompous. He is himself a regular old buck and looks as if he kept himself in a bandbox.' In full dress, Cochrane would have appeared before the merchants of Singapore in a double-breasted coat of dark-blue wool, with twenty brass buttons parading in two columns from neck to waist. A band of gold lace would trim the collar and cuffs of the jacket and, at the shoulders, four eyelets sewn into the bodice would hold the golden epaulettes, insignia of his long service. Those epaulettes survive to this day, the exquisite workmanship of the ceremonial embroiderer, denoting Cochrane's rank.

Such magnificence came at a cost. In 1843 George Gillot, Secretary to the Admiralty, expressed his concerns at the cost of new uniform changes – 'the expense will be the additional gold lace on the skirts of the coats', which he noted would tarnish fast when on, or near, the sea. Embroiderer's bills mounted up for officers in the Royal Navy. Specialists such as Lonsdale & Tyler charged £7 7s. for 'Rich gold "Full Dress" or "Undress" Epaulettes' for an admiral. Cochrane's epaulettes are exemplars of the ceremonial embroiderer's art, the gold silk being embellished with silver-thread purl stars and a red velvet crown worked with silver. Gold braid and purl are twisted at the edge for additional texture, and coils of gold purl cascade from the base to frame the shoulder. Cochrane would have appeared in all his naval glory to the assembled masses at the races and the entertainments that followed, and at some point during this interlude in Singapore he met Anne Sykes, merchant's wife. What their meeting may have looked like it is impossible to know. Did they fall into conversation after an introduction from Adam? Did Anne regale Cochrane with stories of her five years in Singapore? Did she describe to him the contents of her silk-covered album and suggest that he might like to contribute a scrap of cloth to her collection?

~

The activities of pirates would have been an ever-present reality in Anne and Adam's life in Singapore, particularly since merchant ships were often the target of the opportunistic *prahu* boats. Singapore provided rich pickings for the raiders, who often sailed in close to the very harbour of the town itself to take advantage of the variety of shipping that arrived daily. One contemporary observer wrote, 'Thousands of ships from the surrounding countries continually entered the harbour; among them were Arab ships from Java, flying the Dutch flag, and a varied assortment of smaller coasting craft.' Such constant activity, and boats weighed down with all the luxuries of commercial trade, made easy targets.

Each May the direction of the monsoon winds would shift and would bring with them the fleet of maurading boats, perhaps thirty *prahus* with upwards of sixty oars each, rowed with enormous speed and agility. These 'pirate winds' brought months of misery sweeping along the coast, with the pirates' appetite for plunder and slaves. In 1846 Henry Keppel, a captain of the vessels sent to Borneo and Singapore to try and eradicate the pirate threat, wrote of his first encounter with one of the piratical fleets, 'the pirates swept up the river, eighteen prahus, one following the other, decorated with flags and streamers, and firing both cannon and musketry'. He admired their seafaring skills and their passion, whilst acknowledging the suffering they left in their wake. The pirates would chase prized vessels, taking the crew of the ships into slavery to sell further along the coast and stealing the valuable cargo.

Keppel described the goods transported from a wreck that he discovered during his voyages up and down the coast: 'her cargo consisted of red woollens, fine white cloths, Turkey red cotton handkerchiefs, tin, pepper, Malacca canes, rattans etc.' The presence of 'red woollens' might account for the swatch in Anne's album – that fragment of scarlet wool so dramatically captioned. Pirates could fashion flags and streamers from the spoils of their plunder, decorating their ships to further terrify vessels as they rowed towards them. They would keep their hair long in order to let it loose during battle, adding to their ferocious appearance, wielding bamboo shields as they boarded ships. Some trade ships over the years were actually chosen for their ability to deal with pirate attacks: vessels like the American brig *Antelope*, which carried ice and opium. 'She had rakish masts for large amounts of sail and had to be able to outrun oared pirate junks lying in wait along the China coast.'

Traditionally a red pirate flag sent a very clear message of intent – 'no quarter given'. The scarlet banner conveyed to those on board that the pirates would show no mercy: a sight to strike fear into the hearts of passengers and crew as the pirate *prahus* sped towards them. Flags were an important marker of tribalism for the different groups that prowled the China Seas, the colours that they held aloft identifying the origins of their crew. Group identities were a part of the pirates' cultural backgrounds, not only creating fearful reputations, but also binding them together in gang-like territorial groups. Keppel described a gathering of the pirate tribes and the spectacle of their clothing: 'The performer with the Illanuns [the Maranao people of northern Borneo] is decked out with a *fine helmet* (probably *borrowed* from our early voyagers) ornamented with bird of paradise feathers. Two gold belts, crossed like our soldiers over the breast, are bound at the waist with a fantastical garment reaching half way down the thigh and composed of various-coloured silk and woollen threads one above another.'

In a naval context, flags were the pride of any vessel, the unifying banner of identity that rallied the crew. To capture a flag was to strip a vessel of its pride. There is no way of knowing which of the pirate ships Anne's snippet of flag once belonged to, although the practice of taking such items was described by Captain Keppel, following one of the successful raids by the British fleet: 'young Douglas made his appearance, bearing in his arms the captured colours of an Illanun pirate'. The efforts of Cochrane and Keppel were largely successful and, after a series of attacks on pirate forts inland, a truce of sorts was called. Negotiations took place between the officers of the British Navy and the leaders of the pirates, with Keppel noting, 'At the appointed hour the chiefs made their appearance, dressed in their best, but looking haggard and dejected.' By the end of August 1845, Admiral Cochrane was able to report the positive results in the suppression of one of the most prolific chiefs, in his dispatches sent to the Admiralty: 'I consider his influence to be entirely annihilated and his confederacy with various piratical chiefs in the Archipelago broken up.' The *Singapore Free Press* recorded that by 1846 the pirate threat had been radically reduced, much to the relief of the local and merchant community.

Whilst the reasons for a military presence in Singapore were serious ones, such activities within the settlement were not unwelcome. The colour and variety that the officers brought with them offered a welcome diversion amongst the small European and American community, bringing much-needed new conversation to society. Maria Balestier enjoyed such occasions and depicted the pomp of their appearance, should officers visit her in her official role as wife to the American Consul. Following a visit from Captain Younker of the Russian frigate *Abo*, Maria described his magnificent appearance to her sister: 'I admired his splendid crosses and a silver medal with which he was ornamented as well as the superb embroidery on his uniform for he was in his full dress which was of black with massive gold embroidery and buttons with a device upon them which I supposed to be the Black Eagle.' Officers stationed in the town, or visiting temporarily, took part in entertainments or even contributed to them. One of the daily points of interest for European residents was the early-evening stroll along the Esplanade, a place to see and be seen – a site of gossip to enjoy as the heat of the day waned slightly. When the USS *Constitution* was moored in Singapore harbour in 1845 its ship's band played on the Esplanade on alternate days, bringing with it the sound and remembrances of home.

Behind the neat uniformity of Anne's cloth samples there must have swirled a sea of uncertainty. Her album captures friendships and family connections. It does not reveal the burden of anxiety that the couple must have faced. It does not tell of crime; of the smallpox outbreaks that were part of life in the region; or of the fires that ravaged residences and warehouses. It tells us nothing of the poor sanitation, limited access to medical help and struggling infrastructure. Containing fragments of cotton from home and silks from China, it may have been her escape from unfamiliar surroundings – a place to share the beauty of the cloth and those people it represented, as a counterpoint to uncertainty.

There is no other record in Anne's album of anything approaching a
military contribution from those she may have met in Singapore. There
are no swatches of navy-blue wool to claim her association with those
forces making their presence felt, but this is no surprise. The value of
a naval uniform and its sharply tailored lines would leave little excess
cloth. The only concrete evidence of Anne soliciting contributions for
her book is found in her monochromatic silk pictures of Queen Victoria
and Prince Albert that the merchant Mr McMicking had given her. The
McMicking brothers were, like Adam, members of the merchant community and so were part of Anne's social circle. Mr McMicking himself
experienced a different kind of violence that plagued the settlement of
Singapore, piracy of another sort, in the shape of armed gangs whose
attacks on the local population were bold and swift. *One Hundred Years of
Singapore*, an early history of the settlement published in 1921, described
the extent of such robberies: 'This history of Singapore is full of references to gang robberies and some of which attained almost to the dignity
of military operations. In 1842 an attack was made by an armed body of
about fifty persons on a house near the river on South Bridge Road.' Until
1864 the only means of lighting residential areas consisted of coconut-oil
or animal-fat lamps. The resulting darkness provided ample cover for the
organised gangs, and Mr McMicking fell foul of one of these attacks in
1835. It was reported in *The Straits Times* that 'Mr McMicking was nearly
killed by gang robbers in his house, Duxton, an affair that created a great
sensation.' Violence was not, for Anne and Adam, a vague possibility,
but a very real one that merchants of their acquaintance encountered
and lived through.

Her language relating to Mr McMicking's textile swatch is interesting, his 'contribution' suggesting that she spoke of her fabric-collecting
to those around her and welcomed the offerings that might result. Presumably the same was true of Admiral Cochrane, and in lieu of a piece
of his own clothing, he was able to proffer something entirely more

romantic. After almost five years in Singapore, Anne's album was full of the colour of her friends and associates in the settlement. The floral cottons of daytime, and the silks of evening, marked the shape of her days and the passing of the years in cap ribbons and fancy dress, in lace trim and velvet slippers, but Admiral Cochrane's pirate flag spoke of an entirely different side to life in the archipelago. It is the fragment that speaks of uncertainty and danger. Its incongruity jars with the comforts of home, and brings sharply into focus the precarity of their life forged between jungle and sea, tiger and pirate.

CHAPTER 9

Frontier Women

Miss Grant, Miss Connolly and Others

> . . . the luxuriant verdancy, the neat houses of the
> Europeans in the midst of beautiful houses, the
> plantations of the most precious spices . . . the jungle in
> the background, compose a most beautiful landscape.
>
> Ida Pfeiffer, *A Woman's Journey Around the World*, 1852

Nearly 7,000 miles separated Anne from everything that she had known, when she moved to Singapore in 1840 to start a life on the colonial frontier. For seven years she forged friendships and took part in entertainments, decorated her home and contributed to the emerging institutions that were beginning to make their mark on this multicultural landscape. However, it is not just her own experiences that are given voice through the material scraps of her album, but those of a host of other women whose lives intersected in this tropical archipelago.

When Anne arrived in Singapore there were around 200 Europeans living in the settlement, and hardly any of them were women. Having braved the four-month sea journey, she was presented with challenges of an entirely different sort, with only a few other women to share her daily experiences in this brave new world. As she gathered new acquaintances, so she gathered the scraps of their existence in Singapore, carefully saving these pieces of their lives and helpfully labelling them, so that we might reimagine them 180 years later, in the humidity of the jungle-fringed town. Turning the pages, we find a young, motherless merchant's daughter, and a newly wed German couple embarking on a new venture; a doctor's sister travelling to keep house for her brother; the nomadic wife of a sea captain, accompanying him on his travels; and an idealistic young missionary schoolteacher, whose scraps of clothing sit side-by-side those of the American Consul's wife and the grandes dames of the mercantile community. Memorialised, too, are the colourful cloths that passed through the trading post and that capture the vivid cultural backdrop of South-East Asia – textiles that hail from China, India and Java and find their place in Anne's album.

The histories of old Singapore quantify the achievements of the merchants, their columns of figures, their ships full of goods. It is a history that is almost entirely white and male, neglecting the stories of the women and people of colour who lived in the settlement. Popular mythologies would have us believe that upper-middle-class women in the nineteenth century wilted gently, casting themselves along a chaise longue, fan in hand, as they experienced the world in a kind of passive trance. Their clothing was apparently too impractical, their opportunities too limited, their will too weak. Yet the women who populate the pages of Anne's album prove that this was far from the case. This is not to downplay the very real and awful experiences of women in a world in which they were mistreated and marginalised in countless ways; but to cast them as helpless creatures is to do them a gross disservice. The women that Anne met during her years in Singapore were fine examples of women taking on what would be, to us, unimaginable challenges. From the travel itself, to the building of a life against an entirely new geographical and cultural backdrop, with little communication from loved ones, there are stories to be told of everyday courage.

As with the rest of Anne's album, some names feature frequently against the rainbow swatches of cloth, whilst others offer the briefest of acquaintances. Sometimes, however, that is all that is needed. Take Miss Grant. There are just three small airy flutters of ribbed cotton fabric that are associated with her – labelled simply 'Miss Grant', each is a textured white cotton, with colour to add interest. One features a pink resist-dyed floral pattern, another is woven with a purple stripe and the third is printed with a blue leafy repeat. It is her only entry in Anne's album and yet Miss Grant stands out as a pioneering woman. She arrived in Singapore in July 1843 as the representative of Britain's Society for the Promotion of Education in China, India and the East, and her role was to take on the running of the first girls' school in Singapore, the Chinese Girls' School. The establishment housed and educated orphaned Chinese girls, although its chief aim was driven by Christian missionary ambitions. Miss Grant wrote with great passion of her hopes for the life that lay ahead of her as her ship lay at anchor in the harbour: 'There lay before me the land of my future life – or it may be death – the land of my solitude; the land of my labours; but I trust also the land where I may be permitted to gather many a rough unhewn stone, to shape and fit it for a place in the spiritual temple above.' She was very clear from the outset about her priorities. She made a point of meeting other missionary families in the locality, but beyond that, her resolve was clear: 'other society I do not intend to seek, as much visiting only monopolises time and leads off from my one object'. This accounts for the brevity of her appearance in Anne's book. She was not mixing regularly with other women, or looking for their camaraderie, but was intent on the moral and spiritual guidance of the twenty-one girls who populated her school in those early days.

It is no surprise that amongst the women to appear in the album during Anne's residence in Singapore are the wives or daughters of fellow merchants in their community. Miss Connolly, Mrs Behn, Mrs

Clark and Mrs McEwen, all of whom appear in the album, can be traced to their masculine mercantile connections, the very connections that had brought them to the colony in the first place. Seventeen fragments, mostly of colourful cotton with just one or two silks, belonged to a Miss Connolly. The name Connolly relates to one of the oldest firms trading in the settlement, that of Spottiswoode & Connolly, originally agents who had started out in 1824 and, by the early 1840s, were appearing regularly in *The Straits Times*, advertising cargo or with ships at anchor in the harbour. Maria Balestier recorded her impression of the matriarch Mrs Connolly and her home when she first arrived in Singapore in 1834: 'She received us most graciously. We made her quite a long visit and she showed us the arrangement of her house. It is very large and has a very grand scale.' Her choice of the word 'graciously' is suggestive of the condescension of one who has lived in the outpost for some time, welcoming a newcomer who is yet to make her mark. The Connollys had one child, a daughter who was at this time attending school in England, as did so many children whose parents were experiencing the colonial life. Only a few months later, Mrs Connolly died after a short illness. The swatches present in Anne's album belonged to her daughter who, on completing her schooling, made the journey to Singapore to be with her father. The predominance of cotton in the swatches that Anne has recorded would be appropriate for a young woman; lavish gowns of silk would have been deemed inappropriate at this stage of her unmarried life.

In contrast, the page of brightly coloured silks all dedicated to 'Mrs Clark' denote her status as the wife of Mr J. S. Clark, head of one of the oldest European merchant companies trading from Singapore. Six lavish swatches swirl in pinks and glossy greens, boldly striped and shaded. The luxury of the fabric speaks of both wealth and experience. Not for her the ultra-modern and very bold printed cottons of the younger generation, but the more stately sheen of patterned silk. Mrs Balestier was introduced to Mrs Clark in 1834 and later paid her a call at her large house on a hill off Bridge Road that overlooked the town. Her husband's name can be found against the list of donors to various charitable causes, the mark of a respectable and munificent man of business.

Almost twenty years after Mrs Clark first arrived at the settlement, another young merchant's wife appeared in the colony. Behn, Meyer & Co. was established in November 1840 by two friends in Hamburg, Germany. Theodor August Behn and Valentin Lorenz Meyer began to trade in commodities such as coconut oil, copra, pepper, camphor and rattan and later moved into shipping and insurance. The closeness of their working relationship was further enhanced when Theodor married Valentin's sister, Caroline, on 7 August 1844. Four months later, just after Christmas, she arrived in Singapore. She was the first, and for some time the only, German woman to live in the settlement – a stark change to her life in Hamburg. Her wardrobe is vibrant. There are twelve swatches of cloth bearing her name, of which four are silk whilst the rest are beautifully patterned printed cottons, some resist-dyed in complex designs and ombré shades and others decorated with tufted woven spots or hand-embroidered motifs. Such bright swatches dispel the notion of colourless women fading into the background. Caroline might have found herself in a land that was entirely alien to her, unable to speak her own language with anyone but her husband, yet here she carved out a life for herself. Her inclusion in Anne's album at least suggests that she made some friends amongst the other women in the settlement, the community that was replicated in cloth within the pages of the album. Certainly one account appears to confirm that the cheerfulness of Caroline's wardrobe was replicated in her character. The Austrian traveller Ida Pfeiffer, who wrote of her exploits around the world, arrived in Singapore in 1847 and presented herself at the offices of the agents Behn, Meyer & Co., bringing with her letters of introduction: 'Frau Behn would not hear of me lodging in a hotel; I was immediately installed as a member of her own amiable family in their comfortable bungalow on Mount Sophia, not far from Government Hill.' The chance for Caroline to speak German with another woman must have felt like an opportunity not to be missed, but it seems that the women took a genuine liking to one another.

This community was a small one in the 1840s, and so the networks that extend outwards from the silk-covered album are entwined with acquaintances and places in common, stories that begin in one place and end in the bright square of fabric on the pale-blue page. Anne Little was born far from Singapore, in the dreich cold of Edinburgh on 9 May 1822, the daughter of William and Ann Little. Her older brother was a doctor who built a respectable practice in Singapore, and in her late teens Anne decided to make the arduous journey from Scotland to the Far East to keep house for Dr Robert Little in the settlement. Dr Little made the acquaintance of Adam Sykes when he moved into a house that Adam had built and owned, Bonnygrass, one of the large classical residences on River Valley Road, only a few yards from Anne and Adam's own house. Whilst managing the domestic affairs of her brother, Anne met another of the local merchants, Mr Robert McEwen of McEwen & Co., and on her twentieth birthday they married in Singapore. It is likely that Anne Sykes attended the wedding, and in fact on page 94 of the album, framed in one of her customary wax-paper borders, is a cream figured-satin swatch labelled 'Mrs Martin's dress at Mr McEwen's wedding'.

Anne transports us to a time and place full of light and laughter with a fragment from Anne McEwen's wardrobe. A robust white cotton swatch printed with a purple stripe is overprinted with a jagged red repeat, creating what must have been a striking dress. Above the cloth Anne wrote, 'Mrs McEwen wore this at the picnic we had to P_____ S_____.' I couldn't initially make out what those two words might be or where this mythical picnic had taken place – until the moment when I discovered that Anne was living in Singapore for most of the 1840s and that Mrs McEwen had been there too. Once this particular discovery had been made, details like this began to take shape, and by perusing some maps

I discovered that sitting a short pull on the oars from Singapore harbour lies the island of Pulau Selegu. Unpicking Anne's copperplate with that knowledge makes this the most likely translation, although she has spelt it a little differently. Here then is a moment of levity, a happy outing to the tree-clad hilly little island with an intricacy of coves and beaches, within hailing distance almost of the harbour itself. Perhaps, as they all piled into boats, stowing their picnic baskets safely beneath wooden seats and opening parasols against the sun, they revelled in a little sea breeze and trailed hands in the water as they made their way out amongst the merchant shipping at anchor. Was this an unusual trip or a regular occurrence? As the food was decanted from the hampers and the party looked back at the colourful community they called home, did Mrs McEwen smooth down her striped cotton dress and reflect on the fortunes that had brought her to her brother, and inadvertently to a husband?

By the time the 1851 census was taken, Anne and Robert McEwen had returned to England and were living with their two young daughters, the eldest of whom had been born in Singapore, at 33 Finchley Road in London. Less than three years later, Robert died at the age of thirty-eight. Anne's travels had taken her from Edinburgh to Singapore, then to a home in London, but the years of her widowhood saw her return full circle to the land of her birth; and by 1861, as head of her household, she had moved to Hamilton, back in Scotland, with picnics on subtropical islands in striped cotton skirts but a distant memory.

~

Not all of the women who found themselves both in the humidity of Singapore and memorialised in the pages of Anne's precious album were full-time residents of the town. Two swatches catch a Mrs Milward at the very point of her arrival in the harbour. Both are complex and vibrant printed cottons in the brightest of designs, one trailing branches and flowers across a pale-blue ombré background and the other a riot of geometries – stripes and stylised motifs in navy blue, reds and oranges. The first, in Anne's tiniest writing, says, 'The dress worn by Mrs Milward the day she first landed in Singapore Aug 23rd 1842', and the second in similar fashion states, 'The dress worn by Mrs Milward the 2nd time she landed in Singapore August 15th 1843.' It seems curious, initially, that Mrs Milward should be landing in Singapore twice in less than a year, until you read the shipping arrivals printed in the weekly editions of the newspaper. Amongst the ships leaving harbour on 19 September 1842 was the *John Dugdale*, a Boustead-owned ship that was inextricably linked with Adam Sykes's business dealings, and the commander of the *John Dugdale* was recorded as Captain Milward. Similarly, a year later the newspaper reports on 17 August that the *John Dugdale*, commanded by Captain Milward was once again at anchor in the harbour, tying in beautifully with the dresses that Anne recorded as Mrs Milward's choice of landing ensemble. It was, therefore, a nomadic life that Mrs Milward led with her husband. Her first landing saw her stay in Singapore for almost a month, long enough to enjoy the society of women there before onward travels bore them away.

It was not unheard of for women to accompany their husbands on such voyages and in such roles. Later in the nineteenth century Maud Berridge travelled with her husband around the world on a number of trips from ports in England to cities that included Melbourne and San Francisco. She captured life at sea in her journal, charting on-board entertainments, food, passengers and the natural phenomena they witnessed along the way. On 17 July 1880 she wrote, 'The most wonderful and beautiful phosphorescent light is seen in the wake at night, looking over the ship's side one sees all sorts of fantastic shapes in the brightest silver . . .' Only a few weeks later the experience was a very different one: 'We have had some terrible rolling the last three days and nights. No one is able to sleep or in fact do anything but <u>hold on</u>!'

Of course these sea voyages were familiar to all of the women who had moved out to Singapore, with all of the hardships that entailed. Miss Grant, the indefatigable missionary schoolmistress, wrote at one point on her journey to Singapore of a fierce storm, 'Went to bed quietly on Monday night: at four an appalling motion of the ship . . . we were in a deep valley, the sea like perpendicular rocks around us, mainsail split, mainmast snapped, ropes cracking 500 miles from land.' Travelling was still considered to be a risky undertaking in the 1840s, not only physically challenging but morally, too. The author Florence Hartley included a warning to the unwary in *The Ladies' Book of Etiquette, and Manual of Politeness*, published in 1860: 'There is no situation in which a lady is more exposed than when she travels.' Along with tips on punctuality, luggage and the benefits of a strong pocket, she advises her readers on the most appropriate garments for travelling. 'A lady will always dress plainly when travelling. A gay dress, or finery of any sort when in a boat or stage lays a woman open to the most severe misconstruction.' She suggests that garments should be made in 'neutral tints', for ease of care.

Similarly, the intriguingly titled *Travelling and its Requirements – Addressed to Ladies by a Lady* recommends, 'In choosing each item of the travelling costume, care should be taken to avoid everything *outré* or *conspicuous*.' Anne does not include anything in her album that she openly refers to as travelling clothes. Perhaps their functionality made them less worthy of inclusion and therefore they did not warrant a place amongst the pages. What she does include are those garments that were chosen by the women for their arrival in Singapore – moments that were significant enough to be recorded, a new life memorialised in the choice of dress. It was Anne's decision to make that distinction against her own arrival dress that unlocked her diary in the first place, but others are included.

From amongst all her cotton dresses, the only silk garment belonging to Miss Connolly was a shining green taffeta, against which Anne wrote, 'The dress in which Miss Connolly landed in Singapore March 1845', and above a fine cream wool printed with a floral repeat Anne inscribed, 'June 1846 Mrs Martin to be worn on her voyage home'. They were important moments to be captured. Both the arrival and departures marked different experiences – fear of the unknown, the distance from home, the leave-taking of friends and the trepidation of months at sea. To arrive and depart in a garment that was not of the everyday created something of a ceremony, with the sense of donning one's best self, albeit briefly, for that moment in time.

Thanks to Anne's assiduous textile-collecting and caption-writing, these women have been reunited once more. Where once these dresses promenaded in tandem in the cooler hours of evening on the Esplanade or were smoothed down as their wearer took tea with friends, now they are frozen in place, with the merest echo of their former life just detectable from the colourful fibres of cotton and silk. Their experiences were diverse. Miss Grant held dear her ambitions to convert the orphaned Chinese girls in her care without the distractions of 'Society' to deter her. Miss Connolly had lost her mother and perhaps found some maternal figures amongst the established merchant wives. Mrs Milward flitted in and out of the harbour during her annual sea voyages with her husband. And Mrs McEwen married and started her young family in the settlement, finding a life here that was surely unexpected when she arrived to look after her brother. Anne knew them all and invited them to leave a little piece of their lives with her.

Of daily life in Singapore for the European women, we have little to go on, as far as Anne is concerned. Those who feature in her diary come from her own cultural and economic space. There is little by way of diversity within its pages – no colourful Chinese garments or traditional Malay clothing. Her interest in textiles in the abstract does appear to extend beyond her own cultural boundaries at times, however, and in her quest for swatches to fill the pages she pasted in some unexpected samples. Page 46 reveals a brilliant spectrum of silks, all cut into smaller

rectangles and arranged in a sunburst pattern reflective of their bril-
liance. Above these fragments she wrote, 'Syed Omar's dresses, all arab
silks.' Syed Omar was another of the merchants trading out of Singapore, and his contribution brought some geographical variety to Anne's
book. Only a few pages further on, against a splash of resist-dyed brown
cotton, the caption explains, 'Mrs Davidson & Mrs Whittle – Battick [*sic*]
print, printed in Java.' There are Madras and Chinese silks included across
these years in Singapore, the great sea of commodities that flowed in
and out of Singapore trapped here and there in Anne's album, but none
of these are attributed to particular people. Women of different ethni-
cities feature not at all. Anne was a product of the British class structure;
garments worn by women of the Chinese population, or the Malay servants with whom she doubtless conversed at length on a daily basis, do
not find their way into her story. These women appear in the history of
early Singapore only incidentally, hidden in even deeper shadows than
their European counterparts.

CHAPTER 10

Tokens of Friendship

Fanny Taylor

It is hoped that this little volume . . . may prove to many
an acceptable memento of departed dear ones, a
cherished token of that union of hearts that gladdens the
earth with the sunshine of Friendship.

Gift of Love and Friendship, 1845

I can't find Fanny Taylor. I have searched through every configuration of
her name – Fanny, Frances, Francesca – to no avail. I have trawled through
the census records and deciphered parish registers of births. I have run
my finger along countless passenger manifestos and leafed through the
published accounts of *The Asiatic Journal and Monthly Register for British
and Foreign India* in the 1840s. Searches for Miss Fanny Taylor in the
Singaporean newspaper archive have been similarly fruitless. It is not
that there are no Fanny Taylors to be found, but rather that there are
too many. There is an abundance of them – one of whom might be the
very lady I am seeking, but if she is there, then she passes by unnoticed,
one of many amongst all her contemporaries.

However, Fanny looms large in Anne's life, and for five of the seven
years that Anne lived in Singapore, Fanny was very obviously a dear

friend and was thus frequently recorded in the album. The echo of their friendship is captured in a shared material culture. Page after page, pieces of cloth bear both Anne's and Fanny's names – ribbons that they both wore, fabric they purchased together, dresses made from the same cotton. It is a snapshot of female camaraderie, of close bonds that tied these two women together. There is nobody else in the album to whom Anne is so closely connected through dress than to Fanny Taylor. Evidence of female friendship and gift-giving abounds in the dress diary. Such was the value of textiles that to give them to a friend was significant, and Anne acknowledged such gifts in the neat captions appended to her fragments. The album is also in part constructed of gifts – gifts of small pieces of material requested and freely donated to a friend in order that she might construct her unique record of their lives.

There is a single moment in the diary when we can pinpoint Fanny accurately before she dissolves into the shadows. Above a pink silk swatch that swirls with blurry magenta flowers Anne wrote, 'This dress worn by Fanny Taylor Aug 23rd 1842 when she landed in Singapore.' As if to commemorate the significance of the moment still further, Anne pasted a piece from her own garment alongside, a fragment cut to exactly the same dimensions so that they stand side-by-side, in cloth as in life, and she wrote, 'The dress worn by Anne Sykes Aug 23rd the day Fanny arrived in the Jhn Dugdale.' As we have seen, the *John Dugdale* was a ship owned by Edward Boustead, the merchant firm in which Adam was a partner, and plied its trade between Liverpool and the Far East carrying its valuable cargoes as well as mail and passengers. We catch Anne and Fanny at this exact moment in time, Fanny dressed in striking pink silk and Anne meeting her in a lightweight white cotton printed with a stylised blue leaf motif, more suited to the Singaporean heat in which she had already lived for two years by 1842. Did Anne stand on the harbourside straining for a glimpse of her friend as she disembarked, shading her eyes against the sun and the sparkle of the water? There is, of course, no solid evidence that Anne and Fanny necessarily knew each other beforehand, although it seems to be inferred from the captions that Fanny's arrival was an exciting moment for Anne. That she came via the Boustead ship offers a further connection. I like to think that it was a moment long anticipated as the *John Dugdale* weighed anchor. Whilst Fanny's exact origins might be hazy, there are other Taylors in the album that are suggestive of broader family connections – Mercy Taylor, Emma Taylor, Charlotte Taylor and Kate Taylor – perhaps all sisters with whom Anne shared an extended acquaintance.

From her arrival in the August of 1842 there are seventeen swatches of fabric that bear Fanny's name alone: cottons and silks from dresses, snips of bonnet ribbons and flutters of lace trim. More than that, however, there are those pieces of cloth that join Anne and Fanny in their friendship. Sometimes they are dress fabrics, and so the shared cloth might have been pragmatic. Above a plain black satin Anne wrote, 'Fanny Taylor & Anne Sykes 1842'. It is likely that this was a cloth specific to mourning, and so to buy a length of the sombre fabric in order for it to be made into mourning dresses, should the occasion arise, was a decision based on economy of cloth. Others are more frivolous, however. The shared purchase of ribbons seems to tie Anne and Fanny into a silken familiarity, their propensity to choose the same haberdashery reflected in the captions that Anne wrote. Wide ribbons, narrow ribbons, some made with complex floating wefts or warp-printed patterns, jagged-edged or with a picot-looped finish, they all shared similar descriptions. 'Anne Sykes & Fanny 1843 neck ribbon,' reads one. 'Anne & Fanny 1843 sash & neck ribbon,' reads another. With these small cloth tokens, worn tied around the throat, fastening a bonnet or threaded through a fine cotton cap, Anne and Fanny displayed their solidarity as they walked out together along the Esplanade or made their curtsies at the evening Assembly Rooms.

Their unity of dress extended beyond mere trimmings into whole garments as well. One white cotton fragment printed with purple spots and stripes is labelled, 'Anne Sykes & Fanny's morning dresses July 1845'. We cannot know for certain their motives in this instance. It could simply have been a matter of making the most of a length of cloth or it could have been that the general scarcity of fabric limited their choices. It is not necessarily the case that they would have worn the dresses at the same time, although the indication that they were morning dresses places them in a particular time and space. There were, however, precedents for what the scholar Anna Kirk has termed 'like-dressing' as a practice specific to the nineteenth century. Dressing in matching clothes was an expression of kinship in countless photographs from the period. Sisters would be photographed side-by-side in identical garments, not only as small children but into their adulthood as well, although this generally ceased on marriage. It was, of course, much easier to make two dresses from one piece of cloth than go to the trouble of choosing different material with different trimmings, especially if there was a budget to consider. It was intended as a non-verbal indicator of affection as well.

One of the most well documented and public displays of like-dressing took place in 1873, and the protagonists were two of the most celebrated public figures of the day. Alexandra, Princess of Wales and her sister Dagmar, the Tsarina Maria Feodorovna of Russia, spent most of each year separated from each other, their frequent letters expressing the sadness they often felt at such extended periods between visits. In June 1873 Dagmar and her husband were scheduled to make a state visit to London, hosted by her sister Alexandra and her brother-in-law, Edward, Prince of Wales. The sisters determined on a bold plan to enliven their public appearances together, one that was to be a logistical tour de force. For the duration of their visit and to entertain the public, they would dress alike for the entirety of the stay. Their letters were soon spilling over with ideas for garments and accessories and the means by which it could be achieved. When the Russian imperial yacht docked at Woolwich, the young Tsarina walked down the gangplank in a white dress with a straw bonnet trimmed with cherries, to be greeted by her sister wearing exactly the same outfit. It caused a public sensation. One of Alexandra's ladies-in-waiting, Louisa Antrim, wrote, 'The sisters set each other off and became the centre of a glittering crowd wherever they went.' Weeks later the sisters were still maintaining their performance, *The Times* reporting on 2 August, 'HRH the Princess of Wales wore at the last garden party at Chiswick, pale blue silk trimmed with velvet of a darker shade and a bonnet ensuite. The Czarevna was in pink silk made in the same style and a bonnet to correspond.'

Anne and Fanny may not have been biological sisters, but to dress the same could be perceived as an act of sisterhood to the outside world. Even closer are the white cotton dresses with a red woven check, against which fragment Anne wrote, 'Anne & Fanny new on Christmas Day 1845.' That they spent Christmas together and both wore the same dress perhaps indicates that Fanny was actually living with Anne and Adam. Other captions seem to imply this might have been the case. One cotton sample is described as being sent by Mrs Coubrough for Anne and Fanny – not only hinting at a friendship established before their time in Singapore, if Mrs Coubrough is sending cloth from home for them both, but also sending a single length for them to share. A soft blue-and-cream check wool / silk swatch is captioned, 'Fanny & Anne's morning shawls January 1847', and somehow I see them seated side-by-side on the verandah, wrapped in their shawls, before the heat of the day sees them fold the matching wraps and put them away as morning moves towards noon.

Given their apparent closeness, it might be that Fanny helped Anne with the composition of her dress diary. It is possible that Fanny was charged with cutting into shape the fragments that Anne handed to her, or in discussion of their arrangement on the page. This kind of albumisation practice was a female activity that promoted the memorialisation of relationships and connections. Keeping scrapbooks had been fashionable for decades, tokens of all sorts being collected together and offering a narrative on a part of one person's life, whether through autographs, tickets, illustrations, newspaper clippings or stamps. In the early 1870s the American writer Mark Twain, who was a keen scrapbooker himself, patented a self-pasting scrapbook to avoid the mess of home-made adhesive 'mucilage'. His empty albums came with the instruction, 'Use but little moisture and only on the gummed lines. Press the scrap on without wetting it.' Such was the popularity of his books that by the turn of the twentieth century there were more than fifty different choices of album for the scrapbook enthusiast to purchase.

In the mid-nineteenth century the ability to capture photographic likenesses of friends and families saw the emergence of the photo-collage as a creative practice. By snipping around the outline of a figure, the images of loved ones could be pasted into hand-painted scenes, manually Photoshopping them into fantastical backdrops – gathered together in art in ways that might not have been possible in real life. At a time when the creation of public art was the preserve of men, such albums offered women an artistic outlet that was held within the safe space of domesticity. The English poet Charles Lamb described his view of the fashionable lady's album in a short verse from 1830:

> 'Tis a Book kept by modern Young Ladies for show,
> Of which their plain grandmothers nothing did know.
> 'Tis a medley of scraps, fine verse, and fine prose,
> And some things not very like either, God knows.

Although such scrapbooks might have been created in the privacy of the home, that did not necessarily mean they were private objects. In fact these albums were designed to provoke comment and invite conversation and, as such, could act as vessels of social interaction. In 1873 *Chambers's Journal of Popular Literature, Science, and Arts* published an article entitled 'Albums', which looked back at the popular practice of half a century earlier. The author wrote, 'Did any thoughtless young lady exhibit her drawings after dinner to a select circle of friends in the drawing-room, she was immediately besieged by each in turn: "Do allow me, dear Miss Crayon, to send you my album for a contribution." '

∼

Using fabric as a means of memory-keeping, and sharing those memories, with friends was not a new phenomenon. Quilt-making is an art that stretches back for generations, but in the nineteenth century it had become a hugely popular practice undertaken by the women of the new industrial classes, whose domestic tasks included stitchcraft in all its various forms. The leftover fragments of cloth from a dressmaker would be amalgamated into the pattern for a block quilt, and other fabrics would be sourced especially for a particular project. The collaborative possibilities of hand-quilting made it a practice that involved both family and friends. Jane Austen wrote to her sister Cassandra in 1811, 'Have you remembered to collect pieces for the patchwork – we are now at a standstill.'

It took more than one pair of hands to make a quilt, and so the ties of love and friendship were stitched into the polychrome patterns of its many fabrics. Choosing the cloth, deciding on the arrangement of the pieces, cutting the paper templates and, ultimately, sewing them together took time, decision-making and conversation. At the very point when Anne was choosing the arrangement of her own cloth pieces, women in America in the 1840s were designing and making album quilts – individually designed blocks created in different patterns that were sewn together to create a sampler from different sources. Sometimes known as 'autograph quilts', they formed a material commemoration of female friendship networks.

In a sense, Anne's diary is a deconstructed friendship quilt. The pieces might not be sewn together, but they are fastened close, bound to each other within the turn of a page. Within the pink silk of its protective covers, the many hundreds of memories that each cloth sample represents are brought together, part of the lifespan of Anne Sykes and the people who ebbed and flowed around her, from her time as a young, newly married woman to the maturity of middle age. Perhaps in her later years, in their hilltop house overlooking the sea at Bispham in Lancashire, she would take her album and quietly turn the pages, recalling the heat of Singapore, the dress she wore to a ball or the ribbons that she chose with Fanny Taylor. With the passing of the years, and of her friends and her family, her album held fast the colourful remnants of their lives.

In the spirit of friendship, evidence of the exchange of gifts appears throughout Anne's diary. The giving of gifts is a cultural phenomenon that changes in significance across time and place, but within nineteenth-century Western cultures the emergence of mass-produced goods and the growth of disposable incomes meant that the gift-giving attained greater heights than in previous centuries. Although fabric was being produced on an industrial scale, it was still an expensive commodity. Anne records those occasions when she gave textiles to her friends whilst retaining a piece of it to add to the album. In 1846 she wrote above a soft grey figured silk, 'The dress I gave to Anna Coubrough and Isabella Butler.' Since Anna had been one of Anne's bridesmaids and Isabella was Anna's sister, these were relationships of long standing, but enough silk to make two dresses was a generous gift. The same year Anne received some printed cotton from Anna Coubrough, a shaded cotton gauze in gradations of blue and brown diamond motifs. Also in 1846 Anna Coubrough sent printed cotton, this time a diagonally striped pink fabric, above which Anne wrote, 'Anne & Fanny from Mrs Coubrough 1846.' She notes that it came by the 'Med Rose', the name of the ship that had travelled from Anna in England all the way to Anne and Fanny in Singapore.

In this respect, cloth made a sensible choice as a gift. It could be packed easily and was flat and easily stowable, to travel the long distances between these friends. What is difficult to ascertain from Anne's descriptions is the nature of the gift of dress. Although she might write of the dress given to her or the dress that she gave to somebody else, it is important to remember that this relates to the cloth rather than the whole garment.

A similar flow of fabric gifts existed between Maria Balestier in Singapore and her sister back in their home city of Boston. In a letter dated 1841 Maria thanked Harriet for the 'muster cap', the pattern for which she could show and have another made in Singapore. She in turn sent whole garments or cloth back home. On 21 June 1844 she writes that she is 'happy that Mrs C can find a use for the satin I sent' – pleasure found in the knowledge that these materials would meet with family, even if she could not. The safe arrival of textile gifts was not always guaranteed, of course, and in 1845 Maria sent her sister some 'unfortunate silk' that had clearly been damaged in transit, suggesting that it could be dyed and might make 'a convenient dress for travelling'.

The variety of textiles meant that smaller tokens could be exchanged. In July 1845 Anne described a wide pink silk ribbon as 'Fanny's sash given to her by Mr Sykes'. Two small needle-lace trims were apparently given to Anne by Mrs Coubrough – items perhaps small enough to tuck into the folds of a letter as a welcome surprise on opening. Not all gifts needed to be large and costly and, then as now, the labour involved in the making of a gift was a sign of affection and careful thought. The fragment of a ribbed white cotton has a chain-stitch motif hand-embroidered across its surface. Anne wrote against it, 'This dress given to Miss Brennand by Fanny Taylor 1844.' Cloaked in her checked wool shawl and wearing her cotton morning dress, did Fanny sit and embroider the cotton before folding it carefully into Miss Brennand's hands? Another home-made gift is recorded by Anne, the pink silk ribbon belonging to two caps made for herself and Fanny by Aunt Sykes, a handmade token of her affection for them, created in Lancashire and sent across the seas to Singapore.

It was not only women who gave gifts of textiles. There are several instances in the book of gifts presented either by men to the women in their lives or, indeed, to other men. A striking navy-blue ikat cotton bears the caption 'Manila Silk. Mr Wise gave Mr Sykes these two vests in 1844.' A few pages further in and above a plain black velvet Anne recorded, 'The vest Edward gave to Adam April 1846.' Robert Wise was Adam's business partner and Edward Burton was Anne's brother: two different men who both saw the value in gifting cloth from that important male garment, the waistcoat. In gifts that echo across the centuries for their familiarity today, Adam also received birthday presents of a dressing gown from Fanny and some blue velvet slippers from Anne, intimate objects concerned with the comforts of house and home.

Not all gifts are successful ones, no matter how genuine and kind the intent behind them. In one of the most candid of her captions, Anne described the origins of a figured yellow silk. She wrote beneath its buttery floral motifs, 'The dresses given to us by Mr Boustead and which we never wore.' Underneath this, by way of a postscript, she added, 'Changed the above for these'. The two printed cotton swatches, one bearing Anne's name and the other Fanny's, were apparently more to their taste. Poor Mr Boustead: was he pleased with his choice of sunny yellow silk that he presented to Anne and Fanny? Was there a moment of unwrapping when the two women fixed a smile on their faces and thanked him effusively for the gift, before later agonising over his poor taste? Maybe they both hated yellow dresses, or the colour was not an agreeable one against the saturated landscape of Singapore. Swapping silk for cotton might have been more practical for their everyday needs, an exchange that they perhaps had to manage discreetly, given Mr Boustead's standing as one of the more influential merchants in the Singaporean trade. Whatever the outcome, it is another reminder that, however different these women's clothes may appear to us now, the human spirit of giving and receiving and the reactions to those gifts are entwined with anxieties that we would find familiar.

The final description of Fanny in Anne's diary is attached to a bonnet ribbon that they shared in 1847, the year that Anne returned to the UK after seven years of life in the settlement. Fanny is never mentioned again. This is something of a puzzle, given Anne's continued attachment to her friends. Those women who were close to her appear from start to finish in the book, sometimes more often than others, but always a constant presence – the cloth with their name a reminder that they were still a part of her life. I do not know what became of Fanny Taylor. Her complete absence after 1847 might suggest that theirs was a friendship based completely on circumstance, and that for those years in Singapore they were exactly what they needed to be for each other at that time. Yet the frequency of their shared connections makes her sudden absenteeism a curiosity. Did Fanny never leave Singapore? Fever was rife in the humid, jungle-fringed town. There was no hospital, and medical options were limited. I searched with some trepidation for any British nationals by the name of Taylor whose deaths were recorded in Singapore in 1847, and I read the announcements columns of the newspapers and journals, but Fanny Taylor remains shrouded in mystery. If she died in Singapore, far from home, then Anne never alluded to it in her diary.

In an album that is so much a dedication to friendship, to female companionship and to the pleasure of giving a gift, Fanny Taylor stands alongside Anne as her supporter, sharing their lives together, laughing over the haberdashery counter as they picked out new ribbons and sharing a knowing glance as they opened Mr Boustead's unfortunate choice of yellow silk. Fanny might be absent in the formality of the records, but for a few years at least, her presence fills Anne's life with love and friendship.

CHAPTER 11

Goods Received

Margaret Brennand

Received by the last Overland Mail and for sale at the
Singapore Millinery Rooms.

Advertisement, *The Straits Times*, 1847

Against a fine black, blue and cream wool check cut into an octagon,
Anne wrote in the tiniest of scripts around its straight edges, 'July 13th
1846. Mr Sykes's vest bought from Miss Brennand's smallwares.' The day
after his birthday, Adam had purchased this smart cloth waistcoat in Singapore from Miss Brennand's establishment. At the same time he bought
a patterned pink ribbon, with stylised floral motifs dotted across its surface and a pinked picot edge. It was given by him to Fanny Taylor – a
sash for her to wear with one of her white cotton dresses perhaps. Similarly the ribbon originated from 'Miss B's smallwares'. On a warm day
in July, Adam waited in the premises run by Miss Brennand for his purchases to be wrapped, the transfer of goods from one hand to another
that mirrored his own mercantile existence. Anne rarely describes the
act of acquisition itself, and perhaps the exchange of money for goods
was too vulgar a topic to describe in detail, but nonetheless there it is
on every page.

Increased textile production and changing approaches to the way clothing was commodified and consumed in the nineteenth century provided the means by which Anne could catch so much in her diary. Shopping itself was to undergo a radical transformation, moving from a model that relied on drapers and dressmakers to the emerging world of the department store. From the handmade to the machine-made, it was a period of dramatic technological change that brought ready-to-wear clothing to the many, but also witnessed the horrific working conditions of the sweated trades. In Anne's lifetime she would see the emergence of couture, setting Parisian designers at the peak of a fashion industry intent on drawing clientele to their luxury showrooms. She would also witness the opening of vast department stores and public transport systems that brought shoppers to the cities, making the act of shopping a pleasurable activity and not simply a functional requirement. The publication of popular magazines such as *The Englishwoman's Domestic Magazine* reported on fashionable attire, their readers poring over descriptions of the latest styles and enjoying the fashion illustrations that featured alongside them. In our world of fast fashion and easy consumption, to look back at Anne and her friends is to catch those moments where the seeds of mass production were sown.

Miss Brennand is the only link in Anne's book to the world of shopping. No other establishments are ever mentioned; no vendors in Singapore or shops in the UK on her return home are ever discussed; nor are the names of any dressmakers or tailors who might have been responsible for the creation of any one of the thousands of garments that feature in the diary. They remain shadowy figures, implied only by the existence of the cloth they sold – which makes Miss Brennand something of a rarity. She appears with some regularity in the album, the fragments described either coming from her own wardrobe or items that she was selling. She clearly contributed a range of different objects, one plain beige silk scrap being described, 'One of Miss Brennand's old aunts wore this dress.'

Tracking Miss Brennand through the archives, however, with nothing by way of a helpful date or even her first name, proved a challenge. In the end I found her via her brother and uncovered the part of her life that had taken her within Anne's orbit and to the heat and colour of Singapore. As with so many of the people that fill Anne's life in the 1840s, Miss Brennand first appears as a ship's passenger along with her brother Richard. Accounts in the *Singapore Free Press* record Richard Brennand in his role as clerk and aspiring merchant in the late 1830s and 1840s, an unmarried ambitious young man working his way up the traders' ladder between a number of different firms.

Margaret Brennand was born on 6 May 1797 in Prestwich, Lancashire, one of the only records that anchor her to this narrative. She is difficult to pin down, appearing for sure only in the 1851 census when she was either living with, or a visitor in, her brother's house in West Derby, Richard having finally married and settled down in 1846. Beyond these two sparse accounts, and the notes of her arrival on board the ships entering the Singapore harbour, her life is obscured. It is possible that she married, but if so, when and to whom remains her secret. There is a Margaret Brennand of the appropriate age listed on the 1841 census as a seamstress living in Liverpool. The same Margaret Brennand appeared in *Gore's Directory of Liverpool* for 1829, where she was plying her trade from 3 Beresford Street. If this is indeed one and the same Margaret, then it would make for a neat explanation of her role in Singapore, running a smallwares establishment for the European community, making up garments for her customers and selling the ribbons and trimmings with which they might decorate or refashion their existing clothes.

Many of the samples in the album that bear Miss Brennand's name carry an international flavour, being described as Japan silks, China silks or a Mandarin satin. She appears to have cultivated connections in order to supply her European customers with cloth arriving from all over South-East Asia, and not always by boat. Alongside a cream-and-blue checked silk Anne wrote, 'June 1846. Anne & Fanny a sash sent overland by Miss Brennand.' Although ships arrived with increasing regularity with mail and supplies from home, the overland routes were still in operation, providing another means by which goods might reach the settlement.

The acquisition of clothing in Singapore was not always predictable in the 1830s and 1840s, although its growth as a European settlement began to attract entrepreneurial spirits to its shores – characters such as M. Agustine Avizagnet, who placed an advertisement in the *Singapore Chronicle* on 6 November 1834: 'M. Agustine Avizagnet has the honor to inform the Public that he has arrived from France and purposes establishing himself at Singapore in the exercise of his profession of Master Tailor. Having worked for upwards of ten years in Paris he hopes to give satisfaction to every person who will do him the honor of sending employ.'

In the late 1830s the absence of shops meant that long-awaited deliveries via the arrival of ships provided much-anticipated supplies. The excitement of receiving these goods was heightened by the method of their disposal, according to an advertisement in the *Singapore Chronicle* on 3 July 1838: 'To be sold by public auction this day at the godowns, the local term for warehouses or storage sheds, of Messrs. Syme & Co an Invoice of Smallwares.' The merchants themselves, then, were taking on the role of shopkeeper, auctioning from their own premises 'coarse and fine white Tapes, superior Bobbin, white Cotton Braids, colored Worsted Braids, Silk and Cotton Wire Ribbons, White Net, Web and Indian Rubber Braces and Cotton Fringe'.

The European women, long denied new additions to their wardrobes, must have gathered for this exciting deviation from their daily routines. By the early 1840s the needs of the female consumer were being met by vendors who had astutely recognised the gap in the sartorial market. The Singapore Millinery Rooms regularly advertised their wares in the columns of the newspaper, selling everything from fancy trimmed and untrimmed bonnets and ladies' white kid gloves, to coloured muslin dresses, white crape and coloured cambrics for slips. Miss Gow ran the Millinery Rooms for a number of years until February 1847, when the establishment was taken over by Mrs Nugent, who was at pains to reassure the customers of her best intentions: 'Mrs Nugent solicits from the Ladies of Singapore that patronage that has been hitherto bestowed upon Miss Gow to merit which every attention will be paid to their wishes and instructions.'

Other options were available to those who chose to correspond with makers from home. Mrs Fry, who described herself as an English Court Milliner with premises at 5 Lupus Street, Pimlico, London, advertised her competitive package to the women of Singapore. She could send six bonnets, six dresses for morning, afternoon and evening wear and six opera and walking cloaks for the sum of £35, 'only requiring bodies to be made according to printed directions'. For those women who had yet to find a local dressmaker to suit their needs, Mrs Fry's offer must have been a tempting one.

In the absence of many local options, it seems that the women might take it upon themselves to improvise when it came to selling items of clothing. On a page of the diary that is devoted to a variety of coloured ribbons, the schoolteacher Miss Grant appears in a slightly different guise to that of missionary school principal. Above a wide lilac figured-silk ribbon, Anne wrote, 'Feb 1846 Anne & Fanny neck ribbon came from Miss Grant's confectionary sale.' To supplement her relatively meagre income, it appears that Miss Grant was selling smaller items – a 'confectionary' of ribbons – to other women in the settlement. Haberdashery might also be sent for from home at low cost, taking up little room in the hold of a ship. Certainly Anne records on numerous occasions either fabric or trimmings that arrived via the merchant shipping that plied back and forth. An entire page in the album, made up of seven silks and two cotton fragments, was part of a welcome arrival that Anne described: 'All this page came by the John Dugdale 1845.' The Boustead ship with

Captain Milward at the helm carried these treats from home, parcels of textiles to tumble onto the table of their house and imagine into newly fashioned bonnets or cotton gowns to mitigate the humidity. In an expatriate community, these tokens were important threads to connect the wearer with all that was familiar.

Maria Balestier recorded some of the difficulties she experienced in acquiring certain of the wardrobe basics, in letters home to her sister. She also described how other merchant wives fared in the maintenance of their own appearance. Following a visit to the veteran merchant's wife Mrs Clark, she saw on the verandah '. . . the lady's dressmaker, a tall, fine looking man in a coat and turban. He was cutting out a dress and had sathins and under sheers and the various articles for a lady's dress around him.' Shortly afterwards, visiting Mrs Connolly, Maria wrote, 'In a kind of sitting room adjoining her bedroom, there was a very grave looking man seated on a mat, dressed in white, surrounded with articles of female attire, which she very gravely said was her dressmaker that worked for her by the year, and she believed was the best in Singapore.'

~

Change was in the air, however, and by the 1830s there began to emerge a market for some partially made-up clothing. In an 1830 edition of the *World of Fashion*, T. Challinier, whose premises were at 109 New Bond Street, London, placed an advertisement that read, 'Muslin Bodices exceedingly useful to the country trade . . . the dresses can be completed for wearing in a few hours' notice.' A stock of gowns was partially made and could then be fitted to the customer, with adjustments made rapidly for those who were visiting town for a short period. For the vast majority of people, though, it was to their trusted local dressmakers that they turned for the regular construction of their clothing. It was a huge industry, each town and village around the UK recording many women employed as dressmakers. In Pam Inder's unrivalled research into this work, she notes that on the 1841 census there were 89,079 milliners and dressmakers and 17,946 seamstresses in England and Wales alone, catering to all levels of society at the time, from the wealthiest clientele to those on much lower incomes. It encompassed a spectrum of labour from those describing themselves as court dressmakers in the West End of London, to the village seamstress earning pennies for her work.

Relationships with dressmakers varied. Some customers remained loyal to a particular maker for many years, building a rapport that relied on a mutual understanding of a client's taste and pocket. It was an intimate transaction, requiring knowledge of the customer's body and measurements, the changes to her physicality over time, catering to marriage, pregnancy, birth and death in the family. Other experiences were more fraught. Many dressmakers considered their customers to be unfeeling in their behaviour. Mary Carmichael described one of these common experiences in a letter to her friend Elizabeth: 'Had a visit on Saturday afternoon from Miss Bateman, had a cup of tea, just in the midst – walked in Lady Braithwaite – wanted a Bonnet, this was half-past-6 and wanted me to unlock and turn out everything.' Clearly Lady Braithwaite cared not a bit for the inconveniently timed visit or the additional work that she was creating for her dressmaker.

The hours that were expected of dressmakers and seamstresses were extraordinarily long, with exceptionally fast turnarounds on orders becoming the norm. One young apprentice in Glossop in Yorkshire routinely worked a twelve-hour day and often even longer, not finishing until past midnight. She recalled, 'We envied the cotton workers who streamed out of the mill as soon as the "buzzer" went at ½ past 5. At least they knew when their working day would end. We never did.' In recognition of the appalling conditions faced by so many low-paid seamstresses, Thomas Hood wrote his poem 'The Song of the Shirt', which was to become a clarion cry for the labouring women who attempted to

make a living through piece work, sewing trousers and shirts for unscru-
pulous employers:

> With fingers weary and worn
> With eyelids heavy and red
> A woman sat in unwomanly rags
> Plying her needle and thread –
> Stitch! Stitch! Stitch!
> In poverty, hunger, and dirt
> And still with a voice of dolorous pitch
> She sang 'The Song of the Shirt!'

The poem was published in the Christmas edition of *Punch* in 1843
and caused a storm of reaction, but change was not to be swift. Twenty
years later a scandal rocked the world of the high-end dressmaker. In
June 1863 an anonymous seamstress had written a letter to *The Times*
in which she described the terrible conditions in the court dressmaking
establishment of Madame Elise. She wrote, 'I work in a crowded room
with 23 others. This morning one of my companions was found dead in
her bed, and we all of us think that long hours and close confinement
had a great deal to do with her end.' She went on to outline the structure of their day during the busy London Season. The dressmaker who
had died was called Mary Ann Walkley, and she had died of exhaustion
and from poor ventilation in the space she shared for rest. This tragedy
was later captured in an illustration by the artist John Leech entitled 'The
Haunted Lady, or The Ghost in the Looking Glass'. A beautiful young
customer in her new gown turns in front of the mirror, with the owner
of the establishment complimenting her appearance, but all that we see
in the mirror is the cadaverous figure of an exhausted seamstress, pushed
beyond her limits to produce the silky confection. Questions were asked

in Parliament and there was a public inquest into Mary Ann's death, but the pace of change remained slow.

THE HAUNTED LADY, OR "THE GHOST" IN THE LOOKING-GLASS.

Madame La Modiste. "WE WOULD NOT HAVE DISAPPOINTED YOUR LADYSHIP, AT ANY SACRIFICE, AND THE ROBE IS FINISHED À MERVEILLE"

The greatest change that Anne would witness in her lifetime of purchasing cloth and clothing was an invention that would revolutionise garment manufacture: the sewing machine. From the eighteenth century onwards, many had tried and failed to successfully design and bring to market a machine that would speed up the process of making clothes. In 1830 the Frenchman Barthélemy Thimonnier patented the first machine that produced a chain stitch, going so far as to win a contract for producing uniforms for the French Army. He was thwarted, however, by the tailors of France, who raided and destroyed every machine that he had made, and by the 1850s found himself penniless in England, having failed in his attempts to revive the business. Many later versions of the hand-cranked sewing machine were attempted in the first half of the nineteenth century by men like Walter Hunt, who made great leaps in the technology required, but never filed a patent for his ideas. The most successful was to be Elias Howe – like Hunt before him, an American inventor – whose machine was patented in 1846. Howe marketed his machine effectively by promoting a competition between his machine and five seamstresses, whom he beat in a timed challenge. However, a series of unlucky business investments left Howe penniless and unable to continue with the development of his invention. It was soon exploited by other men, who were swift to fill the gap in the market.

The greatest breakthrough came from a young machinist named Isaac Merrit Singer, whose successes came from acknowledging the contribution made by Elias Howe, partnering with other interested parties and patenting his own machine in 1851. His business model would become a tour de force. Determined to make it an affordable domestic appliance, Singer worked to create interchangeable parts for his machines and to mass-produce the components in order to drive down costs. The small machines, which were easily stowable, were marketed for use in the home, with payment plans available, and by 1856 Singer opened his first shop in Glasgow. He might not have invented the sewing machine, but Singer certainly knew how to sell them, and in the second half of the nineteenth century his machines not only revolutionised the factory production of clothing, but also precipitated a boom in the home sewing industry.

Popular magazines began to include dress patterns within their pages, and the paper-pattern industry exploded as dressmaking became an economical hobby for the many. It is likely that Anne's clothes, and those of her friends and family, underwent the mechanisation that was thriving around them by the 1850s and 1860s, but it is impossible to track those changes in her diary. The scraps of fabric are, literally, seamless. There are no telltale construction clues that suggest a hand-stitched garment or one that was made at the turn of a Singer handle, so we can only assume – as the pages turn from the 1840s into the 1850s, and on towards the 1860s – that some amongst those scraps of cloth were the first to have been machine-made, drawing Anne Sykes inexorably onwards from hand-stitched clothes to modern mass production.

Alongside the ambitions of the industrialists ran the changing approach to retail. The great Parisian establishments, such as Le Bon Marché, popularised the notion of the department store, a space where customers might browse with no obligation to buy; where counters were decorated with goods that varied in type, but were all sold under one roof. As the century progressed, innovators began to offer refreshment facilities, restrooms, even lounges where customers could sit and write notes to friends on the store's own headed paper. The flourishing world of the late-nineteenth-century department store was captured in Émile Zola's novel *Au Bonheurs des Dames* – The Ladies' Paradise – modelled on the great emporium of Le Bon Marché. Zola wrote of his ambitions for the novel: he wanted to 'write the poem of modern activity', an ode to bourgeois capitalism encapsulated in all of the lives that inhabited the store, from the shop workers living in the attics and eating in the basements, to the customers who roamed the spaces in between.

In fact the origins of the department store model sat much closer to Anne's own world, placing her once again at the heart of great change. In 1831 a shop calling itself 'The Bazaar' opened its doors in Manchester. In its original advertising it stated, 'Prices shall be marked on all the goods, from which no abatement shall be made.' The traditional model of over-the-counter service was disrupted, allowing customers free will to roam amongst the goods for sale. By 1837 The Bazaar was trading as Kendal, Milne & Faulkner and had expanded into vacant premises next door, allowing for a wider range of items for sale. Their 1847 trade card depicted them as silk and shawl warehousemen, but described their services also as general drapers, with 'funerals completely furnished'. They sold everything from fabrics to parasols and dress 'of every description', to blankets, window muslins and upholstery. More than a decade before the bright lights of the Paris stores, Lancashire had blazed a new trail in retail innovation.

Margaret Brennand was just one of the tiny cogs amongst the enormous wheels of commerce that were beginning to turn with greater force from the middle of the nineteenth century. Her smallwares operated as a miniature version of those establishments that were offering a range of goods and services to willing customers, replacing the old but ancient model of the draper and dressmaker, who had for centuries worked to clothe populations. Miss Brennand appears only once in the diary after her departure from Singapore in 1845. It is an entry dating to some ten years afterwards, picking her up in the mid-1850s, when Anne once again describes her pragmatic approach to dress. Against a fragment of robust red flannel, Anne wrote, 'Miss Brennand, part of her 5 day soldier's shirts.' It is an intriguing caption. Had Miss Brennand joined the ranks of the seamstresses toiling to produce multiple garments for the military in order to pay her way through life? Margaret would have been approaching her sixties by this time, so it is possible that this was a philanthropic endeavour, putting her skills to good use for some charitable cause. It seems a fitting final encounter with this entrepreneurial woman, who travelled to the other side of the world and was determined to carve out her own income in a unique set of circumstances.

Letters from Home

An expanse of crinoline in the 1860s.

CHAPTER 12

The Riot and the Party

Emma Taylor

When at the Guild you do arrive,
Like bees they're swarming all alive,
All kinds of trades are working still,
You'll see, now you're at Preston Guild.

Preston Guild song sheet, 1842

Sandwiched between a brown printed cotton that belonged to a Mrs Unsworth and a sage-green silk floral damask – described by Anne as a Mandarin satin belonging to herself, Fanny Taylor and Mary – is a broad ivory silk ribbon. It has even picot-toothed edges and is embellished with three rows of colourful stylised flowers, a rainbow of blurry blooms woven with an additional weft so that they seem to float on the surface of the creamy background. Unlike so many of the other swatches in the diary, whose origin might be narrowed down to a year at best, this fragment is rooted to a specific time and place. Anne wrote above the bright ribbon, 'Emma Taylor's sash at Fancy Ball Preston Guild Sept 1842.' In a moment it is possible to place the object in the wider context of its use, to begin to piece together a single night in the late summer of 1842 and an event tied to centuries of social history. The fragment itself was one of the pieces that began to situate the album more broadly, when it initially came into my possession. With few clues as to the origins and identity of the diary, this was the first caption that suggested an actual place. There were many Anne Sykes in the whole of Britain in the middle of the nineteenth century, and it was Emma Taylor's sash that helped to narrow the field to one county in England, from which I could begin to search the marriage records.

Emma Taylor's appearances in Anne's diary are infrequent. She appears on just six of the pages, with only a handful of fabrics against her name, unlike others who remain a constant presence in Anne's life. Tracking her down beyond the album itself was a circuitous journey, but thanks to Anne's meticulous record of the Preston Guild – like the fragment of ribbon that memorialised her – at least a part of Emma's story emerges. Owing to the mass digitisation of nineteenth-century newspapers, it is possible to scan centuries-old news stories from the comfort of home, which, as it transpired in the Covid era of 2020, was a welcome resource. As a younger researcher in the late 1990s I had found access to archives of British newspapers a much more troublesome affair. For local publications, a trip to the county record office was the only way to glean the necessary information, whilst for a broader spectrum of news and popular periodicals, a trip to the newspaper archive of the British Library required perseverance and a long tube ride to the far end of the Northern Line, where the archive was situated in Colindale. Mastering the unpredictable microfiche machines that would whizz uncontrollably through years of records with an unwitting turn of the handle was just one of the challenges of the research.

But what of the Preston Guild itself? What was this event marked so assiduously by Anne, and at which Emma wore so colourful a sash to the fancy ball? There are more than eight centuries of history that link the town of Preston in Lancashire to the event that still takes place to this day. In 1179 King Henry II granted the town a royal charter and the

right to have a Guild Merchant. The guild formalised the trades operating in the town, allowing only guild members to carry out their business.
It offered a means of regulating trade quality, licensing craftspeople and
merchants. For a small annual fee and following the close scrutiny of
existing members, a new tradesperson might be admitted to its ranks,
and customers would know that, having been admitted to the guild, the
quality of goods or services was assured. By the sixteenth century Preston acknowledged that this admittance need only be confirmed once in
a generation, and so the decision was taken to hold a ceremony every
twenty years. The numbers of people who gathered in response to this
ensured that it became an opportunity to celebrate the successes of the
town, to feast and make merry – a social event that was to become known
as 'England's greatest carnival'.

The entertainments grew in their ambition and the Guild Mayor
presided over ever more lavish costume balls, sporting entertainments,
processions and dinners, held over several days. What had begun as a
medieval statement of power and control became a celebration of commerce and community. There is a rich seam of records that still survive,
charting the history of the guild. The exquisitely inked Guild Roll of 1742
is an inventory of the businesses trading in the town, an alphabetised register of all the colourful industry: John Arkwright, shoemaker; Thomas
Arkwright, tailor; William his son and Richard his brother. Letters, diaries, receipts, certificates, newspaper cuttings and council proceedings
have all been preserved in a long-standing continuity of one town's pride
across the generations. The planning of each guild became ever more
ambitious, and by the nineteenth century more and more spectacular
elements were woven into the five-day occasion. Balloon ascents were
hugely popular, although at the 1822 guild, disaster struck when the hot-
air balloon of one Mr Livingstone crashed and the pioneering aviator
broke his leg. One of the highlights of the 1862 guild was a performance
on Preston Marsh by the world-famous French tightrope walker Charles

Blondin. Only three years previously he had made international head-lines crossing the expanse of the Niagara Gorge, and here he was at the Preston Guild.

Pomp and pageantry were, by the nineteenth century, a defining feature of civic life in Britain. Communities far and wide celebrated individual features of their geography and industry – celebrations that stretched back in time and had become important dates in the social calendar for rural and urban communities alike. Public ritual was an important demonstration of status in a period when this mattered a great deal to the emerging British middle classes. A romanticised vision of the past was reinforced with sometimes lavish ceremonials.

One of the most notorious of these popular revivalisms was the Eglinton Tournament that took place in Ayrshire in Scotland in August 1839. Conceived by Archibald, Earl of Eglinton, it was intended as a re-enactment of a medieval joust, with all the colour and revelry that the imagination could bring forth. Participants were welcomed from the length and breadth of Britain; tickets were free, and applications were made from as far away as Cornwall, Bath and Norfolk, with the Earl requesting that visitors attend in medieval costumes. More than 100,000 people turned up on the opening day, overwhelming the local amenities. A terrible rainstorm upset proceedings still further and the occasion became something of a washout, but it was testament to the revivalism of the era that desired colourful connections with an imag-ined past. Anne Sykes and her peers would no doubt have read avidly of the Eglinton Tournament, which received huge amounts of press cov-erage, at the same time as being ridiculed by Whig Parliamentarians as a grandiose folly. It was a more publicised version of the smaller acts of historical pageantry with which many communities would have identi-fied at the time.

~

Preparations for the 1842 Preston Guild that Emma was soon to attend were not to run as smoothly as in previous years. The North of England had become mired in protest. An industrial depression had seen wage-cuts to workers that amounted to more than 25 per cent, and the mood was ugly. The year after Anne's marriage to Adam in 1838 had witnessed the rejection of the 'People's Charter', a petition to Parliament signed by more than a million people from the working classes, demanding a more democratic political system. Only four days after Anne and Adam had taken their vows of marriage in St George's Church in Tyldesley, a mass gathering of workers was held nine miles away on Kersal Moor near Salford. Speakers from around the country attended to rally the crowd and exhort the population to demand the enfranchisement of a larger section of society, giving the vote to workers and doing away with the corrupt election of landowning MPs. Parliament refused to acknowledge the requests made in the People's Charter, rejecting it in June 1839. Unrest bubbled around the industrial landscapes of England, Wales and Scotland – a period that was punctuated by violent outbreaks and murmurings of a general strike.

In 1842 a second petition was presented to Parliament, this time containing more than three million signatures, but it was once again thrown out. The Chartist newspaper *The Northern Star* reported, 'Three and a half million have quietly, orderly, soberly, peaceably but firmly asked of their rulers to do justice: and their rulers have turned a deaf ear to that protest.' The ongoing depression and dismissal of the petition prompted a wave of strike action. One of the leaders of the Chartist movement was a Preston hand-loom weaver named Richard Marsden, and in August 1842 the strikes that had swept across the North of England from Manchester, Stockport and Bolton arrived in his home town. The strike commenced on 12 August, after a meeting of more than 3,000 of the town's cotton workers saw participants pledge to 'strike work until they had a fair day's wages'. On Saturday 13 August the town's Mayor,

Samuel Horrocks – a member of the wealthy Horrocks family, whose influence had been secured in the 1790s as cotton manufacturers – read the Riot Act, giving permission to the militia to act against protesters in the Lune Street area of the town. Shots were fired and, tragically, four men were killed; several others were injured. All worked in the textile trades. In an all-too-common paradox, it was the very trades that generated the wealth and renown of the British textile industry that were on the receiving end of such hardship from their employers, who took such pride in the industrial past and the mercantile endeavours celebrated at the Preston Guild.

On the very same day that the Lune Street riot ended so tragically, *The Preston Chronicle* issued its full-page calendar of events for the forthcoming Preston Guild, which was scheduled to start on Monday 5 September. That evening there would be a grand firework display and the following morning would see the ceremonial guild procession. On Tuesday evening a 'Grand Miscellaneous Concert' was scheduled to take place, and on Wednesday morning the Mayoress Procession, 'with ladies', would parade the streets. On Wednesday evening there was to be a dress ball, and on Thursday morning not only was there to be a musical entertainment in the Catholic chapel, but the races and regatta would take place around the environs of the town, followed by another grand concert in the evening. On Friday morning the scholars of the town could expect a 'treat' followed by more races, before the denouement of the week: the grand costume ball. On Tuesday 30 August a correspondent for *The Preston Chronicle* reported, 'Now that the tranquillity of the town and its surrounding districts is perfectly restored, with every probability of its continuance, a great deal of interest is taken throughout the county at the approaching Guild Merchant Festival.' Just how well disposed the workers of the town felt towards the forthcoming guild is hidden behind these optimistic reports. The discontent amongst the working population of the town would not disappear and yet, perhaps for a few days, the Preston Guild and its long-awaited entertainments and spectacles offered a brief respite.

That the guild was enjoyed by the whole spectrum of local society emerges from the broadside that was produced especially for the event. Broadsides were cheap ballad sheets sold in the streets to mark such occasions, and John Harkness was the song's author. It began:

You lads and lasses far and near,
Unto my song pray lend an ear,
The time is come for mirth and glee,
To Preston Guild let's haste away.

As well as acknowledging the presence of the lords and ladies in their finery, the author described the great mix of those who came to see the spectacle:

The factory folks are next in view,
Spinners, weavers and carders too,
The piecers do not lag behind,
Brickmakers at the Guild we find,
Bricksetters, masons two and two
To see them walking in a row,
The men who houses and factories build,
You'll see them walk at Preston Guild.

Nor was the social and political situation left out of the ballad's scope – a lament to working conditions being thrown amongst the colour of the processions:

The times are hard, the wages low,
Some thousands to the Guild can't go,

From Blackburn, Burnley, and Chorley still,
They will roll on to Preston Guild,
From Wigan – Bolton – Lancaster,
From Liverpool and Manchester,
The Railroad brings them on it still,
To see the fun at Preston Guild.

It might have been only a temporary cessation of hostilities, but here were the worthies of the town marching with the factory hands who kept the wheels of the cotton trade turning.

At some point then, in early September, Emma Taylor arrived in Preston to take part in the festivities. Did she witness Mr Bywater's fireworks and cheer at the regatta? Perhaps she processed through the streets as part of the Mayoress's cavalcade of attendees, her costume for the ball carefully laid out somewhere, in anticipation of the grand party at the end of the week. Material survivals of the 1842 Preston Guild are many and varied. The nineteenth century saw a huge increase in the mass production of souvenirs and cheap memorabilia in remembrance of regional and national celebrations. Tied as the nation was to the performance of monarchy, collectable objects were made to celebrate royal occasions. Items as varied as white lustreware jugs and commemorative sewing bodkins were produced for Queen Victoria's coronation in 1838, which took place only three months before Anne and Adam married that September. Decorative ceramics were a popular way of memorialising and displaying to others either attendance at or recognition of a particular occasion, and the organisers of the Preston Guild commissioned their own souvenirs to mark the moment. Hand-painted ceramics were first introduced at the 1822 guild. Survivals of the 1842 event include small jugs and painted tankards, the black lettering proclaiming its origins. Weighty guild medallions were struck and presented by the Mayor, Samuel Horrocks, whilst the streets were filled with the refrain of John Harkness's ballad.

As the guild commenced on Monday 5 September, so *The Preston Chronicle* followed events and reported daily on the various entertainments. It recorded that 'Thousands of persons wended their way in all directions and several of the lines of railroad connected with the town put in extra trains and will continue to do so during the week.' The coming of the railroads for the first time brought mass travel to the event, and so the streets were thronged with additional visitors. The Corn Exchange had been fitted out to resemble a Tudor hall, and a 'fancy fair' with refreshments was held inside. Chadwick's Orchard was crowded with exhibitions and 'there were several amusements in various parts of the town consisting of cricket-matches, wrestling and a boat match'. At least 60,000 revellers were reported to have attended on the second day of festivities, filling the streets with a carnivalesque atmosphere. Bands played, street traders sold food, and various souvenirs were on offer to satisfy the day-trippers enjoying a brief period of levity. Prizes to the value of £25 were available to winners of the regatta held at the Ribble Yacht Club, and the Cumberland and Westmorland Wrestling Club enjoyed a few hours' sport. Mr Bywater's fireworks display was a magnificent one, according to the *Chronicle*'s correspondent, 'in a style rarely attempted out of the metropolis'.

The tradition of completing the Preston Guild with a fancy-dress ball was a long-held one that grew in stature with each event. A surviving watercolour from the 1822 ball, painted by local artist Emily Brooke, depicts around thirty of the guests in diverse costumes. Whilst some chose the conventional historical approach and arrived in the garb of a bewigged eighteenth-century gentleman or a medieval merchant, others were more creative (an owl and a parrot notably feature in Emily's painting).

Whereas Emma's dress itself does not remain intact, there is a sole survivor of the costume ball of 1842. In the collections of the Harris Museum in Preston is an ivory silk gown worn to the same ball at which

Emma sported her floral sash. It belonged to Miss Anne Agnes Addison, daughter of a County Court judge, John Addison. As it remains now, it is a relatively simple affair, the creamy taffeta pleated tightly into the waist as fashion dictated, but with little else by way of decoration. It is likely that this was simply a canvas for the various decorations that would have been added. Within a lengthy description of the costume ball and its attendees in *The Preston Chronicle*, Miss Addison is described as attending as Albreda de Lisours, a medieval lady of Yorkshire, and so perhaps the ivory dress would have been adorned with the kind of drapery deemed appropriate to represent the earliest incarnation of the Preston Guild. It is a rare survival, a gown that swayed to the tunes of the musicians in the Corn Exchange building that evening of Friday 9 September 1842.

Tickets for the event went on sale in August. It was possible to buy either a subscription ticket for £2 2s. – gaining admittance to not only the costume ball, but also to the oratorio, concert and dress ball – or to purchase a single admittance ticket to the costume ball for £1 1s. In the opening description that ran in its weekend edition, *The Preston Chronicle* was lavish in its praise of the costumes on display: 'There were some superb Scotch, Brigand, Robin Hood and similar dresses. The costumes of both ancient and modern times and kingdoms were numerous. Among the Charles's, the Elizabeth's, the Edward's and the Henry's we should have much difficulty in selecting the best.'

It was thanks to this appraisal of the night's entertainment that Emma Taylor was brought more sharply into focus. The report endeavoured to record as many of those persons present as it could, and from amongst the hundreds of names that followed, eventually there she was: listed beneath Edward Birley, dressed as the Barber of Seville, and above Mr Jos. Seddon, a Venetian noble, there is 'Miss Emma Taylor, Clitheroe, Swiss flower girl'. The simple confirmation of her home town not only connected her geographically with Anne, but also unlocked a little of her story. According to the baptismal records of Mary Magdalene Church in Clitheroe, Emma Taylor was born on 30 December 1820. Her mother was Jane and her father, John, was a cotton manufacturer in the town. It seems likely that she was related to Fanny Taylor, whose friendship featured so prominently during Anne's years in Singapore, but what that connection might have been remains elusive – a possible link that is obscured by the all-too-plentiful Taylors littered amongst the public records, hiding in plain sight.

A deed of covenant held in the National Archives seems to point to a connection of sorts between Anne's father, the cotton spinner James Burton, and the Taylors. Dated 1829, it indicates that alongside Jane Taylor, James Burton had been appointed as executor to the estate of the recently deceased John Taylor. As fellow textile manufacturers in the town of Clitheroe, John and James appear to have been friends, the two families joined socially as well as professionally. Her father having died when Emma was still a child, it is impossible to tell how she came to the Preston Guild or with whom she stayed. The costume of a Swiss flower girl was an appropriately innocent one to choose, aged twenty-two and unmarried. According to the weekend press report, the guests began to arrive at 9 p.m. 'and the room kept filling fast until a late hour'. The refreshments were, apparently, excellent and 'dancing was kept up till nearly daylight'.

The Corn Exchange was the chosen venue – an imposing brick-built civic building that was solid in its industrial roots. An engraving of the interior as it appeared for the costume ball took the guests back in time, with banners and decorations proclaiming the medieval ancestry of the event. The image depicts guests in various garb milling around the large hall, which is sparsely populated in order to give full view of the building, although, according to *The London Standard* of 13 September, upwards of 1,000 guests attended the grand finale of the Preston Guild. The same article is effusive about the quality of the costumes on display: 'Many of the uniforms and characters were of the most splendid description, having been used at Her Majesty's Royal *bal masqué*.' The first of the three fancy dress balls given by Queen Victoria and Prince Albert had taken place in London on 12 May 1842, and those guests who went on to attend the Preston Guild were able to reuse their splendid costumes.

The Preston Guild continues to be an important part of the town's heritage, its only interruption taking place in 1942 when war prevented the event. The most recent guild was held in 2012, a week-long celebration in early September, punctuated by many of the same kinds of entertainments that so thrilled the earlier population of the town – an impressive trade procession, thronged streets of visitors from all over the world, musical interludes, sporting competitions and fireworks. So many of the ingredients remain the same, although the costume ball is no longer a fixture. The Corn Exchange itself remains, its rich red-brick façade still welcoming visitors through its doors, a hospitality venue that in the past played host to the likes of The Beatles, Pink Floyd and Fleetwood Mac. So many Prestonian feet have danced in that space.

As the final strains of the music died away, signalling the end of the 1842 Preston Guild, those halcyon days must soon have seemed like another lifetime for the workers of Preston. Six years later the Chartists presented another, final petition to Parliament, this time with more than six million signatures. Once more it was rejected, ultimately marking the end of Chartism. It was not until the Second Reform Act of 1867 that a greater number of the population were enfranchised, giving voice to a larger sector of society. How aware was Emma Taylor of the privations of the workers and of those events that had taken place only weeks before, when the Corn Exchange had witnessed a very different kind of disruption?

I hope that Emma danced until dawn before finding her weary way to bed, untying the floral sash of her costume and laying the dress aside as she hummed the tunes of the evening to herself and reflected on the music, the refreshments, the other costumes she had seen. At some point after the event, she cut a portion of the ribbon and tucked it into an envelope. Maybe she wrote an excited letter full of the sights she had witnessed, folding the ribbon fragment within it and addressing it to Mrs Anne Sykes far away in Singapore – a little description of home for Anne to share, reading the news aloud to Adam and Fanny, before slotting the silky sash into the pages of her diary.

CHAPTER 13

Dancing by Candlelight
The Misses Wrigley

Lace trimmings, diamond brooches, medallion bracelets,
trembled on the bodices, glittered on the bosoms, tinkled
on the bare arms.

Gustave Flaubert, *Madame Bovary*, 1856

The Misses Wrigley feature here and there in Anne's album, their
fragments of silk like butterflies alighting on pages at random. Their
provenance is just as sketchy and indistinct, their identities dancing in
the distance, but never quite forming into clear shapes. As humans, there
are a thousand versions of ourselves, depending on the perspective of
the observer. The Misses Wrigley are never graced with their first names
in the book, and so our view of them is hazy. There are no exact dates
from which they can be rooted to one of those life events captured on
paper in the records. They will be there somewhere, their births, marriages and deaths inked formally in registers. A parish ledger will contain
these Misses Wrigley; a death certificate will outline the point of their
demise. Sometimes serendipity lands in the lap of the researcher, so
that the names begin to form themselves into the shape of a person, but
without Anne's helpful addition of a date, a forename or a place in this

instance, the Misses Wrigley remain just out of focus, blurry silhouettes on the horizon of her life.

The most significant heading associated with them in Anne's book relates to page 79. A heading at the top of the pale-blue page reads, 'The dresses worn at Miss Wrigley's dance January 1845'. Some pages earlier, eight fragments of silk are labelled simply 'The Misses Wrigley'. The proliferation of silk in their wardrobe, and the dance given in their honour in 1845, generates a narrow view of these girls – for girls they are, in my mind's eye. Without more detail, I see them forever giggling in preparation for their ball, tying silk sashes and lacing soft evening slippers, arranging lace flounces over their silken bodices and combing their hair into fashionable chignons. It is the merest sliver of life. One evening is all we have of these particular women: a single chink of a view, with the rest of life inhabiting the shadows of the unknown and unrecorded. That reference, however, is enough. It throws light in a broader direction, onto the etiquette of the ballrooms, dinners and outings that marked the specific context of evening dress in the nineteenth century, when clothes were so codified as to indicate more clearly the times of day that they were designed to be worn.

From the seemingly egalitarian perspective of sartorial life in the twenty-first century it is easy to dismiss clothing etiquette as ridiculous. As the boundaries between work and home, day and night, formal and informal blur in our wardrobes, those stricter demarcations that were so rigorously enforced by 'society' in the nineteenth century seem, from our lofty view, to take on a pedantic hue. Yet for many people these markers mattered a great deal, and successful navigation of such etiquettes might mean the difference between professional success and abject failure. For women, especially, this was their domain. To negotiate socialising was to facilitate marriage, cement friendships and enhance job prospects. It was the women who were the keepers of this knowledge, the arbiters of the invitations, the visiting cards, the friendly (or not) nods in the street, the social constructs that kept the wheels of polite society turning. In his *Memoirs of Life and Literature* published in 1920, the novelist William Mallock wrote that 'Society was a matter as serious as politics or any war' in the nineteenth century, and dress was central to its success.

Evening fashions, *Les Modes Parisiennes*, 1860.

For those living amongst the middle and upper classes, dress had grown increasingly complex as an indicator of time of day and occasion. Consuelo Vanderbilt, a wealthy American who married into the British aristocracy and became the Duchess of Marlborough in 1895, wrote in her memoirs of the complexity that went with a country-house visit. She was baffled by the many changes of clothes – from a breakfast gown to tweeds, then a tea gown for the afternoon, after which came the change into formal evening dress. 'All these changes necessitated a tremendous outlay, since one was not supposed to wear the same gown twice. That meant sixteen dresses for four days.' The Duchess of Marlborough was, of course, operating at the extreme of the social spectrum, beyond the expectations of most, but nonetheless the requirement still existed for many to appear in the right dress for the right time of day.

Essentially by the beginning of the nineteenth century dress had become separated into daywear and evening wear. For daytime, garments of cotton and wool with high necklines were deemed suitable, whilst for evening fabrics like silk or organdie weaves were chosen along with a greater degree of ornamentation, lower décolletage and short sleeves. By the middle of the century different strategies began to emerge for the more practical approach to the change of aesthetic marked by the hand of the clock. Born out of the hectic pace that some women were experiencing, but also from an inclination not to spend too much money, the 'transformation dress' arrived. Fashions of the 1850s consisted of a separate skirt and bodice over which was fastened a matching belt. This flexibility of design meant that it was possible to have two different bodices that could be worn with one skirt. The day bodice would have a modest, round neckline that might be trimmed with a neat lace collar and long sleeves with matching lace cuffs. The evening bodice, made from the same fabric, would expose the shoulders with a low, sweeping décolleté and short puff sleeves. Sometimes the transformation might take place in a different way, with detachable sleeves to change the face of the garment, whisking it from lunch to dinner, from lounge to ballroom. These adaptable ensembles were time-savers and more economical, enabling women to mix and match their clothes, extending their usefulness.

To avoid the potential pitfalls of an etiquette mis-step, manuals were published to help the uninitiated with the rules of the ballroom. *Routledge's Manual of Etiquette* spent its first thirty pages advising women on the shape of their day, from morning calls to the promenade and into the evening. The author advised the reader, 'Let your style of dress always be appropriate to the hour of the day. To dress too finely in the morning or to be seen in a morning dress in the evening, is equally vulgar and out of place.' An entire chapter was devoted to the setting up of and behaviour within a ballroom, from the wearing of gloves to the appropriate length of a skirt in order to dance successfully. *The Ladies' Book of Etiquette and Manual of Politeness*, published in 1860, took the prospective ball-goer through every step of her evening, beginning with her toilette: 'In preparing a costume for a ball choose something very light. Heavy, dark silks are out of place in a ballroom and black should be worn in no material but lace. White silk plain, or lace over satin make an exquisite toilette.' Every action was considered in the volume. 'Your first duty, upon entering the room, is to speak to your hostess. After a few words of greeting, turn to the other guests.'

To add complexity, balls were not the only form of evening entertainment, and different rules applied to different occasions, be it dinner, a musical entertainment or the grander occasion of a ball. Take note, the author advised, that 'Gloves and mittens are no longer worn at table, even at the largest dinner-parties.' A single volume of *The Queen: The Ladies' Newspaper* from 1882 included illustrations of the different degrees of evening dress, which included a dinner dress, reception dress, home dinner toilette, evening demi-toilette, concert toilette, evening dress and ball dress. Each of these garments would be distinctive through a slight variation in sleeve length, plunge of neckline or amount of ornamentation. Such distinctions were necessary for the wearer, who might find their appearance described in one of the society pages of the popular periodicals. In 1897 Mrs Tennant gave 'a pleasant dinner followed by an evening party at her house in Richmond Terrace'. The guests were described in all their finery: 'Lady Conway in a yellow brocade gown with Watteau pleat and ivy leaves in her hair; Miss Green in brightest red chiffon over silk with a gold waistband; Mrs and Miss Channing in pink moiré; Lady Seymour in black velvet and diamonds; Mrs Strachey in pale yellow wearing some pretty old jewels.' Whilst not everybody would find themselves written about in the society columns, there is no doubt that appearances were analysed and gossiped over. Whether in London or Liverpool, Singapore or Tyldesley, the efficacy of local chatter would spread details far and wide.

The London Season had evolved into a very specific and structured round of social events by the mid-nineteenth century. Honoré de Balzac described the Season in his 1837 novel *The Muse of the Department*: 'London is the capital of shops and of speculation, the government is made there. The aristocracy inscribes itself there only during sixty days, it there takes its orders, it inspects the government kitchen, it passes in review its daughters to marry, and equipages to sell, it says good-day and goes away promptly . . .' The Season was determined by a variety of factors, from the sitting of Parliament to the sporting events it encompassed – horseracing at the Epsom Derby and Ascot, the Henley Regatta. Sometime after Easter, until the middle of August, wealthy families would descend on the capital to see and be seen. Daughters who had come of age would be presented at court in all the feathered finery demanded by that particular formality, and dressmakers would work around the clock to cater to the whims of their clientele. It was a huge industry for the UK economy. In the 1851 census the clothing trades employed 28,000 men and 84,000 women as tailors, dressmakers, shoemakers and milliners.

The expansion of the middle classes, and the growing industrialisation witnessed in the nineteenth century with the new money that came with it, meant that in the 1830s and 1840s access to 'Society' was important for a larger number of people, not just those living in or visiting London. As the young wife to an ambitious merchant, Anne would have recognised that her ability to socialise with and entertain other merchants and their wives was invaluable. Certainly the prevalence of fabric swatches that belonged to the other wives in the settlement of Singapore seems to confirm that Anne's friendships had extended from her husband's professional network into her own domestic spaces.

As the etiquette manuals proliferated to cater to this new market, so satirical publications such as *Punch* set the nouveau riche in their sights. In 1841 the periodical ran a series of sketches called 'The Side Scenes of Society', which followed the exploits of a newly moneyed family called the Spangle Lacquers. One of the descriptions observed snidely, 'You will always be certain to meet at the Lacquers' a great many persons with whom you are perfectly well-acquainted by sight, but to whom you can assign no fixed place in society, having generally met them in places where distinction was acquired by paying for it.' However scathing the families of 'old money' might be, British (and in Anne's case for a time, the British colonial) experiences of 'Society' were absolutely vital. For the vast majority of women, their entrance into Society determined the direction their lives would take. The ballroom was a space where marriages were forged and in the mid-nineteenth century, for most women, this was the route that took them away from the family home and into a realm of their own making.

∼

The proliferation of silk in Anne's book certainly indicates that she and her peers were fully engaged with the expectations of Society, whether that took place in the community of Singapore or in the North of England. Far from the pace of the London Season, Anne's requirements and those of her friends could take place at a more measured pace, with dressmakers able to fulfil orders made under slightly less pressure. Balls are mentioned more specifically, presumably because they took place less often than dinners. They were occasions marked by some distinction, as Anne notes above a broad piece of blond lace: 'Blond worn by Anne, Fanny and Emma Taylor at their first ball.' On the same page, above a translucent piece of muslin decorated with woven white spiral spots, Anne wrote, 'Ball dress Fanny Taylor 1842 trimmed with this lace', indicating the white machine-lace trim placed next to the muslin – as close as the two elements of the dress were ever to become again, reunited in Anne's album after the last notes of the ball had rung out and the weary attendees had stumbled home. The dresses worn to the Misses Wrigleys' ball in January 1845 are all recorded carefully on the same page. As per the advice from *The Ladies' Book of Etiquette*, each of the fragments that records this particular party is a pale silk – one a cream satin, another of cream satin figured with a colourful floral brocade, a pale pink silk with cream floral motif and finally a cream figured silk. They belonged to Hannah Wrigley, Harriet Ashton, Sarah Newmann and Jane Sykes respectively – Anne's friends gathered in pale shades, iced with lace.

The years covered by Anne's album saw fashion at its most expansive. Skirts of the late 1830s and into the 1840s began to widen into bell-shaped domes, and by the 1850s and 1860s they had grown more extravagant still, with yards of tiered and trimmed fabric suspended over the fashionable cage crinoline. Bodices were buttoned or laced over corsets; sleeves variously named (the bishop sleeve, the pagoda sleeve) fell over practical cotton under-sleeves or clung to the upper arm in a short puff of silk and net for evening wear. The garments themselves are as unfamiliar now as the etiquette they represented, and yet the control that women maintained over their wardrobes, and how they appeared at any given time of the day or evening, was their place of dominance – a space of control and agency into which men dared not venture – and so it mattered.

Without additional commentary from Anne it is impossible to know how much she or her friends enjoyed these evening entertainments, but the specificity of their mention in the album obviously made them worthy of note. Of a striking pink-and-purple changeant-silk taffeta, Anne wrote, 'Anne Sykes Dec 1847. Dress worn at the Bachelor's Ball May 4th 1848.' The reference to December may be the date it was purchased or ordered, for this kind of garment needed to be present in a wardrobe ready for just such an occasion as the Bachelor Ball. Given that at this point in her life Anne was living in Singapore, her access to dressmakers was more limited, but this vibrant silk met the requirements of a candlelit room with its shift and flicker of light.

Evening entertainments were, for those women living far from all that they knew, an opportunity to replicate the assemblies of home for a few hours at least. Maria Balestier wrote to her sister in 1834 describing a party that took place at Mrs Connolly's. Mrs Connolly's name features frequently in Anne's album, although this party took place six years before Anne's arrival in the colony. 'The party at Mrs Connolly's was very brilliant, the Ladies elegantly drest . . . There are only about fourteen or fifteen visitable Ladies in the Settlement. Their return has been a signal for dancing, and many partys have taken place for them.' The desire to dance, on the part of these young women, leaps from Maria Balestier's pen as, dressed in their finery, they meet beaus and drink tea and wine before a 'splendid supper at twelve'. Maria recorded similar events as the years passed, writing again to her sister of the Bachelor Ball in 1838, which 'as I do not dance is rather a dull affair to me'. Of the more than dozen swatches of fabric that belonged to Maria Balestier in Anne Sykes's album, only one is silk – the material evidence confirming her seeming dislike of the formalities required of a dance.

Although Anne's life in the UK had been dominated by cotton, she actually lived fewer than thirty miles from one of the world's largest producers of finished silks. Raw silk had been imported into Britain from as early as the fifteenth century, but by the eighteenth century Huguenot refugees – Protestants fleeing religious persecution from the Catholic Church in France – had settled in the Spitalfields area of London, bringing their expertise in silk-weaving with them. Steam power in the nineteenth century saw silk production move to the North of England. Thanks to a ban on continental imports, by the late eighteenth and early nineteenth centuries towns such as Manchester and Macclesfield were employing thousands of local people in the silk-weaving trade. From twister to drawer, from dresser to dyer, the combined roles in the silk factories produced some of the finest cloth in the world. Silk has social capital. It operates as a signifier of value, a global cloth that began its life along the Silk Road to China or Turkey, was manipulated from its raw state into a commercial fibre and woven into a rainbow of shades to decorate the houses and bodies of the privileged. Silk communicated wealth and so, for Anne and her contemporaries, the choice of silk for formal occasions – the fragments of which she so carefully preserved in her album – was a marker of their place in society.

It was not only the silk industry that thrived in response to the social whirl of fashion. Evening dress required embellishment. Haberdashers and artisanal studios produced a myriad of trimmings for decorating formal garments. Occasional evidence of this beautiful ephemera finds its way into Anne's book. On a page from the early 1840s filled with bright-shaded cap ribbons is pasted a more textured snippet. Pink-and-white corded silk is knotted and looped into a short length of passementerie – the generic name given to the trimmings that could be purchased by the yard to appliqué onto the silks of evening wear. These were skilled trades in their own right. The art of the cord-spinner, the braid-weaver and the tassel-maker were industries that had been described in the eighteenth century in Diderot's comprehensive encyclopaedia of artisanal practices. By the middle of the nineteenth century some of these trimmings were being made on an industrial scale to meet the demands of a broader market with variable budgets, but the handmade existed alongside the mass-produced. For those with deeper pockets, couture houses such as Worth in Paris collaborated with embroidery ateliers such as that owned by Albert Michonet. From the 1860s Michonet could produce intricate hand-stitched panels, taffeta flowers, ribbonwork roses and gold-bullion tassels to decorate the gowns of the wealthiest couture clients.

The ubiquity of embroidery as a female practice meant that it was also a means of customising dresses uniquely, and affordably, for those women who chose to wield their needles at home. The stereotype of women embroidering at home in the nineteenth century is a pervasive one. Hand-sewing and embroidery formed an acceptable and productive activity for women to undertake in the home around their other housekeeping responsibilities. It has become synonymous with passivity and, across both novel and screen, the mark of a strong and liberated woman lies in how badly she embroiders. Only weak and wilting women are good at embroidery in popular narratives, and yet this dismisses the power of the needle and what it could produce.

In Anne's album there is some evidence of the hand-embellishing of garments for evening wear. Early in the volume on a page of five fragments, all belonging to a Mrs Francis, two samples of sheer white cotton have been hand-embroidered in chain stitch – one with a white vine motif and red flowers, and another with small blue and brown chain-stitch butterflies. Chain stitch, or tambour work as it was popularly known, was a fashionable choice of decoration in the late eighteenth and early nineteenth centuries. It could be worked with a broad hoop and a tambour hook, which enabled the stitch to be worked at speed, with loops of silk swirling in shaded motifs creating unique garments, limited only by the maker's imagination. To dismiss the value of home embroidery is to devalue the labour of generations of women – women like Anne and her peers, who were thoughtful about the contents of their wardrobes and were able to fashion and refashion garments for evening entertainments during a period when it was not feasible to acquire something new for each occasion.

As one turns the pages of the album, the silks still glisten from the paper. Each pale, shining swatch holds the echo of evenings past, of dinners and the chink of glass and cutlery, of concerts with their flutter of fans, and of balls that saw the whisk of a skirt spinning in a quadrille. Society and socialising could be both enjoyable and strategic; a gathering of friends in a strange land as the merchant wives gossiped across the punch bowl in Singapore, but also a means of forging connections, marriages and partnerships – social and political ambitions dancing alongside the frivolous.

We don't know if the Misses Wrigley remained 'misses'. Perhaps at their ball of January 1845, recorded so fleetingly by Anne, and dressed in their ivory dresses trimmed with deep lace flounces, they were introduced to the opportunity of a relationship that would dictate the rest of their lives. Maybe, as the guests finally trickled away in the early hours of the morning and the candles were extinguished, they stepped wearily to their beds, full of the evening's events. As they unlaced their slippers and rubbed aching feet, then stepped out of the shining dresses and loosened their corsets, maybe they were recalling a glance here, a smile there. Or perhaps they were dancing still as they donned enveloping nightdresses and went to sleep with the strains of the music still in their ears.

CHAPTER 14

Wardrobe of Grief

Hannah Coubrough

Many widows never put on colours again . . .

The Englishwoman's Domestic Magazine, 1876

More than 100 pages into Anne's album, a poignant caption identifies three swatches of sombre fabric: 'Anna. Three dresses when in mourning for her mother. 1845.' Two of the fragments are open-weave cotton gauzes in black with a resist-dyed stripe and motif incorporated into the design, and the third is a plain black satin, its sheen still catching the light as the page turns. The three samples are arranged uniformly in a horizontal line, one of the only instances in the book that Anne organised her fabric in this way. They sit like sentinels at the top of the page, the single caption written across all three to unite them in their specific purpose.

Mourning clothes were vital markers of the passage of life and death in the nineteenth century, a series of sartorial signposts that indicated the stage of mourning and the passing of time since the loss of a loved one. Snippets of such loss appear frequently throughout Anne's album, but none are more clearly defined than Hannah Coubrough's. These scraps of her mourning dresses open up a world of strict etiquette, a cult of mourning that grew ever more powerful as the century progressed.

It reached a level of complexity that required etiquette manuals that gave the uninitiated a way to navigate these essential but non-verbal communicators – or risk social criticism. The manuals served a dual purpose of both educating the uninitiated into the rites of mourning, but with an eye to commerce too, promoting the apparatus of bereavement and directing the customer towards the retailer. Our modern understanding of mourning clothes is generally confined to the day of burial, the final farewell, standing amongst others in similar sombre attire. Even this remnant of earlier practices is waning, and brighter colours might be worn instead to celebrate the life that has passed. For Anne and her contemporaries, the outward display of mourning commenced with the final breath and continued on a long journey of weeks, months and even years, with shades of grief marked in cotton, wool and silk.

The friendship between Anne Sykes and Hannah Coubrough was of long standing. Hannah Butler was born on 21 December 1809 in Bolton, making her seven years older than Anne. In the marriage register of St George's Church in Tyldesley, Hannah Butler is listed as one of the witnesses to Anne and Adam's wedding in September 1838, and an entry in Anne's album indicates the closeness of their friendship. Above a piece of cream figured silk, Anne wrote, 'Anna and Mary's dresses when they were my bridesmaids.' Anne habitually calls Hannah 'Anna' throughout the volume. On 10 December 1840 Hannah married Anthony Park Coubrough, a Scottish calico printer. One year later, according to the Scottish census of 1841, the couple were living on Rose Street in Glasgow. They had seven children, and in 1843 their son Anthony was baptised with the middle name 'Sykes'. The families were intertwined, in spite of Anne and Adam's absence in Singapore when little Anthony was born; these were friendships that endured time and distance.

If 'respectability' was one of the key social drivers of nineteenth-century society, then the way dress was woven into notions of respectability naturally offered discernible boundaries to outward appearances. Black, worn as a colour associated with mourning the loss of a loved one, was not a new concept in the nineteenth century, and in European contexts it had been worn for centuries to display grief. Particular to the nineteenth century, however, was the industrialisation of the textile industries, which meant the apparatus of grief was displayed in an ever more varied collection of material goods that were available to a larger section of the population. The social commentator Henry Mayhew wrote in 1865, 'In the present day our ashes must be properly selected, our garments must be rent to pattern, our sack cloth must be of the finest quality and that our grief goes for nothing if not fashionable.'

Mayhew was referring to the new emporiums of fashionable mourning that had begun to emerge in the early 1840s. Jay's Mourning Warehouse was established on the corner of Regent Street in London in 1841, occupying the three large houses of numbers 247, 248 and 249, and sold every conceivable object that might be required for the newly bereaved, from mourning clothes to writing paper. In a sense, it was the forerunner of the department-store model, offering a variety of commodities under one roof, for speed and convenience. Establishments such as Jay's, Pugh's Mourning Warehouse and Peter Robinson's all catered for every requirement and provided appropriately sombre interiors for their customers. Henry Mayhew described '. . . the quietness, the harmonious so to speak hush of the whole place'. He recalled its 'unshoppy' characteristics: the hush of thick carpets to soften the bustle, and the mahogany tables at which clients could sit and place their orders in an environment that was unlike other commercial spaces.

Companies such as Jay's and the Grande Maison de Noir in Paris published etiquette manuals, both to ensure that customers did not make a social faux pas in their outward display of grief and to encourage their custom – to offer the guiding hand of commerce in sympathetic tones. The commodification of mourning on such a grand scale in the mid-nineteenth century meant that such establishments were well placed to

Jay's Mourning Warehouse, Regent Street, 1840s.

come under the eye of the contemporary satirist. The poet and writer Thomas Hood produced *Hood's Magazine and Comic Miscellany* in which he created a fictional mourning warehouse. Customers on uncertain ground were advised by knowing salesmen, in comedic exchanges:

> *Lady.* Is it proper, sir, to mourn in velvet?
> *Shopm.* O quite! – certainly. Just coming in. Now here is a very rich one – real Genoa – and a splendid black. We call it the Luxury of Woe.
> *Lady.* Very expensive of course?

The 'luxury of woe' – a cloth to exhibit both wealth and grief in one bolt of fabric – was a satirical critique of the huge expansion of mourning apparatus that Hood witnessed in London, a comedic wink at the excesses of the elite in their supposedly appropriate expressions of grief. Yet for many, in an era when verbal confessions of emotion were not so easily or freely shared, the nuances of mourning dress enabled the conveyance of circumstances to be silently communicated. For smaller establishments, too, catering to the bereaved would form a significant portion of their work. Local drapers would advertise the speed at which they could produce the necessary accoutrements for those newly in mourning, and the obituary and announcements columns of local newspapers would generally carry an advertisement from the local suppliers to that effect.

For Hannah Coubrough, living in Glasgow, it is possible that she ordered her mourning clothes from a large local draper or even from the emerging department stores that were opening their doors in the 1840s. John Anderson was one of these retail pioneers, selling a range of lines in his drapery shop in Clyde Terrace, before expanding and moving to fashionable Argyle Street with the much grander soubriquet of Anderson's Royal Polytechnic. Having lived in the city since her marriage in 1840, it is likely that Hannah had, by this time, found a local dressmaking establishment she favoured, buying the cloth that she desired and commissioning gowns from these smaller retailers. Given that her husband worked in the calico-printing industry, cloth was woven into their lives and her access to sellers, printers and weavers may have been more personal than was usual.

In the regions, local dressmakers were called upon to act swiftly for clients who could not be seen in anything but black, although until the 1860s there was a grace period of eight days before full mourning had to be adopted, to allow families time to assemble their wardrobe of grief. For those whose income could not support the outlay of new clothes, there might be a single garment that was kept for periods of mourning, but the rising numbers of the middle classes saw a boom in purchasing the material expressions of grief. To be ill-prepared risked social castigation. One of Queen Victoria's ladies-in-waiting wrote home to her husband of her frustration during one of her periods of service at Balmoral in 1889, 'I am in despair about my clothes, no sooner have I rigged myself out with good tweeds than we are plunged into the deepest mourning for the King of Portugal, jet ornaments for six weeks! And he was only a first cousin once removed. So I only possess one warm black dress: the Sunday one is far from thick. It is a lesson never, never to buy anything but black!' Much of the increased codification that surrounded mourning etiquette was due in no small part to Queen Victoria herself, whose decision to remain in mourning for her beloved husband Albert became the defining aesthetic of the rest of her life.

Its complexities became ever more detailed as the century progressed, based on the degree of relationship with the deceased. The hierarchy of etiquette was infused with the aspirations of the emerging middle classes in the UK. The expansion of a sector of the population that had money, but was snobbishly denied access to the aristocracy, created a desire for stratification. If the middle classes could not access the upper echelons of social status, they could at least emulate them, and so the myriad sartorial rules of the period – including mourning – grew ever more detailed. A widow went into mourning for her husband for two and a half years. The first and deepest period of mourning lasted for a year and a day, during which time only the heaviest of black crape dresses might be worn. The process of creating silk crape was a technology that had been industrialised by the company of Courtaulds in London, and between 1835 and 1885 its capital had grown from £40,000 to £450,000. Taking a lightweight, diaphanous silk, the crape process both crimped and mattified the fabric so that it lost its sheen, acquiring a deliberately lustreless surface. In *Middlemarch*, written in 1871 but set in the 1830s, Dorothea's maid Tantripp grumbles about her mistress's prolonged mourning for her disagreeable older husband: 'most thankful I shall be to see you with a couple o' pounds worth less of crape'.

After a year and one day the widow might enter the second stage of mourning, lasting for a further nine months. Dresses with less crape trimming appeared in this stage and some jet ornaments might be added to garments, but it was still an unremitting black. Jet became a highly fashionable addition to the outward display of grief and saw a boom in the industry, which was entirely centred on the northern coastal town of Whitby. Memorial jewellery took a variety of forms in the nineteenth century. In the deepest stage of mourning, only those objects with a matt surface were permitted, in tandem with the matt finish of the dresses they adorned. Anxieties surrounding reflected images of the dead hailed back to ancient times – the Greek legend of Narcissus cautioning against the vanity of the reflection, and water sprites that would drag the reflected soul into the depths. Unpolished jet and fossilised wood were suitably dull materials to this end and added to the growing number of consumables associated with mourning practices.

For centuries jet was supposed to contain magical properties, warding off evil spirits and protecting the wearer, but from the medieval period onwards, it was also appropriated by Christian traditions, with carvings and rosaries sold as souvenirs to pilgrims visiting saintly shrines. Jet is actually a type of fossilised wood, specifically of the monkey-puzzle tree, and in the UK rich black seams of the stone threaded through the cliffs surrounding Whitby. By 1832 there were two jet shops producing jewellery for the memorial and mourning industries, and by 1850 this had risen to seven establishments carving thousands of pieces of jet every year. It became an industry on an international scale, supplying department stores as far afield as New York, and by the early 1870s almost 1,500 men in the town were employed in the industry. The finest jet could be enormously expensive and so cheap imitations began to appear – black cut glass that was given the enticing description of 'French jet' and could appear equally ornate. To discern the difference, you must hold the object in your hand, a lesson that I learned as a young curator. French jet is cold to the touch, the chill of glass unmasking it as an imposter.

Another hugely popular form of memorial jewellery in the nineteenth century was that made from hair. In the twenty-first century the notion of hair jewellery can provoke a slightly squeamish reaction and yet traditionally, and across cultures, hair often acted as a symbol of love. As a material that does not deteriorate, it can be read as a metaphor for enduring love, even when the person has passed away. The fineness and durability of hair meant that it was an excellent material to weave, plait and knot into intricate designs for bracelets, necklaces, earrings and brooches. Sometimes lockets engraved with a loved one's initials would open to reveal a lock of hair, or hair woven into a complex design captured for ever behind a disc of glass. The popular American periodical *Godey's Lady's Book* described the practice in 1860: 'Hair is at once the most delicate and lasting of our materials and survives us like love . . . we may almost look up to Heaven and say "I have a piece of thee here . . ."' It is important not to underestimate the comfort of such material survivals. In a period when reminders of those who were loved were not so easily attainable, when photography was still in its infancy and images of people were less available, hair really was a tangible souvenir of a person departed. For those whose budgets might not extend to the commissioning of hair jewellery, women's magazines sometimes offered articles on how to weave an ornament from hair and create an affordable memorial without the additional cost of a professional maker.

Twenty-one months after the loss of her husband, a widow entered the third or 'ordinary' stage of mourning and, while the palette was still confined to black, additional trimmings of lace and jet might now be added – a hint of light shining through the pattern of lace and surface of a jewel. Finally, after two years of black, the last stage of mourning – known as 'half-mourning' – reintroduced some colour into the widow's wardrobe. Garments made from colours such as lilac, grey, pale yellow and white were permitted, to indicate that a different stage of life was looming. Black might still trim the edges of half-mourning dresses, but it was in retreat.

These strictures were, of course, only possible for those whose pockets were deep enough to adhere to all the purchases required to make such clear sartorial statements, and for large swathes of the working population such etiquette was impossible. The commodification of death tied in completely to the British class system. Understanding the nuances of mourning dress was a way in which to demonstrate your place in society, not only having the financial resources to subscribe to the rules, but practically navigating what those rules were. There are other, less commercially motivated reasons for such stratified mourning dress. Grief, of course, is real, no matter the century in which it is experienced. Whilst mortality rates and life-expectancy levels differed, love and loss were felt as keenly then as now.

Black did, of course, come to be associated with age for a time in the nineteenth century. For older women whose budget and social position were perhaps limited, following the death of their husbands, the continued wearing of black was often a convenient option. James McNeill Whistler's tender portrait of his mother in 1871 is a study in widow's weeds, the older woman depicted in a black dress, her head covered with the kind of accessory that came to be known as a widow's cap. Two of the swatches that appear at different times in Anne's album – one a plain black silk and the other a heavier, ribbed moiré silk – both seem to refer to older women in Anne's circle, labelled 'Aunt Sykes' and 'Aunt Ward' respectively. Widow's caps, white crinkled crape objects with long streamers flowing down the back, were customarily worn by single older women who had never remarried – another object to place a woman in a particular social space.

Perhaps the mourning practice that sits most uncomfortably with modern sensibilities was that of post-mortem photography. From the 1840s onwards, as photographic technologies became more sophisticated, families would often invest in *cartes de visite* to memorialise themselves. A visit to the local photographic studio became more affordable and, dressed in their best, families would sit stiff-backed whilst the long exposure time of the camera worked its magic. It is these formal, sepia-toned portraits that have helped to build the aesthetic of the archetypal Victorian family as unsmiling and grey – a misrepresentation of life, and yet one that has generated a stereotype of nineteenth-century grey-scale sobriety. These portraits were often the only time that a family might capture such likenesses, and so it became a popular practice to acquire one final memorial of the deceased before they were buried. In what would seem, 150 years later, a morbid practice, dead relatives would be taken to the studio, dressed in their best clothes and photographed alongside their surviving family. Infants would sit on their mother's lap, seemingly asleep. A young woman reclining on a couch next to her parents would appear relaxed, resting just for a moment. Anne and Hannah were unlikely to have had access to photography in the 1840s, although both lived through the period of its expansion, the wonderful opportunity to capture a true likeness of family becoming available to them in their middle age.

~

Evidence of mourning dress occurs often in Anne's album. Alongside the colour of floral silks and printed cottons sit the plainer, darker cloth samples, life and death existing side-by-side. In the mid-nineteenth century death stalked families frequently, and the mourning clothes that spoke of life's losses were naturally represented with all of the other life events that Anne included. In the 1830s and 1840s, before mourning dress had become quite so strictly codified, the expectations were not as rigid. If economy demanded, it was common practice to alter existing garments in order that they might be worn as mourning clothes. Early in the album there is a swatch of black floral silk that Anne describes as 'Mary Fletcher. Old Burnous – after it was dyed, also like a dress of mine long ago.' Black was not a fashionable colour in its own right at this time in the nineteenth century, its links to mourning being too deeply entrenched, and so Mary's decision to dye her burnous (a type of cloak) meant that she had an appropriate outerwear garment to wear whilst in mourning. There are more than a dozen examples in the album of plain black garments belonging to the different women of Anne's acquaintance – plain woven fabric being an essential part of many women's wardrobes.

Without additional commentary from Anne, we do not have a voice for those times in her life when she found herself in mourning for family members, other than her attribution of Hannah's loss in the album. For those years that she lived in Singapore she would have only learned of the death of a family member many weeks after it had taken place, when the news reached her via the packet ships or the overland mail route. To convey sadness and communicate feelings at such a distance was a protracted affair, as Anne's friend Maria Balestier articulated after the death of her son Revere. She wrote to tell her sister of his death in 1843, in the knowledge that Harriet would not receive the news for many weeks, and waited for the outpouring of sympathy that would arrive by the return vessels many weeks later again.

Such extended expressions of sympathy taking months of back-and-forth communication took their toll on Maria's own health. She wrote in September 1844 of a visiting captain who had purchased some items for her from Calcutta, expanding her wardrobe in her hour of need. He brought 'just such things as cannot be purchased here, darning silk, mittens, gloves, narrow ribbon for my gown and cap and a very nice muslin cape trimmed with black which he bought from a French milliner which she told him was for deep mourning'. Evidence that Anne shared fabric that might be made into mourning clothes is hinted at in those black fabrics that bear her name. Above one scrap of black satin she has written, 'Fanny Taylor and Anne Sykes 1842' – the suggestion here perhaps that Anne and Fanny paid for a length of the plain cloth between them in order to have appropriate garments, should the circumstances require.

The facility to trim garments with black is also evident from the sundries that feature: narrow lace edges, inky black ribbons and other woven haberdashery that might be ordered from home and sent in small parcels, a relatively inexpensive way to indicate a degree of mourning, stitched onto garments and handkerchiefs, black-edged clothes and accessories that outlined the body of grief.

The three fragments of Hannah Coubrough's that remain in Anne's album indicate a range of aesthetics, the sartorial journey through grief in cloth, sitting side-by-side. Mourning for a mother required a different degree of mourning from that of a husband. But the complexity permeated every familial relationship to a greater or lesser degree. Published in 1840, *The Workwoman's Guide* stipulated mourning expectations. Mourning for a parent was expected for upwards of six months to a year, brothers and sisters for six to eight months, whilst an aunt or an uncle required three to six months. Cousins or those family members connected by marriage only required a six-week to three-month show of mourning. These intricate nuances were, however, only displayed by women.

Mourning for men in the nineteenth century was far less prescriptive and by 1860 the most obvious sign of mourning exhibited in menswear was the addition of a black armband. Similarly, a widower might marry again whilst still in the official first period of mourning for his first wife, whilst a widow was entwined in varying shades of grief for years. Magazines catering to a middle-class audience, such as *Sylvia's Home Journal*, would recommend the degrees of dress and the passing of time deemed appropriate for each costume change, and this was reflected in Hannah's choices. The plain black satin placed in the middle of the three swatches reflects that first and most immediate expression of her mother's loss. Flanking this, on either side, are two woven gauzes that are lighter, both physically and chromatically. The shadow of black is still present, but paler stripes in one and ellipses of mauve and cream in the other offer a sign of change. For Hannah to have sent these pieces to Anne is a poignant reminder of life's journey and of the relationship the two women shared. Wordlessly, they tell a part of Hannah's story that she has passed to Anne, who would have understood the significance of each gown they belonged to. Although separated geographically, they share this moment in their friendship – one that is so carefully recorded by Anne in her copperplate caption.

From the columns of church registers and death certificates it is possible to pinpoint those dates in Anne's life when she herself experienced the loss of a loved one. The bare facts of date and cause of death, the announcement in a newspaper, the absence in a census record, cannot record the human experience. If the album adds a little of the material expression of sadness, it does not give voice to the void created by death. Hannah Coubrough was an important person in Anne's life, and although Anne was not able to comfort Hannah in person when she lost her mother, Mary, she has indicated the significance of the event and memorialised her in those three uniform scraps of cloth. Those pieces of fabric associated with mourning do, however, shine a light into that corner of her world and that of those around her, with the inevitability of time passing and people leaving. In a sense the album is itself a memorial.

CHAPTER 15

A Grand Masquerade

Hannah Wrigley

It was a wonderful season for fancy dress balls, Mrs
Arthur Paget leading the way before Easter with her very
successful poudré dance, and Mrs Oppenheim following
suit with her flower ball.

The Woman at Home, 1897

Where there are some names in Anne's album that shape themselves into
actual people and whose lives give up at least some of their secrets to the
seeker, others remain frustratingly tight-lipped. Hannah Wrigley is one
of those names. Presumably she is one of the Misses Wrigley who appear
dancing frivolously in evening wear at various intervals in the album, but
more than that it has proved impossible to discern.

Hannah Wrigley's name is attached to one of the most vibrant and
culturally colourful fragments in the album, a lime-green brocade woven
with a large white floral repeat – the scrap itself larger than most, presumably to accommodate the pattern. It was cut into an unusual shape,
a larger kite-like swatch positioned at the top of its page, seemingly
pointing downwards. The caption above, in a bigger flourish of Anne's
handwriting, reads, 'Hannah Wrigley Fancy Ball dress for the character of

"Dolly Varden" '. Most helpfully, Anne appended the name of Hannah's chosen character to the fragment of her costume, allowing the window to widen still further and take in a vista of Charles Dickens, royal costume balls, professional costumiers and whimsical garments that amounted to a craze for the sartorially creative as the century progressed.

Hannah's absence is both frustrating and liberating. The thrill of research lies in the small and often unrecognised victories that emerge from hours of trawling through documents – newspaper accounts, passenger manifests and census records, the silent vessels of information that harbour a wealth of detail. Discoveries are, by definition of historical methodologies, made in solitary spaces. Many have been the eureka moments in my research projects, celebrated in the silence of an archive or a library – the lone thrill of pieces slotting together and uniting to tell a story long forgotten. With Hannah Wrigley, that moment was not to be. Like Fanny Taylor, hers is a name all too common in the census records of the 1840s, and if she was based in Singapore, then she is even more difficult to find. There are no other helpful markers to steer a line of enquiry, and so hers is one name amongst many that remain almost anonymous, but for these tiny, fragmentary remnants. A few square inches of wool, silk and cotton are all that are left of this woman who once danced in fancy dress, swished in white satin and black lace, promenaded in cream gauze and tied her bonnet with a bright checked ribbon. Having dealt with the disappointment of her relative anonymity, liberation lies in the speculation that follows. Her life now becomes a subject of wonder, a fairytale of possibilities untethered by known facts, and so it is possible to imagine what Hannah might have been.

So what do we know about Hannah Wrigley? Her acquaintance with Anne Sykes seems to have been of fixed duration. Her name is recorded on seven of the more than 400 pages of Anne's album and amounts to twenty-two different fabric samples. Of these, four are directly associated with evening entertainments of some kind, and sixteen seem to fall into the category of daywear, given the fibres from which they are woven. The final two are snippets of silk ribbon, that ubiquitous fabric of the well-stocked nineteenth-century haberdashery that permitted versatility of accessories with a relatively cheap re-trim.

Hannah does not appear again in the album after Anne and Adam's return to the UK, but their association seems to have been a friendly one. Above a fine purple wool twill Anne wrote, 'Hannah Wrigley called this a family affair.' Both of the other two pieces of fabric on this particular page, one a grey-and-blue striped cotton and the other a white silk gauze, also refer to a 'family affair' – an in-joke that is difficult for us to decipher. Maybe it referred to a dress that was long worn and so not fit to be seen beyond Hannah's immediate household? It could perhaps have been a way of describing more than one garment made from the same fabric. It was more economical to buy fabric to make two dresses, especially for sisters, and so are these garments that Hannah shared in style with her sister or sisters? We know that there were sisters, from other snippets of writing in the album that refer to the 'Misses Wrigley', so Hannah was not alone.

There are no other anchor points to which we can fix Hannah's life. These small pieces of bright cloth are all that we have to record her existence and the part she played in Anne's world, drifting into her orbit for a while and then leaving it again. Then as now, there are people we meet throughout our lives who are briefly significant, whose company we enjoy and whose stories we could tell, but who are only temporary figures in the interlocking circles of friendships as life shifts and moves. Hannah was, it seems, one of those people. It might have been that their association was one or two friendships removed, that she sat at the periphery of Anne's network, willing to contribute to her project, but not a close connection in any other respect. The degree of friendship is a closed door to us, looking on now – were they smiling acquaintances or fond confidantes? Alas, we will never know . . .

Fancy balls were a feature of the emerging lifestyle of the merchant community in Singapore in the early 1840s. The first-ever fancy-dress ball was held over New Year to coincide with the much-anticipated horse-racing events. It was described in the *Singapore Free Press and Mercantile Advertiser* on 2 January 1840, with the author reporting that 'Too much cannot be said of the ladies almost all attiring in fancy dresses.' A year later, a letter to the editor described the scene at the second New Year fancy-dress ball and the colourful panoply that filled the rooms: 'First and foremost bloom the Rose, Thistle and Shamrock, blending their respective charms in harmony . . . such is the throng that meets your untiring view.' Maria Balestier wrote to her sister about the same evening and the efforts of their guest, a young Mr Phillips, as he put together his costume for the ball. He 'borrowed a most costly and beautiful Chinese dress to wear' and 'seemed to enter into the fun with great interest'.

It is likely that Anne and Adam Sykes would have attended such a prominent event in the settlement. Having arrived only two months earlier, it may have been their first significant social gathering, and we can only imagine the excitement (or perhaps the trepidation) that Anne felt at the prospect. Whilst the details of her costume on this occasion are absent, the glimpse of Hannah Wrigley's offers a colourful insight. Although an exact year is not recorded by Anne for this particular fancy-dress costume, it is possible to place it within certain parameters. Hannah attended her unnamed ball dressed as the character Dolly Varden. In 1841 Charles Dickens published one of only two historical novels that he was to write. Appearing as a weekly serial, *Barnaby Rudge: A Tale of the Riots of Eighty* was set during the anti-Catholic Gordon Riots that took place in London in 1780. Amongst the colourful cast of characters are the Vardens – Gabriel, a London locksmith, and his beautiful and vivacious daughter, Dolly.

Like the fandoms of the twenty-first century, and those who use clothes to emulate their pop-culture heroes, fancy dress offered a place to be that which was far distant in everyday life. With her bright cotton polonaise skirt and her flattened straw hat, Dolly Varden's appealing historical aesthetic was seized upon, following the novel's publication, as a popular fancy-dress costume choice. The description of her character too, in the episodic publication, was engaging, with a flourish of purple prose. Dickens did not hold back with the warmth of her attributes: 'When and where was there ever such a plump, roguish, comely, bright-eyed, enticing, bewitching, captivating, maddening little puss in all this world as Dolly!' Fashion of the 1780s was distinctive for its polonaise skirt – an overskirt that could be ruched up below the hips to reveal the underskirt beneath. Given the popularity of the weekly instalments of the story, the soap-opera structure of its day and the easy colour of Dolly herself, it was a costume that could perhaps be relatively easily fashioned for a costume ball, with colourful swags around the hips and a plaited straw hat tied beneath the chin. These markers would have provided the shorthand that was recognisable to an audience well versed in the vocabulary of dress and popular literature. Hannah Wrigley's sharp green brocade with its busy florals was the perfect interpretation of Dolly's roguish personality. Since the novel was published between February and November 1841, it is not possible for Hannah to have chosen to appear as Dolly Varden until at least 1842, and by 1847 Anne and Adam's lives would take them away from the bustle of Singapore. Somewhere between 1842 and 1847, then, Hannah Wrigley decked herself out in her cheerful swag of silk as the coquettish Miss Varden.

As a relatively minor character in one of Charles Dickens's less popular novels, Dolly Varden was to enjoy a long life in the public imagination. By the late 1860s there was a resurgence of interest in her sartorial style, and the mid-nineteenth-century obsession with historicism prompted a revival of the Dolly Varden dress in more mainstream wardrobes, rather than within the confines of fancy dress. Decorative draped paniers could be found upon more conventional daywear in contrasting fabrics, and the flat straw bergère hat, originally fashionable in the eighteenth century, found favour once more. In 1872 Alfred Lee's novelty song 'Dolly Varden' became a popular contemporary ditty and referred to her quaint appearance:

Have you seen my little girl? She doesn't wear a bonnet.
She's got a monstrous flip-flop hat with cherry ribbons on it.
She dresses in bed furniture just like a flower garden
A blowin' and a growin' and they call it Dolly Varden.

Dolly Varden would in fact make a later appearance in Singapore. On Saturday 10 November 1877 the newspaper printed the programme of entertainment in the Town Hall Theatre. The Misses Ford begged to thank the local theatre-goers for their patronage and looked forward to welcoming them with a variety performance that included a song and dance by Miss Flora Ford, in the character of Dolly Varden. The subsequent review described Miss Ford's characterisation as 'given with a droll humour and verve which took greatly with the audience'.

The implication, drawn from Dickens's own writing and these many subsequent manifestations of Dolly Varden, is bound up with nineteenth-century attitudes to class. Essentially, Dolly is viewed, by the bourgeoisie, as a bit common. With her too-colourful clothes, her plump comeliness and her ultimate position at the end of *Barnaby Rudge* as landlady of the Maypole public house, she is a happy-go-lucky, but perhaps not quite respectable, likeable miss, bright-eyed and blousy. Hannah Wrigley's choice of Dolly Varden as a fancy-dress costume reinforces this, for to wear fancy dress at this time was to experiment with 'otherness' – to present yourself as that which, in real life, you were not. Hannah presumably occupied a space within a well-to-do merchant's family, and Dolly was deliberately different.

~

The act of dressing up for the purpose of a public ball or a private entertainment had become hugely popular by the middle of the nineteenth century. The art of the masquerade witnessed by travellers to Italy in the eighteenth century was to be replicated in London. Masked men and women would promenade around the pleasure gardens of Vauxhall, delighting in the freedom that disguise gave them to make mischief – something that the contemporary social commentator Horace Walpole decried. Writing from Florence, he observed, 'What makes masquerading more agreeable here than in England, is the great deference that is showed to the disguised. Here they do not catch at those little dirty opportunities of saying any ill-natured thing they know of you, do not abuse you because they may, or talk gross bawdy to a woman of quality.' Masquerading offered guests the chance to cast off social norms and to subvert the status quo, their anonymity covering a multitude of sins. For some, it was a chance to be less visible than they would normally be. One summer's evening in the mid-1870s Lord Esher described a *bal masqué* held at Strawberry Hill at which Alexandra, the popular Princess of Wales, and her friend Helen Standish attended in the same cloak, like 'dominoes': 'the Princess and Mrs Standish, dominoed alike, led the baffled dancers into endless confusion'.

As the century progressed, the masks and dominoes were replaced with character-driven fancy dress that fell broadly into two categories: either allegorical figures such as Summer and Time or actual characters from history and literature. One of the most famous and well documented of these character-driven *bals costumés* took place on 12 May 1842, held in Buckingham Palace by Queen Victoria and Prince Albert. The motivation that drove this elaborate occasion was a show of support for the flagging British silk industry. Two thousand guests were invited to attend this sumptuous ball, with the request that their costumes were to be accurate representations of any historical period, the materials for which had to be sourced from British textile manufacturers. The Queen and Prince Consort chose to attend as Queen Philippa and Edward III, who had themselves been renowned for their patronage of local weavers. Their lavish medieval-esque costumes have not survived, but the Edwin Landseer portrait commemorating the occasion depicts the costly fabrics that were chosen for the Royal couple. The costume historian James Robinson Planché was invited to advise the Queen on the details of the garments, although, in line with most fancy-dress costumes of the period, they managed to channel some medieval qualities whilst adhering steadfastly to the contemporary 1840s silhouette. The ball received widespread attention in the press, helping to cement the already burgeoning interest in fancy-dress parties. To further satisfy the public appetite for the royal spectacle, the dressmakers responsible for Victoria's and Albert's costumes, Vouillon & Laure, were granted permission to exhibit the Queen's dress at their premises on Hanover Square the day before the ball was due to take place. According to reports, more than 250 carriages and countless pedestrians paraded past for a glimpse of the gorgeous garments.

Attention to detail was crucial. By the late 1870s the appetite for variety in the realm of the costume ball gave rise to the publication of manuals to inspire the would-be attendee. The most famous of these was Ardern Holt's colourful volume *Fancy Dresses Described; or, What to Wear at Fancy Balls*. First published in 1879 by the department store Debenham & Freebody, it was so popular that it ran to six editions, the last issued in 1896. It was a smart marketing strategy on the part of Debenham & Freebody. In the preface they reminded the reader that 'A glance through these pages will enable readers to choose the [costume] which will best suit them, and learn how to carry it out.' All materials could, of course, be purchased from them, and indeed for the less confident dressmaker amongst their customers, the costumes themselves could be made up to order.

13. Di Vernon. 14. Diana. 15. Dresden China. 16. England.

Some suggestions for fancy dress costumes in Ardern Holt's
Fancy Dress Described or What to Wear at Fancy Balls, 1887 edition.

The descriptions were detailed. For the character 'All is Not Gold
That Glitters' the text suggests 'Dress of gold coloured satin, with gold
stars and gold lace. Crescents and stars cover the front of the costume
and a cap of cloth of gold is adorned with diamonds. Shoes and stockings worked with gold sequins.' A more ambitious guest might attempt
'Aquarium': 'The idea of this dress is taken from the anemone tanks of an
aquarium. The dress, pale shot coralline and green satin; the trimming;
fringes and groups of natural seaweed, all of the most delicately-tinted
kinds, small pearly shells, coral and large pink anemones, imitations of
the real actiniae with their spreading tentacles placed here and there all
over the dress – on the shoulders, front of bodice and in the hair (interspersed with seaweed) and looping up the satin skirt. Shells, coral and
silver fish ornaments.' The *pièce de résistance* for a 'realistic rendering'
was the headdress: 'a miniature aquarium with water and fish'. Whether
it was a hornet, Lady Macbeth, a bunch of sweet peas or Anne Boleyn,
Fancy Dresses Described catered to the whim of every customer across
its more than 300 pages, twenty colour plates and forty black-and-white
illustrations.

Marie Schild's comprehensive volume *One Thousand Characters Suitable for Fancy Costume Balls* included listings for those suppliers that could assist customers with the best materials for the job. For trimmings, the firm of Stagg & Mantle sold tinsel, silver stars and silver brocade suitable for the character of 'Night'. Wigs could be purchased from Clarkson's, C. H. Fox Ltd or Simmons & Co. Boots and shoes were a speciality of Burnet & Co., whilst B. J. Simmons & Co. hired out complete costumes, wigs included. The services offered grew in line with the popularity of the entertainment. An advertisement in the *Liverpool Mercury* on 10 September 1863 ran: 'J & W Jeffery & Co. have the pleasure to announce that they have succeeded in obtaining a very large and select assortment of fancy dress costumes embracing a great variety of historical, theatrical, naval, military and foreign costumes, court dresses etc. Showrooms lighted with gas will be appointed for their display.'

Prior to a mayoral fancy-dress ball in the city, the firm J. A. Bioletti stated its intention to engage special assistants from Paris to teach ladies how to dress their hair; and his period moustaches were guaranteed not to fall off. Some of these firms would set up temporary premises to help with the preparations for particularly large events. Fancy dress offered participants a chance to be other than what their daily dress allowed them to be. In an era when divergence from the sartorial norm was to risk the censure of those around you, a costume party offered freedoms that were otherwise unthinkable. The writer and art critic Lady Eastlake wrote in her essay on fashion in 1852, 'Every fancy ball brings out some striking or interesting face, generally in some such head-dresses as these, which the day before, seen in its own scanty suit, was overlooked as plain.' For one evening only it was possible to be Cleopatra or Mary, Queen of Scots, or to appear more whimsically dressed as a bottle of champagne or a deck of playing cards. Whatever the choice, it was a step outside the rigid respectability and codified strata that dress inhabited in the mid-nineteenth century – to play at subterfuge and play-act at subversiveness whilst drinking punch and dancing a quadrille.

Well-established theatrical costumiers turned their attention to the amateur market in the nineteenth century – including firms such as Nathan's, established in 1790 in London to dress the theatres of Drury Lane, but which, in the nineteenth century, opened a separate fancy-dress department to cater to those keen fancy-dress-ball guests. Some of the most renowned fashion houses were also prepared to design fancy-dress costumes for their best clients. The House of Worth created a number of garments for the famous Devonshire House Ball of 1897, the event given by the Duchess of Devonshire to commemorate Queen Victoria's Diamond Jubilee. One of the guests, Lady Randolph Churchill, recalled of the preparations, 'Historical books were ransacked for inspirations, old pictures and engravings were studied and people became quite learned in respect to past celebrities of whom they had never before heard.'

The ubiquity of fancy-dress entertainments was not confined solely to the wealthiest members of society, however. Such costumed entertainments were popular across the social spectrum, a home-made and ad hoc approach suiting more modest budgets. Such was likely to have been the case for the residents of Singapore. Some entertainments were easy to mark. For the Feast of St Andrew in 1835, ladies were asked to attend the celebratory ball with a tartan scarf in recognition of the occasion. The chance to make mischief after long months at sea was part of the life of the officer in port, attending these parties in Singapore. Anne must have attended the fancy ball given in 1842 for the officers of the USS *Boston*, after which one of the sailors wrote of another guest, 'one gentleman dressed as a lady who acted his part so well that I did not recognise him till I saw him in a side room smoking and drinking brandy and water'.

Only four months after this, another fancy-dress ball was given to celebrate the visit of a dignitary from Hong Kong. The newspaper reported that, 'Dancing commenced soon after nine' and represented were '. . . sultanas, burgomaster's ladies, Switzeresses, quakeresses, ladies of the olden time, nymphs, Greeks, Turks, Egyptians and Knights of Malta'. The festivities continued for most of the night: 'After supper dancing was resumed and continued until 4 o'clock, when the guests again repaired to the festive board; and after several Scotch and Irish songs separated a little before 5 o'clock.' How these costumes were achieved is difficult to establish. Although the mercantile community was growing rapidly in the 1840s, the opportunities to purchase fabric, trimmings and accessories were still relatively limited. It is likely that with some imagination, some begging, borrowing and altering, costumes were conceived with the ingenuity born of necessity and a lack of any other option.

That colonial Singapore embraced the trend for fancy dress that was already sweeping across communities in Europe and North America is evident from the colourful press reports and occasional references in letters home. These early entertainments coincided with the opening of a theatre in 1842, for which Adam Sykes was listed as one of the first subscribers. The chance to engage in amateur theatre, either as player or observer, was clearly a popular development, with regular updates published, listing the productions that were to be put on. The Singapore press were still printing their reports following the *Twelfth Night* fancy-dress ball as late as the 1950s, the tradition continuing across more than a century of colonial expatriate experiences.

Hannah Wrigley's Dolly Varden costume was certainly of a vibrancy that might suggest that it had been made professionally. The fabric is deliberately gaudy, as befitted the colour of the late-eighteenth-century character it represented, but there are limits to the tales that this lime silk fragment can tell. Anne chose not to record in her album any of her own forays into the realms of fancy dress. We can't tell if she loved or loathed these entertainments, adopting another persona grudgingly or with enthusiasm. Certainly these balls were a way of uniting a small

European community in a space far from home, bringing to this commercial outpost entertainments that were fashionable thousands of miles away. But we don't know whether Anne danced as a queen or a flower or a milkmaid, and we can only imagine the preparation that went into the creation of costumes with limited resources.

Without those certainties, Hannah's costume opens up a world of possibility. It lifts the corner of a curtain, revealing the fancy-dress ballrooms of 1840s Singapore and Britain – a small glimpse into the candlelit brightness populated by an unexpected array of characters. Hannah's bright silk also bears witness to the role of fancy dress in the nineteenth century as a liberator, taking conventional folk and making them 'other' in ways that were problematic from within the confines of their society. As the band plays and supper is served, Hannah Wrigley and Anne Sykes spin across the dance floor out of sight, the sharp green of the Dolly Varden costume flashing as they go.

CHAPTER 16

Missing Moments

Anne & Adam Sykes

There are no foreign lands. It is the traveller only who is foreign.

Robert Louis Stevenson, *The Silverado Squatters*, 1883

After seven years as a merchant's wife, living amongst the challenges of climate and the colour of unfamiliar cultures, Anne and Adam Sykes boarded the P&O steamship *Pekin* on 8 August 1847, their departure captured in a single line of the *Singapore Free Press and Mercantile Advertiser*. It is a reference as fleeting as that of their arrival. There, listed under Departure of Passengers, is simply 'A. Sykes'. They were bound, not for home, but for adventures new. Adam's merchant interests forged their path, and we can only imagine how Anne felt as she left the Singapore harbour for the final time, watching the sampans disappear into the distance and spying the thread of the Esplanade as their ship sailed away. She left with her book in her trunk, tucked amongst her clothes on her way to another distant shore.

An early photograph of the *Pekin* shows the long, low lines of a steamship that still also relied on sails, a form of hybrid technology that meant the captain of the vessel might avail himself of either sail or steam, depending on the conditions and to ensure consistency of travel. Modern though the ship may have been, less than three years later the German traveller Ida Pfeiffer boarded the *Pekin* and was less than complimentary about the facilities on board: 'The furniture was of the most common description, the table covered with stains and dirt and the whole place was one scene of confusion.' Ida had to pay the sum of $13 a day for the provisions, such as they were. For this she was forced to use a single dish, broken knives and forks and to share one spoon with other passengers. The evenings were also grim, since 'The only light we had was from a piece of tallow candle that often went out by eight o'clock. We were then in the necessity of sitting in the dark or going to bed.' Her final observation of the experience was scathing: 'there is an old opinion that the English are, above all other people, justly celebrated for their comfort and cleanliness . . . never did I pay so high a price for such wretched and detestable treatment.'

Did Anne suffer a similarly miserable trip on board the *Pekin*? It must have been a difficult journey, in more ways than one. Perhaps deprivation of that kind is more bearable if the ship is carrying you home, but the P&O steamer was taking Anne and Adam Sykes away from the friends they had made in Singapore, not to the familiar lines of the Lancashire landscape, but to the vastness of China. Once more it was Adam's career that had determined the direction of their lives, and so they landed again in harbours new, this time the recently opened port of Shanghai. Following the First Opium War, the 1842 Treaty of Nanking had permitted the opening of five Chinese ports to British commerce, one of which was Shanghai.

I was fascinated by this development in Anne's life. Over a period of five years I had made several trips to work in Shanghai, teaching Chinese students about developments in Western fashion over the centuries. It is a city of unimaginable vastness, the seemingly endless suburbs of super-high-rise apartment buildings dizzying in their continuousness. So recent is most of its architectural emergence that trying to see a trace of old Shanghai is difficult at times. Down on the riverside Bund the remains of late-nineteenth-century Western commerce are writ large in the stone-stuccoed edifices. But trying to imagine Anne's view is almost impossible, with the blinking lights of the Oriental Pearl Tower and the twist of the city's tallest building, the Shanghai Tower, whose upper floors are often obscured by clouds of pollution. Even in the 1970s these buildings, built on Pudong on the far side of the Huangpu River, did not exist. Pudong was still an area of farmland, flat and fertile. To see Shanghai now is to see a transformation of epic proportions.

In 1847 it was immeasurably different. A contemporary painting of that year, taken from the water and likely Anne's first view of mainland China, shows a walled harbour full of a variety of vessels, from small sampans being poled across the water to larger sailing ships. The many-roofed traditional pagoda is the only building of any height, with low tiled buildings scattered behind the more substantial harbour wall. Mountains rise in the distance, stretching away to the unknown.

Of Anne and Adam's life in this colourful and diverse port we know almost nothing. Unlike the pages filled with the everyday of their world in Singapore, there are no indications of what their two years in China brought them. Anne did not share any helpful pointers that might link them with any of the communities in the region. She occasionally includes a large swatch of patterned silk labelled simply 'China silk', but there is no evidence to suggest that she acquired it during her time in Shanghai. The only garment that might be positively tied to the port is a plain black silk scrap, above which Anne noted, 'Mr Sykes's vest China.' It is the only acknowledgement of their relocation. I don't know where they lived or how Anne spent her time in this vast country; whether she ever explored beyond the limits of this emerging commercial space or gained a sense of the cultural diversity of China.

The only clue that places them there at all comes from Adam's obituary. *The Preston Herald* reported on 17 October 1888 that Mr Sykes had 'resided seven years in Singapore and two in Shanghai'. Long after their return, Adam maintained his business interests in Shanghai, appearing as one of the signatories on a deputation protesting against unequal trading in the mid-1850s and, according to the contents of his will, he had retained a property in the port. The *Northern Daily Telegraph* noted the disbursement of Adam Sykes's assets in its 12 January 1889 edition: 'All his real estate including that at Bolton-by-Bowland in Yorkshire & his property at Shanghai, the testator bequeathed to his nephew Adam Sykes.'

Perhaps the absence of material reminders of Shanghai suggests that Anne was unhappy there. She does not record the dress of acquaintances, as she had done so frequently in Singapore. She does not include swatches of her lounge curtains or drawing-room furniture. There are no ribbons pasted in from a shopping trip or a fragment of a friend's gown. It is curious, also, that Anne chose not to record the rich cultural diversity present in the Chinese textiles that she must surely have encountered. This is true of so much of Anne's album. With the exception of a single swatch of Javan batik and a handful of China silks, Anne did not seemingly make any efforts to acquire examples of indigenous textile traditions during her time abroad. Perhaps this was because her book was really about people rather than place.

Whatever her reasons, the two years that she lived in China are almost entirely absent from the diary. She does not memorialise the dress she wore when she arrived or when she left. It is an interruption in the book, an interval during which time we can only imagine the life she led. This interruption draws to a close in 1849 when Anne and Adam left China and, for the first time in almost a decade, made the long journey home.

Return

The bustle of the 1870s.

CHAPTER 17

Home Comforts

Sarah Newmann

> Home is a name, a word, it is a strong one; stronger than magician ever spoke, or spirit ever answered to, in the strongest conjuration.
>
> Charles Dickens, *Martin Chuzzlewit*, 1844

Covering the entire width of one of the album's pages, a bold floral glazed-cotton sample dominates, with blousy pink printed roses nodding heavily on thorny stems, lush green leaves unfurled around other stylised florals in outline – a riot of shape and colour whose large repeat cannot quite be captured by the boundaries of Anne Sykes's album. Above the large piece of cloth Anne has written, 'Mrs Newmann's drawing room covers 1851.'

In a volume dominated by fabrics that adorned the body, there are only eight pieces of cloth that capture domestic furnishing textiles in Anne's album but, like dress, these were the very domains over which women were able to assert their influence. The inclusion of them in Anne's album – most of them after her return to Lancashire in 1849 – gesture towards conversations between communities of women about home furnishings and an interest in each other's domestic spaces. For

Anne and her contemporaries, furnishing a house was one of the most significant roles upon their marriage, consulting those around them as well as popular periodicals that were beginning to appear, catering to the home-maker and the ambitions she had for her house. Emerging from the sparser interiors of the eighteenth century, the first half of the nineteenth century witnessed a softening of interior spaces as textiles began to play a more important part in the decoration of the home. Drapers advertised their furnishing fabrics to a newly engaged audience; advice manuals offered aesthetic tips; and papers like the *Magazine of Domestic Economy* presented their readers with regular updates on household necessities.

Sarah Newmann's busy print, chosen for her drawing-room furniture in 1851, is in keeping with mid-nineteenth-century trends for floral chintz covers. There are seventeen pieces of cloth in the album that belonged to Sarah Newmann. Sixteen of them are dress fabrics, leaving just this one colourful cotton to represent the realm of furnishings. In all the captions, she is referred to as 'Mrs Newmann'. This indicates a formality of sorts, a relationship that never reached the more intimate state of Jane Sykes or Fanny Taylor, those women of Anne's world with whom she was comfortably on first-name terms. Yet on the census of 1851, in a happy stroke of luck for me, Charles and Sarah Newmann are listed as visitors in Anne and Adam's house on the night of 31 March, the very day that the census was taken. Had they not chosen that particular date to visit, they would have been swallowed by the weight of potential records, impossible to pinpoint amongst the dozens of Newmans, Newmanns and Neumanns – their name spelt using all three of these spellings in different places. Additionally, Sarah's maiden name appears as both Ashton and Ashten in parish records and it is likely that, were it not for the 1851 census tethering them to the Sykes family, their history would have been carried away on a wave of misinformation.

Anne and Adam had returned from Shanghai only the year before and were living in the district of Pendlebury in what is now Salford, in the heart of the flourishing textile trades. Old maps of Salford show that their house on Mode Wheel Road – only ten years earlier the site of a flour mill – was by the 1850s surrounded by cotton mills, dye works and calico printworks, threaded with a growing network of railway lines. They lived near the Broad Oak works, from where some of Anne's printed cottons originated, and were only a few miles from her home town of Tyldesley. Sarah's husband, Charles, was a merchant, and so it is likely that he and Adam knew each other in a professional capacity. Given the formality of Anne's captions, perhaps the two women saw their relationship as similarly work-related – a friendship born of necessity through their respective husbands, rather than through choice. Sarah was just two years older than Anne, born in Hyde in Cheshire in 1819. She was the daughter of a prominent cotton-factory owner, Thomas Ashton. Well known for his philanthropy, Ashton invested in housing, libraries and schools for his workers at a time when this was not universally the case. Sarah's brother, Thomas, continued the family business and in the early 1860s, when the cotton industry underwent a slump, kept on all of his workers, running at a loss for a time, when other factories had laid off hands.

Sarah's life as wife to a relatively comfortable merchant saw her rooted in Lancashire, their residences changing over the years. Sadly, we have no address for the house they lived in during 1851, the house of the chintzy drawing-room covers. By 1861 Charles had retired and they were living at 6 Allerton Road, a smart suburban villa near Liverpool. The census is taken once every ten years, providing a snapshot of a person's life, including their name and occupation. Really, though, the census is all about houses: a story of the walls that sheltered the inhabitants. If the searcher is lucky, then those residences might still stand and it becomes possible to imagine these past lives within them. All too often they are not, however, and only the address itself remains, the building discernible solely through the cold outlines of a contemporary map. In a sense, the census records and their fragmentary information mirror those brief encounters of lives offered by Anne through her album. She unwittingly drops a clue into her sparse caption-writing – a person, a place, a time, ever so briefly – and then it is gone, and we are left wondering.

In the 1871 census, Charles and Sarah were still living in Allerton Road, but had moved to Wyndcote House, where they would both remain for the rest of their lives. Wyndcote was demolished in the early twentieth century, but according to the Ordnance Survey map of 1893, the year that Sarah died there, it was a sizeable property, with outhouses and a large garden wrapping itself around the house. Like the small swatch of her furniture chintz, we see the briefest moment of Sarah's domestic life in a textile and on the bird's-eye view of a map. But that is all.

Control of domestic spaces, both in the way they were furnished and in the daily functions within the home, fell under the remit of women. To support them in their endeavours they could consult a growing number of publications aimed at advising them on cooking, household economy and furnishing and decorating the house. In *Beeton's Housewife's Treasury*, published in 1865, the reader is taken through each room of the house and, as the pages turn, she will learn what furniture best suits which room, how to choose carpets, how to hang curtains. Chapter 12 is devoted to the furniture to be displayed in rooms used by day, directing the housewife towards the fixtures and fittings suitable for the breakfast room, the dining room or the drawing room.

Every one of the eight furnishing textiles in Anne's book relates to drawing rooms, those public-facing spaces where visitors would be seated after dinner or over tea. Given their very specific purpose, early manuals indicated that they ought to be decorated accordingly. Mrs William Parkes wrote in her book *Domestic Duties; or, Instructions to Young Married Ladies* in 1828, 'The dining room, the place of rendezvous for the *important* concerns of the table, should not be furnished in the light and airy style which you may adopt in your drawing room.' Floral chintz fabrics were the perfect realisation of this imperative, although the light and airy materials also needed to be hard-wearing. Beeton's treasury noted of the drawing room, 'The upholstery of the furniture too is also a material that may quickly soil or tarnish, or a colour that may be easily spoiled by untoward usage.' With this in mind, drawing-room furniture textiles, as they appear in Anne's album, are all glazed cotton, to mitigate 'untoward usage'. The glazing of these cotton fabrics consisted of a particular finishing process called calendaring. The cotton cloth would be passed through rollers under pressure, which would flatten the fibres and, depending on the speed or heat of the rollers, the cloth would then develop a lustre. Additional robustness could be created by adding a filling to the process as well – a wax or a resin that would become embedded in the fibres, filling the spaces and contributing to the shine that all of the furnishing fabrics in Anne's book display, an unexpected glint that slides with light across the surface of the cloth as the page turns.

The drawing room was a predominantly female space, which accounted for a choice of style that was considered suitable by society at large: of textiles, furniture covers and curtains in lighter colours and floral prints, over which afternoon tea and after-dinner chats might be taken on the settees and suites of chairs, resting cups and glasses on small occasional tables. Ottomans and footstools, all in matching textiles, formed part of the aesthetic of the mid-nineteenth-century drawing room, jostling for position amongst the sewing tables, screens, writing desks and stools that formed the roll call of drawing-room furniture, according to the appropriate good taste of the period. The drawing room was the best public room in the house and Mrs Panton, in her 1888 publication *From Kitchen to Garret*, warned her readers that 'It is on little things that our lives depend for comfort, and small habits, such as a changed dress for evening wear with a long skirt, to give the proper drawing-room air, the enforcement of the rule that slippers and cigars must never enter there.'

The artist Mary Ellen Best rented a house in York and painted a picture of her drawing room after she had decorated it to her own taste. She captured a room of chintz covers, long draping tablecloths and patterned wallpaper, which gave the room a quintessentially 'Victorian' ambience, with its cluttered stereotype intact. And in 1877 Mrs Lucy Orrinsmith wrote an entire book on the decoration and furniture of the drawing room, underlining its importance as a space within the home, although taste is, of course, entirely subjective. On visiting London in the early 1890s, the young American Sara Duncan wrote of her horror at the extravagant decoration of a British drawing room and the textiles that seemingly adorned every surface: 'The flower pots were draped, and the lamps; there were draperies around the piano legs and round the clock; and where there were not draperies there were bows . . . The only thing that had not made an effort to clothe itself in the room was the poker and by contrast it looked very nude.'

Given the centrality of the drawing room in women's lives, it is no surprise that the furnishing textiles in Anne's album all inhabited a variety of these rooms, whether it was an exuberant spotted floral cotton described as 'Mary's Drawing Room Chintz', the stylised red-and-brown floral cotton that was 'Alice Burton's Drawing Room' or that most bold of leopard-print swatches that graced Anne's furniture in her Singapore home. An especially intriguing swatch is one of the later examples, dating to 1864. Rather than the floral chintz that was especially popular, 'Mary's Drawing Room' was altogether more biological, but reflective of the nineteenth-century desire to categorise the natural world. Motifs that captured the detail of flora and fauna abounded. 'Mary' chose a particularly striking pattern: branches of coral in tones of brown and pink. There is something ventricular about the design, so that it might as well depict an anatomical illustration, capturing the contemporary thrill of new discovery.

~

There is little to be learned about the first house that Anne and Adam resided in on their return to Lancashire in 1849. There is a dark-green, leafy waxed-cotton fragment that may have decorated their Mode Wheel Road residence, although the label is slightly curious. Above this particular furnishing textile Anne wrote, 'Drawing Room Adam Sykes 1850'. Is it possible this indicates a fabric that Adam himself chose for their house? Given the room's female associations, it seems something of an anomaly that the room is linked to Adam. It might suggest the sharing of decisions between the couple – that theirs was not always a partnership so strictly demarcated by convention. By the date of the 1861 census Anne and Adam had moved almost forty miles away to the village of Bashall Eaves and the large detached property of Colthurst Hall. The report of a commemoration day in 1856 for the Clitheroe Grammar School refers to the presence of 'Mrs Adam Sykes and party Colthurst', so they were well established at the hall by the time of the 1861 census.

The swatch that Anne had included is another waxed cotton, but unlike the animal print found in the Singaporean drawing room, this is a more conventional floral print, with large sprays of pink roses and foliage set against a speckled cream background. It is captioned, 'Colthurst Drawing Room 1859'. Aged forty-two, Anne was by now an experienced, and presumably confident, home-maker. Adam, at fifty-two, had retired from trade, and Colthurst Hall was the exterior marker of the fruits of his mercantile labour. On the electoral register, Adam was still residing at Colthurst Hall in 1875, making it the home that he and Anne lived in together for the longest period during their marriage. We even know that whilst living at Colthurst they had a dog, according to a report in *The Preston Herald* on 29 June 1863: 'LOST on 28 June a large SHEEP DOG, black body, gray legs and face; answers to the name of "Tyro". Had on a leathern collar marked "Adam Sykes, Colthurst nr Clitheroe".' Adam's fondness for Tyro was marked by the promise of a generous reward.

Whilst he may have retired from the bustle of merchant life by the

1860s, Adam was not averse to new ventures. Amongst the many advertisements in the *Derbyshire Times and Chesterfield Herald* or the *Manchester Courier and Lancashire General Advertiser* the partners of the Manchester and County Bank (Ltd) included Adam Sykes of Colthurst, describing himself now as a 'gentleman'. It was an important descriptor, one that marked his shift away from industry – the greater the distance from labour, the higher up the social ladder it was possible to climb. Removal to the grey-stoned uniformity of Colthurst, with its tenant farmers, its sturdy slate roof and its symmetrically numbered white sash windows overlooking lush meadowland, conveyed to the world that Adam Sykes was indeed a gentleman. The Manchester and County Bank was established in York Street in Manchester in 1862 and operated as a joint-stock bank, encouraging investors to buy shares in stock, in the details of which these retired merchants were very well versed.

The 1840s and 1850s had seen a surge of interest in interior design. Female consumers were able to frequent the growing number of furnishing drapers springing up around the UK, businesses such as Eld & Chamberlain in Birmingham, whose mid-nineteenth-century trade cards depicted women on the threshold of their shop, on their own and ordering the furnishings for their homes. In *Gore's Directory of Liverpool & its Environs*, published in 1853, there were 138 furniture brokers listed, catering to the desire to present a tasteful and respectable home to family, friends and acquaintances.

Other external forces drove these new ambitions. In the summer of 1851 the Great Exhibition of the Works of Industry of All Nations had taken place within the impressive Crystal Palace, a show of imperial force certainly, but also a space to exhibit the wares of Empire to a captivated audience. More than six million people visited the Great Exhibition, comprising more women than men and offering a vision of the decorative arts in all its many forms. There was an expanding vocabulary of consumerism, with a growing sector of the population becoming well versed in its intricacies. If visiting a furnishing draper was not possible, and if attending the Great Exhibition was out of reach, then the flurry of trade catalogues that were appearing could help the keen householder. These illustrated catalogues listed all the many furnishing options to appropriately fill the home. The increased spending capabilities drove the desire for goods to reflect status, and so it became possible to decorate and furnish an entire house from within the pages of one of these catalogues.

The interior furnishings and the homes of Anne Sykes, Sarah Newmann and their contemporaries are stories of ambition and of moving up in the world. Sarah's chintz covers, chosen for her home in 1851, may have graced her Allerton Road villa, but it is likely that she chose something new for their move to the much grander Wyndcote House. For Anne and Adam, their homes chart their path through the world. They began their married life in the humidity of Singapore, with Anne furnishing a house unlike anything she would have experienced during her early years in Lancashire. On their return they found themselves in a generous house on Mode Wheel Road, but were surrounded with the trappings of industry – the very mills, dye and printworks upon which their respective family fortunes had emerged. They moved again, from industry to landed gentry and the leafy surroundings of Colthurst Hall in Lancashire's Ribble Valley, where Anne decorated her drawing room in a rose-sprayed chintz and attended agricultural shows.

Colthurst was not to be their final home. It was the residence in which they lived the longest together, inhabiting its wood-panelled spaces and taking in the long pastoral view from its front windows for almost twenty years, but they were destined to move again, to take in new vistas. The album accompanied Anne to each of her homes during the half-century of her marriage to Adam. Today it resides in a house devoid of glazed cotton chintz. It sits on a table from Ikea in a small South Devon town, a world away from its beginnings.

CHAPTER 18

Sisters in Style

Emily & Alice Burton, Charlotte Dugdale Sykes

'For there is no friend like a sister
In calm or stormy weather;
To cheer one on the tedious way,
To fetch one if one goes astray.'

Christina Rossetti, 'Goblin Market', 1862

What was Anne really like, I often wonder? Did she have a sweet tooth? Was she fond of Dickens and loathed Shakespeare? I can tell where she lived, what pattern she chose for her chair covers and what dress she wore in 1856. I know the name of her dog, the size of her greenhouse and the sum of money that she and Adam gave to philanthropic endeavours. But I don't know what made her laugh. I don't know whether she was sad that she never had children or relieved. I don't know if she missed her years in Singapore or delighted at the comfort to be gained from the familiarity of home. I don't even really know if she and Adam were happily married.

That is the paradox of the album. It offers such intimacy through the very fabrics that clothed their bodies, but in fact reveals so very little. What I can say from the diary alone is that from the 1860s onwards, when Anne had reached her forties, she lacked the same enthusiasm for recording the sartorial lives of those around her. The shaping of the cloth was less precise, the writing larger and the detail absent. Had the album become something of a chore perhaps? Maybe she kept it up for form's sake, or because the family kept on presenting her with pieces of cloth after all these years of collecting and she didn't have the heart to ask them to stop. Certainly during these latter years and later pages, those swatches that are present come from the inner circle of family – a sisterhood of sorts, comprising her niece Charlotte, whose baby clothes filled an early page of the diary so many years before, and her sisters-in-law, the women who had married her own and Adam's brothers.

Charlotte was a young woman whose fabrics were fashionable, with similar styles still surviving in garments that have been collected in museums around the world and which testify to the modishness of her choices. At the age of eighteen in 1854 she wore a white checked cotton printed with a pale-blue rose repeat. Stripes, checks and florals in purples, blues, golds and pinks filled her world, folded carefully no doubt in wooden presses in her bedroom at 70 Garston Old Road in Liverpool, where she lived with her mother Jane, who for more than twenty years had been head of her household. Charlotte's grandmother, Mary, lived with them as well, a household of women making their way in the industrial world of mid-nineteenth-century Liverpool.

At another address in Garston, a long, low villa called Aigburth Hall, lived John Edward Sheppard. John had been apprenticed to a prominent cotton brokerage at the centre of Liverpool's port trade, working for the firm of Littledale & Co. from 1851, before later striking out on his own. Given the proximity of their accommodation, perhaps Charlotte and John met at a local social event or at church? Perhaps they strolled around the green spaces of Garston as their courtship developed, with Charlotte looking proud in her rose-printed cotton or maybe even her best gold-and-green striped taffeta.

On 15 October 1862 Charlotte and John married in St Mary's Church,

Grassington. Surprisingly, given Anne's propensity to memorialise wedding dresses in her book, there is no pale snippet of wedding silk bearing Charlotte's name. How she appeared on her autumnal wedding day is lost to us. Her change of status brought with it a change in her sartorial choices, based on the fragments that remain from the years following her wedding. The printed cottons were replaced by a proliferation of silk in browns and blues, fashionable colours for the decade that saw the arrival of the broadest of crinoline skirts in the mid-1860s. One sky-blue silk features a large black warp-printed carnation, the size of the flower too large for the swatch that Anne included, so that only a part of its nodding bloom is included. The dress in its entirety would have been a swish of flowers, the expanse of silk a broad canvas for the size of the pattern. Charlotte Sheppard was a young wife whose clothes demonstrated that she was fashionable and understood the changing tempo of cloth and silhouette. Charlotte and John did not have children immediately. Five years after their marriage, their first daughter Constance was born, and only a little over a year later their second daughter Isabel arrived, the family living comfortably in the up-and-coming professional suburbs of Liverpool, at 8 South Bank Road in Garston.

The continued closeness of Charlotte to Anne and Adam Sykes appears in the happy coincidence of the 1871 census, those moments frozen in time that catch people during one evening in March every decade, wherever they might happen to be. The March of 1871 found Anne and Adam Sykes staying in the Imperial Hotel in Blackpool, an imposing red-brick establishment on the North Shore, which only two years earlier had played host to Charles Dickens during his literary tour of the North of England. Along with Anne and Adam were Charlotte and John Sheppard, accompanying them on their seaside break – Anne and Charlotte doubtless gracing the sweep of staircase in the hotel with their silk polonaise gowns as the cycle of fashionable female dress turned once more to herald the first hint of the bustle era.

The 1870s witnessed the last entries in Anne's album. Charlotte appears only twice – the name C D Sheppard attached to a pale-lilac silk faille, not dissimilar to her mother's wedding dress of forty years earlier, and to the striped silk that she gave Anne. The records, however, continue to catch Charlotte and her family and, according to the 1891 census, the four of them – Charlotte and John with both of their girls, Constance and Isabel, now aged twenty-four and twenty-three – still lived at 8 South Bank Road, enjoying a prosperous life that included five domestic servants and a coachman. John had retired from cotton brokering in 1885, and by 1901 his standing in the community was such that he had become a magistrate and alderman, a pillar of Garston and an archetypal Victorian gentleman, made from his early apprenticeship in the world of cotton.

Neither Constance nor Isabel features in Anne's album, the evidence of her great-nieces' material lives absent from her collection. In 1896, at the age of twenty-eight, Charlotte's youngest daughter Isabel died and was buried in the cemetery of the parish church at Halewood. Constance remained at home and was to continue as her mother's companion. The three of them moved to a larger house by the turn of the new century and, with John a respected magistrate, they now occupied Eastfield, a larger house in Garston. At the age of seventy-one John was a Victorian success story, a man who built his fortunes on cotton and took on the civic duties that would have been expected of a man of his ambitions, keen to leave his mark on his community as a respectable gentleman. In December 1901 he died at the age of seventy-two, leaving behind Charlotte, his wife of almost forty years. Charlotte and Constance returned to 8 South Bank Road, the house in which the four of them had lived for so long in happier times, and there they stayed until Charlotte's death in 1917.

Charlotte might have adopted the richer silks that befitted her role as the wife of a magistrate, but Anne's book will forever capture Charlotte's youthful wardrobe, her brightly sprigged floral cottons in which she toddled about as the precious only child of her young widowed mother. We can see the fashionable light white cottons that witnessed her coming of age and her courtship with John as they promenaded together around Garston, the suburb of Liverpool that was to be their home together for the rest of their lives. I like to think that Anne was a fond aunt; that she wrote often to Jane and Charlotte whilst she was in Singapore, describing the multicultural world before them and waiting eagerly in her turn for the snippets of dress they would send her to remind her of the vibrant world that awaited her back in England.

~

Anne's connections were forged through the women who passed through her life and, increasingly, these networks came via the wives of her brothers – namely Emily, Edward's wife; Alice, who married Oliver; and Ellen, who was married to James. The two sisters-in-law who appear with the greatest frequency in Anne's diary are Alice and Ellen, and they both married into the Burton family a mere week apart in June 1851. Ellen Dugdale married James Burton on 4 June, and Alice Proctor became Oliver Burton's wife on 12 June. Throughout the 1850s and 1860s both women presented Anne with regular fabric contributions that she could add to her album, each demonstrating a familiarity with the fashionable mores of the day. Their kaleidoscopic wardrobes included bright corded silks, plaid wool, sheer figured gauzes and, of course, cotton aplenty. The boldly striped printed cottons favoured by Alice in the early 1850s, shortly after her marriage, need to be imagined as a layered skirt made *à la disposition* in ever-increasing flounces to the hem. The wax-resist dyed cloth of Ellen's wardrobe in pink and blue made for striking ensembles, when the three-inch squares of cloth are expanded in the mind's eye to sit over the newly fashionable cage crinoline. The scale of these patterns might be better appreciated hanging in folds, the yards of cloth suspended from the waist and coming to rest at the ankle.

As the wives of cotton manufacturers, Ellen and Alice lived comfortably. Anne offers few details at this point in the diary, only the name of the wearer and the year, but the vast majority of the swatches relate to the main garments of both daywear and evening wear as being appropriate to the role they would have played in their immediate communities. Unusually for Anne, she does describe one changeable greenish-black taffeta as 'Alice's mantle', attributing an actual garment type to a fragment. It refers to an enveloping piece of outerwear that was popular at the time, and generously proportioned in order to fit over the top of the broad skirts beneath. Anne rarely makes these distinctions, and this is one of the only times she does so. A sense of closeness seems to connect Anne and Alice. In the more than forty samples of Alice's clothing that Anne included, many of them also bear Anne's name – the use of dress to bind family connections recorded in their names written side-by-side above the cloth. Alice liked purple gingham and geometric prints. She wore the floral cottons and diaphanous striped gauzes that were popular for evening wear in the 1850s, where the generous skirts might acquire a sheen against the candlelight of assembly rooms or supper parlours.

Anne and Alice did not always live close to each other. In the 1850s and into the 1860s Oliver ran Atherton Mill and lived in Westfield House in the parish of Atherton with Alice, so for the first decade at least of their married life they were within visiting distance of Anne and Adam. But change was to come. Oliver took his prosperity to a new life in Wales. He and Alice moved to the leafy rurality of Gwaenynog Hall in Denbighshire, a rambling stone building with beautiful gardens, where he sat as a Justice of the Peace and involved himself in the local community. So far-reaching did his influence become that in 1881 he was elected to the office of High Sheriff of the county, with Alice doubtless attending civic functions at his side in garments that by then went unrecorded by Anne. Visitors received by Oliver and Alice, recorded in the careful handwritten script of the 1871 census, reveal more connections with Anne's album – happy coincidences that join the threads of previously unknown connections, linking names and families together.

In March 1871 Gwaenynog Hall played host to three visitors – Humphrey Gregg, Mary Gregg and Eliza Ward. The spark of recognition was immediate: I had seen those names before. Both Mrs Gregg and Eliza Ward appear in Anne's diary, Mrs Gregg with great frequency amongst the 1850s and 1860s pages of the album. Tracing the records backwards, I found that Mary Gregg was called Mary Proctor before her marriage. She was Alice Burton's sister. Mary married Humphrey, a solicitor, and lived with him in Kirkby Lonsdale, where he practised. The connection with Anne is more tenuous – were they friends through their shared association with Alice, or did Alice simply request snips of fabric from her sister, knowing of Anne's endeavour, that she could pass on to her sister-in-law? Sometimes these glimpses are frustratingly brief. Doubtless Anne and Adam visited Oliver and Alice at Gwaenynog Hall, so perhaps they made the acquaintance of the Greggs there. Whether it developed into a friendship or whether Anne was simply grateful to have the many swatches of Mary's garments for her book remains a mystery, but none-theless the jumble of names that appear without the context of family in Anne's diary is at least partially untangled by these revelations.

Oliver Burton died in 1883, but rather than sell his Welsh home, his brother Frederick moved there himself with his wife Harriet. It is here that an unexpected connection with one of Britain's best-loved children's authors overlaps with the family of Anne Sykes. Frederick's wife Harriet was the aunt of Beatrix Potter, her sister Helen Leech having married Rupert Potter. The young girl would visit her Burton aunt and uncle in their rambling house and gardens at Gwaenynog Hall, and from the veg-etable garden and potting shed in its grounds she created the domain of Mr McGregor, whose nemesis would become the naughty Peter Rabbit. Whether Anne ever met the young Beatrix Potter it is impossible to know, but it is an intriguing thought.

Other women do appear in the diary during these years, but the lack of a helpful detail to locate them beyond the pages of the diary ensures that they are all but anonymous. Who was Mrs Robinson in her corded purple silk dress? Where does 'Florence', with her wardrobe of small sprigged cotton frocks and warm woollens, fit into the web of Anne's life? For all of the stories that can be told, there are countless others that remain a mystery, just a tantalising glimpse of an acquaintance here and there. Perhaps Anne didn't even like her sisters-in-law and tolerated them for the sake of family harmony. What is a certainty is that Anne's diary reveals less and less as the years pass. What is also apparent is that only women were present in its final years. Without knowing anything about the nature of their relationships, this much at least is true.

CHAPTER 19

Upstairs, Downstairs
Margaret Charnock

> Some ladies stand very much in awe of their cooks,
> knowing that those who consider themselves to be
> thoroughly experienced will not brook fault-finding . . .
>
> *The Servants' Practical Guide*, 1880

There is a female experience caught in the pages of Anne's album that reaches beyond her own middle-class comfort – a world that is perhaps best reflected in a solitary fabric swatch belonging to a woman different from those Anne most often included in her diary. Anomaly though it might be amongst the pages of Anne's peers, it opens up a world beyond her own, a space that briefly intersected with hers, but which was vastly different at the same time.

At the bottom of a page filled with fabrics variously belonging to Ellen and Alice Burton there is a striking printed cotton in shades of brown. A geometric repeat is broken by a broad stripe of autumnal shaded leaves, tendrils that curl in a vertical trellis. It is captioned simply, 'Margaret Charnock'. In the first instance, it meant nothing and related to nobody that I knew of, but the more I discovered about Anne, the more I began to find out about the women around her. Re-evaluating the names some months later, I stumbled across Margaret Charnock's name in the diary once more, and this time it struck a chord. I had seen that name somewhere. Revisiting the all-important census records taking household snapshots once a decade, there she was. At the bottom of the 1861 census that accounted for everyone living under Anne and Adam Sykes's roof in Colthurst Hall, there was Margaret Charnock. She was their cook.

The cook: an often-anonymous domestic servant, one of the tens of thousands of working-class women occupying the homes of their wealthy employers and whose lives, and clothes, are infrequently documented in detail. Ironically, this makes Margaret Charnock's sharp printed cotton one of the rarer fragments in the album, the wardrobe of a cook traditionally receiving little attention.

On 2 January 1831 little Margaret Charnock was baptised in the parish of Whitewell in Yorkshire, a daughter to John and Catherine. John was a farmer and Margaret's childhood was a rural one, growing up in a small hamlet in the Ribble Valley, a landscape of rolling hills, stone walls and farmland that existed just beyond the reach of the industrial sprawl to its south. The nearest town was Clitheroe, the town of Anne's birth. As with so many young women in her economic position, Margaret would very quickly have reached the age where she was expected to make a financial contribution to the family coffers. The occupations most widely available to her would have been as a factory hand or a domestic servant. Both consisted of long hours and back-breaking work, but perhaps Margaret saw the possibilities of advancement in the domestic-service route, for that is the direction she chose. Maybe it was chosen for her, the network of patriarchal connections reaching out to find families who might wish to recruit a young housemaid.

In 1851, aged nineteen, Margaret moved thirty miles south of her rural Yorkshire upbringing, leaving the farm behind, to live in the household of Joseph Henderson, a cotton spinner, and his wife Jane, who lived in the small village of Clayton-le-Moors, only two miles north of the industrial landscape of Accrington and nearby Burnley. She was listed as a servant, one of three in the household and the youngest. The other two servants, William Naylor and Mary Whalley, would most likely have acted as a butler and cook respectively, meaning that Margaret was a maid of all work, undertaking a whole variety of tasks.

In 1825 Samuel and Sarah Adams had published an instructional volume aimed at assisting both household servants and their employers in the world of domestic service. *The Complete Servant: Being a Practical Guide to the Peculiar Duties and Business of all Descriptions of Servants* brought Samuel and Sarah's own considerable experience of a life in service to the next generation. They began with a table that outlined how many servants a household ought to employ, depending on income. Joseph and Jane Henderson fell into the category of a comfortable household without children, and so would require two female servants and one male. The book endeavoured to give advice to those young people entering service for the first time: 'They will probably find every thing different to what they have been accustomed to at home, or in common life; and as their mode of living will be greatly altered, if not wholly changed so must be their minds and manners.'

The volume continues with a list of duties and tips, beginning at the apex of the service hierarchy with the housekeeper and moving down towards the other positions. In the large country houses, service would have been strictly demarcated between different statuses of maids, with those allowed above stairs compared favourably to those whose roles kept them strictly below. However, for a relatively small household such as the Hendersons, Margaret would have been expected to take on all and every job required, from keeping the house and its fixtures and fittings clean, to laying the fire, making beds, assisting with laundry, washing the kitchen dishes and perhaps even serving food, if required. In their summary of the 'servant of all work' duties, Samuel and Sarah Adams were breezily optimistic: 'Industry and cleanliness, with a determination to be useful, and to please, will speedily overcome all difficulties.'

Clothing domestic servants was one of the concerns that mistresses of a larger household would have been expected to manage. Male servants, who might be seen in the public area of the house at mealtimes, for example, wore livery. This kind of especially old-fashioned garment was essentially a throwback to feudal times in centuries past, when families would have their own heraldic markers to denote those serving under their allegiance. Large country and town houses in the nineteenth century maintained this unusual sartorial tradition, sending away to ceremonial embroiderers to have jackets embellished with the colours and motifs associated with their name, emblazoned in gold. Young Frederick Gorst recalled the livery he wore as a footman for Lord and Lady Howard in the 1890s: 'My dress livery for the London house was also a novelty. I had never before put on blue plush knee breeches, white stockings, and pumps with a silver buckle. I also was expected to wear a claret coloured swallow tailed coat with silver buttons, a claret waistcoat and a stiff, white shirt.' Housemaids whose duties took them above stairs were generally expected to wear a uniform that consisted of a black cotton dress with white accessories, a lace-trimmed apron and a white cotton cap – the female equivalent of the more ornate livery.

For women working behind the green baize door that separated the world of upstairs and downstairs, the requirements of dress were not so much formal as practical. Patterned cotton washing frocks were the most popular garment: sturdy dresses that might be easily laundered. For smaller households especially, meeting the cost of these garments was the responsibility of the servants themselves. Housemaid Harriet Brown wrote to her mother in 1870, 'I do not know how to thank you for your kindness in doing the aprons for me. I should never have got them made myself for I have not made the print dresses yet that I told you about when I was home last.' Margaret Thomas described working small jobs minding children from the age of fourteen in order to save for her service clothes: 'Eventually I saved enough and got my uniform:

print dresses, morning aprons, black dress, afternoon aprons, stiff collars and cuffs all packed into a tin trunk.' If their employers were generous, servants might expect gifts of fabric for clothing as a Christmas present. The department store D. H. Evans included an advertisement in their mail-order catalogue of 1901 entitled 'Christmas Gifts for Servants'. Small swatches of sample cloths included 'English prints (fast colours)' for maids and 'Oxford shirtings (for hard wear)' for men.

The irony of these ubiquitous garments today is that they are incredibly rare. The museum curators of the late nineteenth and early twentieth centuries were tasked with collecting objects that were the rarest and most beautiful of their type. From the perspective of clothing, that invariably meant Parisian couture and London court dressmakers, exemplars of embellishment and adornment. The cheap cotton frocks of a housemaid were then of little interest to the keepers of the arts. In more recent years, with a growing emphasis on more diverse social histories, the material culture of domestic service is sought-after but scarce. These dresses were rarely kept, but were worn and worn, eventually entering the second-hand market or being cut up into cleaning cloths and dusters. They were certainly not preserved for posterity by their owners, who would no doubt have been scornful of any scholarly interest in their everyday garb.

~

Margaret Charnock was not destined to remain a general dogsbody and, over the course of the next decade, learned the skills required of a cook. By the early 1860s at the age of twenty-nine, she was cook to Anne and Adam Sykes in their country home of Colthurst Hall, a bigger household than that of her former employers, the Hendersons. Here she worked alongside the housemaid Elizabeth Richman, a 'waitress' called Ellen Thompson, the dairy maid Catherine Pinder and the coachman Thomas Leeming, who lived in the lodge house of Colthurst. *The Complete Servant* was emphatic about the role of the cook. 'On her first going into a family the Cook will do well to inform herself of the rules and regulations of the house – the customs of the kitchen – the peculiarities of her master and mistress, and above all she must study most sedulously to acquire a perfect knowledge of their TASTE.'

What were Anne and Adam's tastes? Had they acquired an interest in different food after their years in Singapore and China? Did they surprise Margaret with unusual requests for dishes that she had to research, or did they run to plainer fare, maintaining a safe table that Margaret could cater to in appropriate style? As well as *The Complete Servant*, by the 1860s Margaret would have had recourse to publications such as *Mrs Beeton's Book of Household Management*, which was also published as *The English-woman's Cookery Book*. Her intention, she stated in her preface, was to 'help Plain Cooks and Maids Of All Work to a knowledge of some of their duties and to assist them in the important task of dressing and serving daily food'. It was a comprehensive volume that took the cook from the arrangement of the kitchen and the necessary utensils, to recipes for fish, game, meat, the preparation of preserves and the baking of biscuits.

A large part of the cook's job involved liaising with her mistress to approve daily menus, and so regular conversation would have formed the basis of a working relationship between Margaret Charnock and Anne Sykes. The nature of such relationships goes largely unrecorded. Domestic servants rarely had the time or the means to share their thoughts and feelings about the realities of their lives. A rare survival in the V&A uses a textile to record an experience of service. On a piece of plain white cotton, the servant Elizabeth Parker cross-stitched her woes in fine red thread, telling a tale of hardship and misery. It was stitched in 1830, just a year before Margaret Charnock was born. Elizabeth used stitch to write of the treatment she received at the hands of her mistress where she served in London as a nursery maid, 'with cruelty too horrible to mention'.

Whilst these kind of material artefacts are few and far between, there is a cook's uniform that has, in fact, survived and is now in the collections of Manchester Art Galleries, mere miles from the various homes in which Margaret lived with Anne and Adam over the course of her service. Dating to around 1890, it is a pink-and-white striped cotton ensemble of the style advertised by D. H. Evans. Perhaps it started life as a length of fabric, given to the employee by her mistress, which she then turned into the high-collared blouse and matching skirt that remain. It is recognisably fashionable. Practical though the fabric might have been, the style of dress includes a slightly gathered waist, a puff at the sleeve-head and a small frill at the collar, which showed an awareness of prevailing trends and, without being too showy – which would have been unacceptable – weaves those details into the construction of the uniform.

The dress that belonged to Margaret Charnock and which Anne included in her book is almost certainly not that which she would have worn in the course of her duties for the Sykes. The striking printed cotton, with its broad stripe of autumnal-shaded leaves, is too decorative for the kitchen. It seems unlikely that Margaret would have been prepared to share her workwear with her employer and so, given its style and the conditions of their relationship, it is more likely that this was Margaret's best dress, one that she wore to church on Sunday and for outings to the seaside on her occasional half-day off, a dress that she liked and was happy to share.

For Anne to have acquired a little swatch of Margaret's dress, perhaps we might view their association in a more favourable light. Friends they may not have been, but Margaret remained in the Sykes household for more than twenty years, moving with them from Colthurst Hall and beyond as they prepared to relocate to a different home. In 1885, at the age of fifty-two, Margaret Charnock got married. Did a now much frailer Anne and Adam attend the nuptials of their long-serving cook? I hope that they did. Margaret married Joseph Whalley, a builder and widower seven years her senior, and so after almost forty years of living under the roofs of her employers, Margaret came to cook in a kitchen of her own – her feet under her own table, mistress of her own household. Sadly, it was to be a short-lived period of domestic change. Margaret died just three years after her wedding to Joseph. She was fifty-five.

I wonder how Margaret felt about contributing to her employer's album of fabrics? Class boundaries in nineteenth-century Britain were riven with complexity, and with notions of place. They generated snobberies that live with us still. My own grandmother was always desperately anxious about class, about knowing her place. She hated having to invite my grandfather's friend, a local landowner, into their small, immaculate terraced house, for fear of serving the wrong biscuits. As a child of the 1920s, she was only one generation away from the Victorian hierarchies. Her own sister was a 'tweenie', a between maid – meaning a maid of all work in the local country house in the dying years of domestic service. It was a job she despised, and as a family they held that kind of wealth and power in disdain at the same time as being intimidated by it.

Margaret was a servant to Anne. She would have to have 'known her place', and yet at some point Anne perhaps called her upstairs to discuss the week's menus. Whilst they were discussing what to eat on Wednesday, maybe Anne was busy arranging some newly acquired fabrics on the page of her fabric-filled album and showed Margaret the fruits of her endeavours. Then perhaps Anne said that she ought to have a piece of Margaret's clothing to add to this record of her world. Was Margaret embarrassed or flattered? I hope there was a warmth between these two women who lived in the same space, but occupied different worlds. For a moment and in a swatch of cloth they exist side-by-side. Were it not for Anne's decision, then Margaret's tale would never have been told, hers just another faceless employee lost in the vastness of the broader domestic-service story. But there she is, in her bold printed cotton taking a turn on the sea front alongside Joseph Whalley, no longer as a cook but as a married woman.

CHAPTER 20

The Brightest of Hues

Bridget Anne Peacock

purple hands wave from open carriages – purple hands
shake each other at street doors . . . purple striped gowns
cram barouches, jam up cabs, throng steamers, fill railway
stations: all flying countryward, like so many purple birds
of migrating paradise.

'Perkins's Purple', *All the Year Round*, 1859

Almost exactly halfway through Anne's album of fabrics there is a shift. Creeping across the pages, a new addition to the aesthetics of nineteenth-century dress makes its presence felt, a splash of vibrancy here and there that speaks of science at work and the thrill of the new. Aniline dyes began to alter the sartorial landscape from the mid-1850s onwards, washing the fashionable landscape in a haze of purple. This trend is reflected in Anne's collection, a mark of both her own and her friends' eyes being focused firmly on emerging changes.

Innovative dye technologies and the colours that they produced could stand as a metaphor for the pace of nineteenth-century change in general. The quest for the unexplained, the uncharted and the unmeasured was a part of the life scientific at this time – be it in an exploration of the natural world or of the industrial one. New discoveries were applied rapidly to lived experiences, so that one man's chemistry experiment might find itself clothing the women of a nation in a very short space of time. Such experiments were not without their risks and, in an unregulated environment, fashionable hues became perilous during those years when Anne was recording these vivid changes in her volume. To explore the world of nineteenth-century dye techniques is to capture the zeitgeist of a century that was forever testing the untested.

One of the samples in the diary is a bright-purple corded silk, a small swatch that in just a few inches can still convey the rich lustre of both colour and cloth. It glows from its pale-blue paper canvas. The caption informs us that this luminous fragment belonged to somebody called Bridgetanne in 1862. Unusual names are the researcher's dream, their unique nomenclature allowing them to shine like beacons amongst the millions of names populating census records, parish registers, marriage certificates and probate entries. Bridgetanne appears with regularity in the dress diary, and on page 217 a large sample of pale-lilac moiré silk proclaims to be 'Bridgetanne's Wedding Dress 1864'. Elsewhere, captions offer her surname. She was Bridgetanne Peacock, the name appropriately capturing something of the brightness of her wardrobe as it features in Anne's arrangement of swatches. The gift of both her full, slightly unusual name and the year of her marriage illuminates those parts of her life that were a matter of public record, and she emerges in all her purple glory.

Bridget Anne Peacock was born in 1815, baptised in the parish of Bolton-le-Sands near the city of Lancaster. Her father, John, was a squire and her mother was Sarah. Bridget Anne was the youngest child of three and the only daughter to John and Sarah. Unlike many of the other women to whom Anne was connected in her diary, Bridgetanne appears to have no obvious link to the textile industries and so the root of their acquaintance is shadowy. There is a hint that they had either travelled together or met up in Malta in 1839. A leap of the imagination is sometimes required from the scant captions offered by Anne in the album. One of the early references to Bridgetanne is attached to a figured beige silk that bears the label 'Bridget Ann Peacock wore this in Malta.' As early as page 9 of the album, Anne had noted three dresses that she described as 'Anne Sykes Malta May 1840'. Further circumstantial evidence appears a little further on. Against a black printed cotton with a pattern of red branches Anne wrote, 'Bridgetanne 1839'.

The placement of the fabrics and the brevity of their descriptors nonetheless builds into a network of connection that seems to suggest that Bridgetanne and Anne Sykes found themselves in Malta at the same time in 1839 and 1840, although the purpose of their visit remains shadowy. Did they travel together, a newly married young woman and her unmarried friend? Perhaps they met on the island and discovered that they both hailed from Lancashire, forging a geographical bond that developed into a friendship lasting more than forty years. Bridgetanne was a single woman at this time and so the ability for her to travel freely and unchaperoned would have been compromised by her marital status, unless she was in company with a married woman or in the employ of somebody in Malta.

That her friendship extended to others in Anne's circle is apparent from the 1861 census, where she is to be found as the house-guest of Jane and Charlotte Sykes. When Bridgetanne stayed with Jane and Charlotte in 1861, she was forty-six years of age and as yet unmarried. By the standards of the day she would have been considered a spinster, a woman who had missed out on her chance to marry and have a family, and who might prove financially burdensome to her family unless she happened to be able to support herself independently, thanks to some generous bequest or allowance. Even then she might not possess her own property, but would find herself in the unenviable position of nomadic female guest or full-time occupant of another family member's home, the archetypal older unmarried-aunt figure who reached her apotheosis in the character of Miss Havisham – Charles Dickens's unflinching depiction of a jilted bride doomed to a life unwed.

Elizabeth Gaskell brought these women out from the shadows in her creation of *Cranford*, published in the early 1850s in *Household Words*. Of the unmarried women with whom she populated the village of Cranford, she wrote, 'Cranford is in the possession of the Amazons . . . all the holders of houses above a certain rent are women.' Whether Bridgetanne was a Cranford woman or a Miss Havisham woman in the early 1860s is impossible to know, but in 1864 she underwent a change of status just before she turned fifty. On 2 July 1864 Bridgetanne Peacock married the widower James Maychell Harrison, a solicitor with three children. James and Bridgetanne were similar in age and her three stepchildren, Mary, Elizabeth and Robert, were eighteen, sixteen and fifteen respectively when she married their father.

It is intriguing to speculate about their meeting and subsequent marriage. Given their closeness in age, we might hope that this was a marriage based on a fondness for one another following the death of James's first wife, Ann. It is entirely feasible, however, that Bridgetanne was in search of some financial stability in her life and a household of her own, and James might have welcomed a mother figure to see to the fledging of his three children. Once again there is a hint of closer ties, thanks to Anne's memorialisation of these women, however sparse the information. Towards the end of the album are pieces of cloth that bind stepmother and stepdaughters together. A bright-blue twill-weave swatch is captioned, 'Mary and Lilly Harrison 1875'. Here are Bridgetanne's stepdaughters, themselves unmarried at the ages of twenty-nine and twenty-seven, captured by Anne amongst fabric belonging to their stepmother – the shortening of Elizabeth to Lilly a mark, surely, of a closeness between them and of an enduring friendship with Anne Sykes. The family lived in Flookburgh Lodge, the house that James had inhabited for many years before his second marriage, and the house that Bridget-anne continued to live in as head of the household into the early 1880s after James had died, with all three of his children still sharing the home in which they had grown up.

The vibrancy of Bridgetanne's wardrobe, as portrayed by Anne in the pages of her album, sketches the outline of a woman of fashion rather than the colourless spinster of Victorian stereotype. Bridgetanne was embracing the possibilities offered by the new synthetic dyes in all their peacock-like splendour. The craze for the colour purple has deep-seated associations that reach far back into the annals of dress history. Since a material attains value through scarcity, Tyrian purple was the mark of an accidental discovery from obscurity. Purple had long been a notoriously difficult colour to fix to cloth, unstable dyes leading to patchy results and unsatisfactory shades. The secretions of a small sea snail, the murex, was the ancient world's answer, a discovery made in Ancient Greece that was adopted by the Romans. Labour-intensive and thus highly prized, the dye that could be produced from the accumulated murex snails produced the rich shade of Tyrian purple. Such was its value that only the impe-rial family was permitted to wear the purple cloth, and the seeds of its associations with royalty and with the Church were sown. It remained a shade beyond the reach of most ordinary folk. The colour became the subject of sumptuary laws, legislation that, over the centuries and in dif-ferent social and political contexts, was used to control the availability of certain sartorial choices. Purple might only be worn by those at the top of the social hierarchy, and to do otherwise was to risk all manner of consequences. Today, purple still maintains its regal associations in the ermine-trimmed violet velvet of ceremonial robes.

Along with the crimson of cochineal (another animal dye that was hugely labour-intensive to produce), Tyrian purple was prohibitively expensive and so, for the vast majority of any population, cloth was dyed using well-known vegetable dyes, predominantly madder and indigo.

Processes remained largely unchanged for centuries. Combinations of woad, saffron and turmeric might vary, but the raw ingredients prevailed. None of those combinations were able to produce a shade of purple that did not fade, blotch or fail to fix to the cloth, and so purple retained its lofty place in the dress hierarchy, the preserve of royalty, law and religion. Some developments took place in France in the eighteenth century, and in the early years of the nineteenth century an American scientist working in London, Edward Bancroft, published his findings relating to new natural dyes that he had developed and patented, including the golden yellow of quercitron, obtained from the bark of the Eastern Black Oak, a tree cloaking the hills and mountains of North America. Colour-fast purple remained the holy grail of the colourist's art, but the eventual solution to this colourful conundrum was to be entirely accidental.

William Perkin was a young chemist in the early 1850s with a makeshift laboratory set up in the upper storey of his father's house in London. Only eighteen years of age, he had been working on synthesising quinine so that the treatment might be more readily available as a treatment for malaria. Coal tar was one of the ingredients that was central to his thesis, the addition and subtraction of substances forming part of his experimental alchemy, one of which was aniline. Whilst the synthesised quinine evaded him, the residue from his trial with aniline – a substance that one of his detractors was to call 'purple sludge' – would make his fortune. Perkin noticed that this by-product dyed cloth a solid and vivid purple that did not fade in sunlight or when washed, and he began to wonder if there might be a market for such a product, recalling later, 'After showing this colouring matter to several friends I was advised to consider the possibility of manufacturing it upon the large scale.'

He contacted large dye manufacturers and received encouraging feedback. Buoyed by the responses, he acted to protect his invention and in August 1856, still aged only eighteen, he filed a patent for his miraculous dye, mauveine. His serendipitous discovery could not have taken place at a better time, as far as the British textile industry was concerned. The production in cotton-spinning, silk-weaving and calico-printing had increased enormously from the early nineteenth century, with many companies employing their own industrial colourists to push the boundaries of chemical knowledge. Those surviving pattern books that rest now in institutions across the north-west of England attest to the quest for new pigments in their daily endeavours. Perkin had some reservations about the potential barriers to the success of his invention. The traditional processes that were so entrenched in textile-dyeing manufacture had been practised for so long that Perkin feared this new synthetic approach would fall at the first hurdle. If he failed to persuade the manufacturers that this new technique was the future, then there would be no market for mauveine.

His fears came to nothing and by the summer of 1857 Perkin had found premises for his product, purchased equipment and ingredients and went into production. By 1858 the colour mauve was sweeping fashionable metropolitan spaces. In 1859 the popular periodical *All the Year Round* wrote, 'you Mr Perkins [*sic*] . . . can itinerate Regent Street and perambulate the parks, seeing the colours of thy heart waving on every fair head and fluttering round every cheek!' In August 1859 *Punch* announced the arrival of an epidemic – the 'Mauve Measles' – the symptoms of which 'consists in the eruption of a measly rash of ribbons, about the head and neck of the person who has caught it. The eruption, which is of a mauve colour, soon spreads, until in some cases the sufferer becomes completely covered with it.'

This was to be the triumph of William Perkin's life, bringing him wealth and celebrity that remained with him into old age, when he undertook a speaking tour in America at the age of sixty-eight in 1906. The taste for mauve was not confined only to fashionable urban centres, but could be found across the country, reminding us that, then as now, fashion did not just 'happen' to those living in the cities. Bridgetanne Peacock caught the mauve measles. Six swatches of her silk dresses in Anne's diary from the early 1860s are fashionably purple, and we might imagine this single woman, in her forties, wearing clothes that are anything but the sober garb of a shrinking spinster. Peacock by name and, it seems, peacock by nature, Bridgetanne was unafraid of colour and was happy to appear as a stylish and modern woman in her middle age. Anne herself was not immune to the charms of synthetic dyes, according to the swatches in the album, with several of the intense aniline fragments belonging to her.

~

Whether synthetic or not, colour of course sits at the heart of Anne's endeavours with her diary. Before the pages are even turned, the silk cover cries out for attention. The bright shocking-pink silk was originally cut a full five inches larger than the size of the marbled paper-covered volume. The book was placed in the centre and then the edges of the cloth were folded inwards, stitched down neatly to form three sides of a square. The bottom edge of the brilliant-coloured silk has frayed now, suggesting that for some time in its trajectory of survival it stood on a shelf, a brightly hued curiosity amongst other more sober-looking book spines.

If Adam bought the ledger for Anne on their marriage, then presumably it was Anne who chose to personalise it in this way, obscuring the masculine aesthetic of a leather-bound accounting book and making it her own unique object. The choice of such a vivid pink silk was an invitation to its contents. Perhaps Anne wanted to ensure that her album was unmissable so that her friends and family were reminded of its purpose: to memorialise their own colourful lives through dress and to chart their world through a spectrum of shades. Whether printed cottons, silks or the less frequent woollens, the tides of colour in the diary point to shifting tastes across the almost forty years of its scope. The kaleidoscope of the nineteenth century rotates before our very eyes with each whisper of a turning page, the colourful women sharing a part of their lives across decades of experience.

If William Perkin and his happy chemical accident stand as one of the success stories of the era, then the unregulated nature of other aspects of colour and fashion meant there was a darker side to such invention. The craze for artificial foliage to adorn the heads and dresses of women of fashion in the mid-nineteenth century had seen the proliferation of flower workshops, where young women in their hundreds laboured to produce the lifelike green leaves and blooms that would make a fetching headdress or would trail becomingly across the bodice of a gown. The lushness of the green was achieved by the application of a powder, a pigment that was created by mixing copper and the highly toxic chemical, arsenic trioxide. The physical effects of working with this poisonous compound were horrific. Contemporary medical drawings depict the green hue of the skin and dreadful open lesions on the hands of the maker, whilst the daily gradual ingestion of the powder by the flower girls was eventually fatal.

Arsenic was not only confined to the artificial decorations and accessories, but was woven into the very fabric of the gowns themselves. The dress scholar Alison Matthews David collaborated with scientists who tested contemporary garments in museum collections and found high arsenical levels in a number of mid-century green gowns. Anxiety about these toxins found their way into the popular press, and in 1862 *Punch* published a cartoon entitled 'The Arsenic Waltz or The New Dance of Death', in which two well-dressed skeletons are about to take to the dance floor. The cartoon was dedicated to the green wreath- and dress-mongers whose lives were held in scant regard by the industries that hired them.

Other colours across the spectrum of fashion were also found to be problematic. As experiments continued in the wake of Perkin's aniline discovery, different combinations were trialled using additional

THE ARSENIC WALTZ.

THE NEW DANCE OF DEATH. (DEDICATED TO THE GREEN WREATH AND DRESS-MONGERS.)

ingredients alongside the aniline. A bright-magenta hue was achieved by adding arsenical-based chemicals to existing aniline dyes, brightening the already luminous shades – but these left residues themselves, along with a toxic labour trail in their wake. Although there are no swatches of socks or stockings in Anne's diary, these too were part of the poisonous recipes of the era. As the vogue for brightly coloured striped socks grew, there was some alarm that the number of examples of chemical burns or serious skin irritations on the lower legs and feet was growing. Colours such as the bright reds and magentas of fuchsine were often the cause, creating horrible skin conditions on coming into direct contact with the body. One report described the eczema that had erupted in stripes around the legs of a man who had purchased stockings on a trip to London. The stripes of eczema correlated with the dyed stripes of his socks, the potent chemicals reacting painfully against his skin.

When Lewis Carroll published *Alice's Adventures in Wonderland* in 1865 he introduced a character whose personality had been irrevocably affected by toxins in the fashion industry. The Mad Hatter, whose distinctive style has become a cultural icon, derived his name from the mercurial poisoning that was a devastating reality of the hatter's trade. Mercury was a quick and easy way of turning stiff and unworkable furs into a softer material that could be more easily shaped into the felted hats that were a ubiquitous part of the male wardrobe. As well as physiological impacts, the effects of mercury poisoning could be neurological as well, resulting in the colloquialism 'as mad as a hatter'.

It was not until the latter years of the nineteenth century that chemicals in the textile industry began to be more consistently regulated, after the many and varied reports undertaken over the course of decades demanded legislation. Although the reports into working conditions in factories had begun to highlight some of the most iniquitous practices from the 1830s, and despite increasingly vocal diatribes in the popular press, it took many decades for big industry to take the health and safety of its employees seriously. The flower girls, the hatters and the seamstresses of some of the more cheaply made accessories were, for too long, taken for granted, their life-threatening labour a requisite of the capitalist commercial juggernaut that careered through the nineteenth century.

Even in the twenty-first century, however, such practices have not disappeared, but have simply shifted out of the geographical line of sight. Today the quest for swift chemical solutions to some of fashion's more ubiquitous styles sees similar toxic processes dog the industry. Lest we imagine that these were practices that plagued the past, cheap denim production still poisons waterways and the communities they serve in less developed countries – those that have become intrinsically bound up with the production of fast fashion. Regions of China, India and Bangladesh continue to suffer from the realities of water pollution, with environmental agencies estimating that 70 per cent of Asia's lakes and rivers have been contaminated by more than two billion gallons of toxic waste-water. If public outrage eventually forced legislation around toxic fashion when it was on the doorstep of the Western consumer, it did not disappear altogether, but was rather pushed away to unseen spaces. Thankfully, as more of a spotlight is shone into those dark corners of the fashion industry, a greater awareness about methods of production, as well as the need for a sustainable and ecologically sound approach to garment manufacture, is beginning to change the sartorial landscape.

If we were able to see Anne and the people who inhabited her world, we would see colour. There is no way of visualising any of these women through photographs or painted portraits. I don't know what colour Anne's eyes were or the shade of her hair. I don't know if she was fair-skinned. I don't know if she was tall or short, slim or more generously proportioned. I have no idea how these women moved through their world in a physical sense. And yet here they are in all their colourful choices, in the purples of the unmarried Bridgetanne, the shades of mourning that carried Anna Coubrough through her grief, the pale celebratory wedding dresses and the jewelled silks of evening wear. The faces of these women are a mystery, but a little part of them has survived.

Bridgetanne continued to enjoy a colourful life in dress after her marriage. As the 1860s moved towards the 1870s there was a shift in her aesthetic. As we might look at old photographs and marvel at the clothes we once wore, so did her aesthetic move away from the aniline dyes of her younger years towards the newly fashionable vogue for black dresses decorated with colourful floral motifs. After half of her lifetime as a brightly hued singleton, Bridgetanne found another place in the world as the well-to-do wife of a professional man. She died in October 1886, aged seventy-one. Her financial legacy can be quantified in the stark columns of the probate records, leaving the sum of £1,360 – more than £188,000 in today's currency. Thanks to Anne Sykes, Bridgetanne leaves an entirely unexpected legacy, one of swirling purple silk.

CHAPTER 21

Seaside Retirement

Anne & Adam Sykes

The idea of seeing the SEA – of being near it – watching
its changes by sunrise Sunset – moonlight – & noonday –
in calm – perhaps in storm – fills & satisfies my mind.

Charlotte Brontë, 1839

'The Knowle, Bispham-with-Norbrick about 1½ miles from Blackpool – To
Be Let with immediate possession, the above desirable country residence
containing drawing, dining and breakfast rooms, eight good bedrooms,
kitchens, coach-house, three stalled stables and other outbuildings with
extensive gardens in excellent order, croquet lawn, vineries, greenhouses
and a close of land.' Thus was Anne and Adam's final home advertised
in *The Preston Chronicle*.

This was where the fruit of their labour and decades of married life
had carried Anne and Adam – this comfortably proportioned detached
house with sea views in the distance. I picture Anne sitting in her extensive gardens, looking across the fields that fall away to the beach and the
waves. By the time she and Adam had moved to The Knowle, Anne no
longer filled her diary with bright flashes of fabric. There are plenty of
empty pages, so it was not for want of space in the album. More likely

she was less interested in her wardrobe and even less so in those of her friends. It is not universally the case that we cease to take an interest in clothes as we get older – far from it, for many people – but it is possible that the labour involved in memorialising cloth and recording its owner became too much. As friends and family died, it is likely that Anne and her friends spent longer periods of time in mourning and so the opportunity to record colourful cottons and sparkling silks was also dwindling.

Certainly by the later years of the nineteenth century, more and more clothing was purchased ready-made or at least partially made, with customers attending a dressmaker or department store for one fitting only, for the garment to be altered prior to purchase. This meant that those chances to take a snip of cloth were much reduced. It was a changing world, one in which the relationship of textiles and the clothes they made was beginning to see the disconnect that would only accelerate with the new century. Gone are the vibrant fabrics of Anne's youth, and so we can only imagine how she decorated her house or clothed her body, but tucked away into one of the rooms of Knowle House, wrapped perhaps in brown paper or stored at the back of a drawer, was her album.

It is possible to find the Sykes here and there, through records of their charitable donations and connections with local institutions, but of their life in these years of their retirement the book is entirely silent. Newspaper reports capture mere moments of Anne and Adam enjoying their retired existence in their penultimate residence near Preston. *The Preston Chronicle* reported on 8 February 1879, 'During the past week Adam Sykes Esq of West Beach Lytham, has presented to the Institute Library several valuable books, the cost of which was something like £30.'

Nearing the conclusion of Anne's story and my own part in it, it became increasingly important to me to find her beyond the covers of her album. Whilst I held this intimate glimpse of her life in my hands, the pandemic that struck us all in 2020 meant that I was unable to take in those vistas of her world that I knew still existed. Before I finished the pages of my own book, I wanted to follow in Anne's footsteps and see if I could find her for myself. Writing a life story during the pandemic meant that so far I had discovered Anne and her world in my imagination, from my desk in Devon. I escaped into her story between online teaching sessions and the painful reality of home-schooling teenagers. Anne Sykes became my sanity and salvation as I pictured her amongst the factories of Tyldesley, on the Esplanade of Singapore, beside the harbour of Shanghai. Her world opened up as ours shut down.

So, on an unexpectedly sunny day in early January 2022, I took to the road and ventured north in search of Anne and her family. Rather like the dress diary itself, it was a journey of fragments. Trying to capture another age against twenty-first-century landscapes that have either erased or encroached upon the past requires another leap of imagination, but there was enough. I walked along the church path of St George's Church in Tyldesley and I knew it was the route Anne would have taken on that September day in 1838, the day she married Adam. The church is a golden Gothic edifice, squarely no-nonsense, as befitted its industrial setting perhaps. What I had not realised was quite how close Factory Street and Anne's home were to the church – a mere three-minute walk – and so Anne must have made that journey from Burton House, with the church spire always visible, perhaps even from her bedroom window. Modern red-brick houses are all that remains of Factory Street now. James Burton's mills are long gone and in this quiet residential space it was impossible to see their walls, to hear the clatter of the power looms or the daily spill onto the streets of the mill hands at the end of their shift.

I found Anne's parents in St George's churchyard. The long, flat stone of their memorial was framed with wind-blown grass. There was nothing to indicate the impact that James Burton must have had on the town of Tyldesley and its inhabitants. His occupation was not given, and his family had chosen not to give him a vertically dramatic headstone, but rather a horizontal slab under which he and his wife Alice would lie together. My husband fetched water and we cleaned the stone until it shone under the January sun, each word now legible for the first time in who knows how long. I imagined Anne standing in that very spot after her father's death, Adam at her side.

An hour further north towards Clitheroe, I looked beyond the modern to the horizon and the escarpment of Pendle Hill, trying to spy features that were unchanging and would have drawn Anne's own eye as she bumped in a horse-drawn carriage towards her home at Colthurst Hall. The forty-mile trip would have taken most of the day, I calculated – perspectives of space, travel and speed at odds with our own trip. We drove through the picturesque village of Waddington near Bashall Eaves, in search of Colthurst Hall, Anne and Adam's home for twenty years. I realised as we drove through that here was the church they would have attended; here were the paths they trod on Sunday strolls; and finally here was the gateway that framed a tree-lined drive to the house itself, a mile or more from the village. I couldn't resist a view of the property and so, with some trepidation, I walked along the driveway, planning to take just a peep at the walls of Colthurst and maybe the view from their front windows.

Fortune favours the bold, I decided, and seeing lights in the windows, I knocked on the door. The delightful owner was kind enough not to be irritated at this completely unannounced visitor and, following my doubtless garbled summary outlining my quest, she invited me into the house to see Anne's domain. It was an unanticipated joy. Wood panelling and stone-flagged floors, original corniced ceilings, stained glass. Here was the room for which Anne had purchased her rose-printed furniture fabric in 1859, and there were the stairs down which she would have rustled in silky crinolines to greet guests. We were led through the front door and out to the beautiful lawn with a sweep of a view down the Ribble Valley, empty and unchanged. For a moment I could see Anne's world exactly as she would have seen it, the comfortable symmetry of

Colthurst opening onto a scene of pastoral calm. Is this what drew them to this quiet corner after the heat and noise of Singapore?

I desperately wanted a glimpse of the industry that formed the backdrop to Anne's upbringing, but the closure of so many mills in the twentieth century and the subsequent dereliction and demolition have changed that landscape. One survival in Clitheroe, however, tied that world to the Sykes, to Anne's diary and to me. The Primrose Printworks, where Anne's brother-in-law William worked as a designer prior to his untimely death, is rising from ruin. Those complex printed cottons that were so technologically modern in the 1830s and that Anne had included and labelled in her diary were created within its walls, and on the edge of Clitheroe between a residential area and some industrial units there sits Primrose Mill. Clad in scaffolding, it is undergoing a resurrection, saved from collapse and bearing advertising boards welcoming tenants to apply for studio spaces. Perhaps it will once again become a creative hub, humming with the force of artisanal skills that once fuelled the industry of this town.

And so to our accommodation for the night: the imposing Victorian solidity of The Imperial Hotel in Blackpool. It was here, in March 1871, that Anne and Adam were recorded as guests on the census, staying with their niece Charlotte and her husband, John Sheppard. Whilst Blackpool might be unrecognisable to Anne – the illuminations and arcades fantastically bleak in the emptiness of a rainy January, and the tower not then anticipated – the hotel itself remains steadfastly the same. The striking red-brick building that had only opened some four years before Anne and Adam's visit, its white-painted stonework framing each window, looks today much as it did in early photographs of the establishment, photographs that now line the walls of the hotel lobby. Subsequent decades would see politicians and pop stars stay within its walls. I looked at the darker grey of the sea against the paler grey of the sky and I wondered what brought Anne and Adam here? Simply a holiday or were they in search of a new home?

The next day, in driving rain, we went in search of one of those homes. Further south along the coast, the small town of Lytham has been preserved in Victorian aspic. The estuary-like mudflat and the lack of golden sands presumably account for its survival as a quieter resort, and here again it was possible to find Anne. West Beach looks out over an expanse of grass-flanked promenade, the ebb and flow of the tide visible from the windows of their tidy brick-built villa. They lived at number eight for an indeterminate number of years, possibly even as a holiday residence, but it no longer survives. Instead a 1960s apartment building sits in its place, awkwardly situated between two Georgian terraces and a grander porticoed house. It looks rather uncomfortable, like a teenager who has turned up to their grandparents' house in unsuitable clothes. The original building was another of the Georgian terraces, with a wrought-iron balcony ideally placed for watching life on the water. I see Adam there, watching the world go by. On a street behind West Beach, a small florist had trays of early primulas laid outside in rows and I bought one to take to our final destination on this odd pilgrimage. And so to Bispham, our last stop – and Anne's too.

Like so many buildings that were part of an earlier, less populated town, All Hallows Church in Bispham is now marooned, an island in a many-roofed sea of houses and metal-framed industrial units. The rain had eased and, armed with my small potted primula, I ventured into the churchyard, prepared for the zigging and zagging required in order to locate one person amongst so many. And then there they were. Beneath an impressive and ornately carved Celtic cross they lie: 'In Memoriam. Adam Sykes. Anne Sykes.' At the foot of the stone I scratched out a gravelly patch of soil and planted the scarlet primula from Lytham, a token of another place in their lives and one that connected us all at that moment. I had spent so long following the clues of Anne's life in the scraps she left behind. I had journeyed with her to far-flung corners of the globe. I had seen the bright gauze of her dress whirl across an assembly room, and had felt the smooth surface of the morning robe she had worn before the day proper began. But Anne had always been just out of reach, disappearing from the corner of my vision when I turned my head to look. I still don't know what she looked like, but I had found her at last.

The headstone of Anne and Adam Sykes, All Hallows Church, Bispham.

In each of the communities in which they lived, from Colthurst Hall in the 1860s to seaside retirement in Lytham and finally their hilltop residence in Bispham, Anne and Adam were visible contributors to local charitable causes in those last years of their lives, activities that were seen as appropriate at that time to their status in the world as a wealthy retired couple. It seemed to be a genuine but quietly managed philanthropy. At the beginning of October 1888 Adam died, at his and Anne's final home overlooking the sea. Their marriage had lasted half a century, taking them from the industrial North of England to the pepper plantations of

Singapore and the port of Shanghai, before returning to Lancashire in 1849 to live the rest of their lives variously in the world of the merchant, the benevolent squire and the retired gentleman. Moving to the coast, Adam spent his last years overlooking the sea and the stretch of water that had carried him to distant shores as a younger man.

The Preston Herald ran a description of his funeral that succeeded in capturing some of the most illuminating characteristics of Anne's husband. The arrangements for the funeral were 'of the simplest character, unostentatious and in keeping with the character and wishes of the deceased gentleman'. His standing in the community was notable, according to the writer, with a genuine fondness for Adam emerging from the report: 'It is a saying that a good man's name may wear out, but at each of the above places where Mr Sykes has been a resident his name is still fresh and green, and on account of his benefactions and benevolent disposition will remain so in the memories of the people.' He is described as 'quiet but earnest' amongst those who knew him, and the report concludes: 'He has been a great benefactor in a quiet way to many people.'

What did Anne do with Adam's clothes after he had died? Maybe she left them for a time, reluctant to part with the familiar suits and the comforting smell of his laundered shirts. In time perhaps she folded them carefully and donated them to a good cause, to pass them on to somebody who needed them, continuing that quiet benevolence that seemed to be such a characteristic of Adam Sykes, Esq. Did Anne turn the pages of her diary and recall the youthfulness of Adam in his bright vests; remember him buttoning up his floral silk waistcoat and arranging his cravat for an evening at the theatre; or picture him tying his striped silk dressing gown for breakfast in the bright sunshine of Singapore? Theirs was a half-century of shared life, captured in fragments by Anne in her diary, but consisting of a varied and colourful experience that saw them travel around the world together and spend their final years overlooking the sea. Merchant to gentleman, husband and uncle, Adam left his mark on the world, and in Anne's album, the creator of and contributor to her unexpected legacy.

Anne Sykes died on 31 January 1890, less than eighteen months after she had buried Adam. She was seventy-three years old. The executors of her will were her brothers Edward and Frederick Burton, charged with the dispersal of her personal estate, valued at almost £32,000, equivalent to the enormous sum of £4.4 million today. Her bequests reflected the philanthropic shape of their retirement as practised by Adam in his later years. She gave £4,000 to Bispham Church, where she would be laid to rest alongside her husband. She left generous legacies to nieces and nephews, female friends and other relatives. She had dictated that 'to each of my present female servants in case she shall be in service at the time of my death the sum of fifty pounds', but poor Margaret Charnock had pre-deceased her former employer of such long standing by fewer than two years. In the final paragraph of her will Anne instructed that 'I give and bequeath all the residue of my personal estate and effects whatsoever and wheresoever unto my two brothers Edward Burton and Frederick Burton for their own use.'

Here must lie the fate of Anne's dress diary. Amongst all the personal mementoes of her long life, the pink silk-covered album arrived in the life of either Emily or Harriet Burton, the wives of Edward and Frederick. Harriet never appeared in the volume, so perhaps it was with Emily that the book rested for a time. At what point the book left the care of the Burton family and found its way onto the flea-market stall of a London trader in the 1960s is a journey lost. It had been judged by somebody to be of little value, an anonymous book of scraps and notes. No provenance or context travelled with it, and so the slightly battered volume with its frayed pink silk cover washed up in a city far from its creation.

But when Anne sat on her verandah in the shimmering Singapore humidity, snipping fragments of cloth to size, or looked out at the wintry Lancashire landscape outside the drawing-room window of Colthurst

Hall whilst pasting in her colourful octagons of cloth and carefully labelling each one, she could not have anticipated the world that she was preserving. Each swatch was unwittingly telling the story of a life, however fragmented. Without her endeavours, those stories would be lost. Stories of merchant life, of pirates and princesses. Stories of birth, marriage and death. Connections forged around the world, friendships made and lost, and relationships that endured.

Anne's story is both remarkable and ordinary. She gave voice to the women in her world. She caught a tiny piece of them and protected their colourful variety in her most unusual of diaries. Not through her written word do we find these women, and Anne Sykes herself, but through these precious pieces of cloth.

We hope you enjoyed *The Dress Diary of Mrs Anne Sykes.*
Discover more pictures – and mysteries – from the diary here . . .

Acknowledgements

I started to write this book in the before times, only a few months before the pandemic changed our lives in March 2020, and so all of the plans that I had to visit collections and archives on the quest for Anne Sykes had to take another form. I was so very fortunate to encounter online support at every turn. Archivists, authors and curators did everything they could to provide information at a distance. Caroline Alexander, curator at the Harris Museum, sent me collection records, images and database information and even offered to try and look at objects via Zoom, such was her desire to help as much as she could. Kate Hurst, genealogist, gave me invaluable advice and were it not for her expert digging, I would never have found Anne and Adam on the 1871 census, living it up in the Imperial Hotel in Blackpool. Archivists at the Massachusetts Historical Society were helpful in directing me to their digitised collection of Maria Balestier's letters as were those managing the digital newspaper archive in Singapore. For her expert analysis of the free labour cotton movement and her thoughtful read-through of my chapter on cotton, I sincerely thank Anna Vaughan Kett. The kind of unselfish collegiality that she demonstrated fills me with warmth. I want to thank the Paul Mellon Centre for the invaluable opportunity the award of their Research Support Grant gave me and the chance to visit Lancashire in Anne and Adam's footsteps.

I also want to thank those women who have been enormously influential to me in my career to date. Maria Hayward, Barbara Burman and Lou Taylor believed in me when I often didn't believe in myself. Shelley Tobin taught me that to be a dress historian is a special thing and introduced me to the way that objects can tell stories. My agent extraordinaire Clare Alexander offered her wealth of expertise and knowledge to bring Anne Sykes to the world and I feel incredibly lucky that our paths crossed. To Clara Farmer, my editor at Chatto, I thank you for deciding in the earliest days that this was a tale worth telling. It has been a joy to work with you. Amanda Waters, your editorial contributions have been thoughtful and made a world of difference. Mandy Greenfield provided careful copy-edits for which I am very grateful. Thank you also to Carolyn McAndrew and Vicki Robinson. The entire team at Chatto & Windus and Vintage have helped immeasurably – thank you Victoria Murray-Browne, Isobel Turton and Carmella Lowkis for all of your wonderful input. For a book that emerged from a beautifully visual object, Kris Potter and the design team worked their magic to bring this to the reader. Thank you all.

This is a book all about networks of female friendship and companionship and for the duration of my research and writing I was surrounded by groups of women who were supportive at every turn. To the wonderful 19th century ladies – Robyne Calvert, Hilary Davidson, Lynn Hulse, Veronica Isaac, Suzanne Rowland, Hannah Rumball, Anna Vaughan Kett and Kim Wahl – through lockdown and beyond you have been a tonic. We have not all met up in real life yet, our little community coming into its own through COVID, but your friendship has seen me through some tricky moments. Thank you to my wonderful academic sisterhood, my friends alongside whom I have taught and laughed for more years than we should count – Julie Ripley, Lizzy Orcutt and Monica Fischbein. I could not have maintained sanity without you. My very dear friend Alison Matthews David was my constant champion; her counsel was wise and despite living in different time zones we have always made time for tea.

My three dearest friends have been here throughout, listening to discoveries, to losses, to frustrations and excitements. Amanda, Amy and Lu you are a trio of treasures. In the earliest days of this, in the weeks before lockdown hit, I turned up with laptop in hand to write at Lu's house and was treated to soup and chat, talking about the expanse of Anne's world just as ours was about to shut down. Thank you.

~

Anne memorialised family as much as she did friends and I hope in some way I have captured those relationships as I reflect on my own. Sheena, you have always brought so much enthusiasm and encouragement, thank you. I am lucky enough to have parents that always told me to be whatever I wanted as long as I was happy. Mum and Dad, this is for you and for being there every single step of the way. Finally, for my boys – for my sons Iwan and Elis and my husband Stuart. There are not really any words that are enough. But I hope you know.

List of Illustrations

Plate 8: The swatch of pirate flag given to Anne by Admiral Cochrane sits on the same page as a pair of blue velvet slippers that belonged to Adam, a birthday present given to him in 1846.

Plate 9: Anne recorded the garments worn by the women she came to know as they arrived in Singapore. On this page are swatches from the dresses of Fanny Taylor and the sea captain's wife Mrs Milward.

Plate 10: Miss Brennand ran a 'smallwares' shop in Singapore. On this page Anne includes a blue and white check sent overland from Miss Brennand and a wool swatch which was 'Mr Sykes's vest bought from Miss Brennand's smallwares.'

Plate 11: Sandwiched between two brown swatches, this floral ribbon captured a particular event. Anne wrote, 'Emma Taylor's sash at Fancy Ball, Preston Guild 1842.'

Plate 12: The four silk swatches recorded on this page are all associated with evening dresses, garments that are described as having been 'worn at Miss Wrigley's dance, January 1845.'

Plate 13: At the top of a page consisting of various fabrics sit three swatches sent to Anne by her friend Hannah Coubrough. The note reads 'Anna. Three dresses when in mourning for her mother, 1845'.

Plate 14: The large green swatch at the top of this page of four fragments bears the note 'Hannah Wrigley's Fancy Ball dress for the character of "Dolly Varden." '

Plate 15: At the bottom of a page filled with mixed fabrics and shades sits a printed floral cotton in cream and brown captioned 'Margaret Charnock'. Mrs Charnock was Anne and Adam's cook.

Plate 16: Four of the six brightly shaded swatches on this page bear the name Bridgetanne Peacock, the friend of Anne's whose colourful dresses matched the new synthetic dyes of the 1850s.

TEXT ILLUSTRATIONS

p. x: *Le Follet Courrier des Salons*, 1838, No. 621: Chapeau en paille de riz, published by Dobbs & Co, © public domain. Gift from the M. A. Ghering-van Ierlant Collection to the Rijksmuseum; **p. 5:** Pancratium Maritinum (Hexandria Monogynia), formerly in an album (Vol.VII, 45); *Sea Daffodil.* 1778 Collage of coloured papers, with bodycolour and watercolour, on black ink background. By Mary Delany, © The Trustees of the British Museum; **p. 13:** *O Recreio, Jornal das Familias*, November 1840, No. 11: Grinalda de froc (. . .), © public domain. Gift from the M. A. Ghering-van Ierlant Collection to the Rijksmuseum; **p. 38:** Woman using Spinning Jenny – Invented by James Hargreaves (c 1720 – 87) in 1764. Wood engraving c 1880, © Photo 12 / Alamy Stock Photo; **p. 40:** The new industrial landscape of cotton, from Edward Baines's *The History of Cotton Manufacture in Great Britain*, 1835, © public domain. Shared by the University of California Libraries; **p. 43:** The power loom, from Edward Baines's *The History of Cotton Manufacture in Great Britain*, 1835, © public domain. Shared by the University of California Libraries; **p. 78:** 'The Calico Printer'. Engraving from *The Book of English Trades and Library of the Useful Arts*, C&J Rivington, London, 1827, © public domain. Shared by the Getty Research Institute; **p. 85:** *Le Follet*, 1855, No. 1971: Chapeaux Mme Naudé, after drawing by Anaïs Colin-Toudouze, © public domain. Gift from the M. A. Ghering-van Ierlant Collection to the Rijksmuseum; **p. 90:** 'View of the town and roads of Singapore from the government hill', by Robert James Elliot R. N. (1790 – 1849), taken from *Journal of an Embassy from the Governor-General of India to the Courts of Siam and Cochin-China* by John Crawfurd, 1828, © public domain; **p. 155:**

'The Haunted Lady, or The Ghost in the Looking Glass', *Punch Magazine*, 4 July 1863, © public domain; **p. 159**: *Cendrillon*, 1866, No. 28: Journal des petites Demoiselles, © public domain. On loan to the Rijksmuseum from the M. A. Ghering-van Ierlant Collection; **p. 177**: *Les Modes Parisiennes*, 1860, No. 887: Robes de Gagelin (. . .), engraving by Préval, following a drawing by François-Claudius Compte-Calix, © public domain. On loan to the Rijksmuseum from the M.A. Ghering-van Ierlant Collection; **p. 190**: Jay's Mourning House, from p. 914 of *The County Families of the United Kingdom; or, Royal Manual of the Titled and Untitled Aristocracy of England, Wales, Scotland, and Ireland*, by Edward Walford, 1860, © public domain. Shared by Allen County Public Library Genealogy Center; **p. 209**: Fancy dresses, from p. 69 of *Fancy dresses described or, What to wear at fancy balls*, by Ardern Holt, 1887, © public domain. Shared by the California Digital Library; **p. 219**: *Le Journal des Dames et des Demoiselles*, 1875, No. 1249e: Jupons et Corsets, engraving by A. Bodin, following a drawing by Jules David (1808-1892), published by Ad. Goubaud et Fils © public domain. On loan to the Rijksmuseum from the M.A. Ghering-van Ierlant Collection; **p. 256**: 'The Arsenic Waltz', *Punch Magazine*, 8 February 1862, © public domain; **p. 265**: Headstone of Anne and Adam Sykes, All Hallows Church, Bispham © Kate Strasdin.

Notes on Sources

Preface

4 For a detailed biography of Mary Delaney, see Molly Peacock's *The Paper Garden: An Artist Begins Her Life's Work at 72*, Bloomsbury, London, 2011.

5 There is a facsimile of Barbara Johnson's entire album edited by Natalie Rothstein: *A Lady of Fashion, Barbara Johnson's Album of Styles and Fabrics*, Thames & Hudson, London, 1987.

9 Kay Staniland, *In Royal Fashion*, Museum of London, London, 1997, p. 13. Written as an exhibition catalogue to accompany the garments on display, this is one of the most comprehensive volumes on nineteenth-century royal dress.

1 My Charming Anne

16 Thanks to the digitisation of so many records, it is possible to track UK residents through the online census records. I used Ancestry.com, which gave me access to birth, marriage and death records, census entries and electoral registers. It is a wonderful resource, accessible to all for a monthly subscription.

27 Cited in Viscount Esher, *The Girlhood of Queen Victoria: A Selection from Her Majesty's Diaries Between the Years 1832 and 1840*, Longmans, London, 1912, p. 318.

28 Edward, Lord Brabourne (ed.), *The Letters of Jane Austen*, Little Brown, Boston, 1899, p. 39.

29 Florence Hartley, *The Ladies' Book of Etiquette, and Manual of Politeness*, G. W. Cottrell, Boston, 1860, p. 259. This is just one etiquette manual amongst a range of different publications.

29 Anon., *The Englishwoman's Domestic Magazine*, May 1862, one of the earliest affordable periodicals for women.

29 & 30 Margaret Smith (ed.), *The Letters of Charlotte Brontë: Volume 3, 1852–55*, Oxford University Press, Oxford, 2004, pp. 244, 266.

2 Spinning into Gold

36 Sir John Mandeville, *Mandeville's Travels*, British Library, translated from the French manuscript, 1919, original *c.* fourteenth century.

37 Edward Baines, *History of the Cotton Manufacture in Great Britain*, H. & R. Fisher, London, 1835, p. 162, based on the author's own description of the inventor.

44 Edward Ward (ed.), 'The Spittle-Fields Ballad or the Weavers' Complaint Against the Callico Madams', in *The Northern Cuckold: Or, the Garden House Intrigue*, London, 1721, stanza III, pp. 10–12.

46 Letter from Lydia White to William Lloyd Garrison, 9 May 1831, Boston Public Library, Anti-Slavery Collection.

47 Samuel May is cited in Julie L. Holcomb, *Moral Commerce: Quakers and the Transatlantic Boycott of the Slave Labor Economy*, Cornell University Press, New York, 2016, p. 170.

3 A Lady's Laundry List

55 It is an enormous volume, but you can find the advice given here in Isabella Beeton, *Mrs Beeton's Book of Household Management*, Ward, Lock & Co., London, 1906 edn, p. 1786.

56 Anon., *Enquire Within Upon Everything*, Houlston & Sons, London, 1894. There are numerous volumes of this book, published frequently and running to many hundreds of pages – quite tricky to navigate, but full of unexpected tips.

57 There are many examples of this kind of domestic detail in Flora Thompson's semi-autobiographical novel *Lark Rise to Candleford*. My edition was published by Penguin Modern Classics in 1974.

57 Beeton, *Mrs Beeton's Book of Household Management*, p. 1786ff.

59 Eliza Warren (ed.), *The Ladies' Treasury*, Ward, Lock & Co., London, 1857.

4 Cobwebs of Fashion

69 Samuel Pepys's diary, Wednesday 21 May 1662. There are many online sources via which a reader can explore Pepys's diaries for this kind of detail.

70 John Heathcoat cited in William Murphy, *The Textile Industries: A Practical Guide to Fibres, Yarns & Fabrics*, Gresham Publishing Co., London, 1910, p. 94.

72 Letter from William Wills to Mary Tucker, 1863, Devon Record Office. There is a whole host of papers relating to this family, and indeed to Honiton lace generally, in the archive.

5 The Chemistry of Calico

77 Godfrey Smith, *The Laboratory; or, School of Arts*, J. Hodges, London, 1756.

79 Joseph Dodson Greenhalgh describes James Thomson in *Memoranda of the Greenhalgh Family*, T. Abbatt's, Bolton, 1869, p. 104.

6 The First Dress I Wore . . .

97 Letter from Maria to her sister Harriet, Sunday 6 January 1839, Maria Revere Balestier Papers, Massachusetts Historical Society, www.masshist.org/collection-guides/view/fa0175. The letters have been digitised but are quite difficult to read, especially where they have been cross-written to save paper.

97 George Bennett, *Wanderings in New South Wales, Batavia, Pedir Coast, Singapore and China*, Richard Bentley, London, 1834, pp. 202–3.

7 An American Abroad

103 John Turnbull Thomson, *Some Glimpses into Life in the Far East*, Richardson & Co., 1865, p. 14.

103 Maria's frustrated letter is cited in R. E. Hale, *The Balestiers: The First American Residents of Singapore*, Marshall Cavendish, Singapore, 2016, p. 18. The

other quotes from Maria's letters in this chapter can be found in the Maria Revere Balestier Papers, Massachusetts Historical Society, www.masshist. org/collection-guides/view/fa0175.

8 Pirates!

112 Thomson, *Some Glimpses into Life in the Far East*, p. 16.

113 All of these personal and not very complimentary reminiscences are cited from the *Dictionary of Canadian Biography*, www.biographi.ca/en/bio. php?id_nbr=4903.

117 George Gillot's concerns are cited in Amy Miller, *Dressed to Kill*, National Maritime Museum Publications, Greenwich, 2007.

117 The remaining citations on pirates and boats during the period come from James Brooks and Henry Keppel, *The Expedition to Borneo of HMS* Dido *for the Suppression of Piracy*, Chapman & Hall, London, 1846.

121 Roland Braddell et al., *One Hundred Years of Singapore*, John Murray, London, 1921, p. 330.

9 Frontier Women

125 Miss Grant's letters were published in the *History of the Society for Promoting Female Education in the East*, Edward Suter, London, 1847; extracts from her letters p. 210ff.

127 Ida Pfeiffer, *A Woman's Journey Around the World*, Office of the National Illustrated Library, London, 1850, p. 118.

130 Cited in Sally Berridge, *The Epic Voyages of Maud Berridge: The Seafaring Diaries of a Victorian Lady*, Bloomsbury, London, 2018.

131 Hartley, *The Ladies' Book of Etiquette, and Manual of Politeness*, p. 34.

131 Anon., *Travelling and its Requirements – Addressed to Ladies by a Lady*, London, 1878, p. 11.

10 Tokens of Friendship

138 Anna Kirk, ' "Composed of the same materials": Like-dressing and the

dress of the doppelgänger in Victorian art and culture; *c.*1855–1885', unpublished PhD thesis, The Courtauld Institute of Art, London, 2013.

140 E. V. Lucas (ed.), *The Works of Charles and Mary Lamb, Volume V*, Methuen & Co., London, 1903. There are a number of different album verses written by Lamb from p. 43 onwards.

141 R. Johnson (ed.), *The Letters of Jane Austen, Volume 2*, Frank S. Holby, New York, 1906 edn, p. 152.

11 Goods Received

153 Pam Inder's *Busks, Basques and Brush-Braid: British Dressmaking in the 18th and 19th Centuries*, Bloomsbury, London, 2020, offers a wealth of detail about the dressmaking industries. Letters from dressmakers are cited here from Pam's book, which includes extensive research of documents from a whole host of different archives.

12 The Riot and the Party

165 *The Northern Star*, Chartist newspaper, 20 August 1842.

167 John Harkness, 'A New Song on the Preston Guild', Church Street, Preston, 1842, Bodleian Library Ballad Collection, BOD2673.

169 *The Preston Chronicle*, 10 September 1842.

For all sorts of material relating to the Preston Guild, the Harris Museum in Preston is a fount of all knowledge.

13 Dancing by Candlelight

177 William Mallock, *Memoirs of Life and Literature*, Harper & Brothers, London, 1920, p. 96.

177 Consuelo Vanderbilt Balsan, *The Glitter and the Gold*, George Mann Books, Maidstone, 1973, p. 93. Many of the nineteenth-century socialites began to publish their memoirs or letters in the mid-twentieth century, so there are plenty of fascinating accounts.

178 Anon., *Routledge's Manual of Etiquette*, Routledge, London, 1860, p. 12.

179 Hartley, *The Ladies' Book of Etiquette and Manual of Politeness*, pp. 166–7.

179 *The Queen: The Ladies' Newspaper and Court Chronicle*, Saturday 17 April 1897, p. 755.

180 Honoré de Balzac, *The Muse of the Department*, Gebbie Publishing, New York, 1899 edn.

14 Wardrobe of Grief

189 Henry Mayhew, *The Shops and Companies of London*, Strand Printing and Publishing Company, London, 1865, p. 67.

190 Thomas Hood, *Hood's Magazine and Comic Miscellany*, Volume 1, H. Renshaw, London, 1844, p. 192.

191 Victor Mallet (ed.), *Life with Queen Victoria; Marie Mallet's Letters from Court, 1887–1901*, John Murray, London, 1968, p. 32.

192 George Eliot, *Middlemarch*, Penguin Classics, London, 1985 edn, p. 847.

15 A Grand Masquerade

204 The letter to the editor can be found in the *Singapore Free Press and Mercantile Advertiser*, January 1841.

204 Charles Dickens, *Barnaby Rudge*, Chapman & Hall, London, 1913 edn, p. 286.

206 Alfred Lee, 'Dolly Varden', sheet music published by Oliver Ditson & Co., Boston, 1872.

207 Peter Cunningham (ed.), *The Letters of Horace Walpole*, Volume 1, Clarendon Press, Oxford, 1903, p. 49.

207 Reginald, Viscount Esher, *Cloud Capp'd Towers*, John Murray, London, 1927, p. 163.

208 Ardern Holt, *Fancy Dresses Described; or, What to Wear at Fancy Balls*, Debenham & Freebody, London, 1879, p. 1. Holt's publication ran to many editions over the course of more than a decade, so there is a variety of changing options, depending on the volume and date.

210 Marie Schild, *One Thousand Characters Suitable for Fancy Costume Balls*, Samuel Miller, London, 1884.

210 Elizabeth, Lady Eastlake, *Music and the Art of Dress*, John Murray, London, 1852, p. 88.

211 Mrs George Cornwallis-West, *The Reminiscences of Lady Randolph Churchill*, Edward Arnold, London, 1973, p. 301.

211 Anonymous account cited in Hale, *The Balestiers*, p. 157.

16 Missing Moments

216 Pfeiffer, *A Woman's Journey Around the World*, p. 118.

17 Home Comforts

224 Isabella Beeton, *Beeton's Housewife's Treasury of Domestic Information*, Ward Lock, London, 1865.

224 Mrs William Parkes, *Domestic Duties; or, Instructions to Young Married Ladies*, J. & J. Harper, London, 1828, p. 173.

225 Jane Ellen Panton, *From Kitchen to Garret: Hints for Young Householders*, Ward & Downey, London, 1888, chapter on the drawing room, pp. 78–90.

226 Lucy Orrinsmith, *The Drawing Room: Its Decorations and Furniture*, Macmillan, London, 1878.

226 Sara Duncan, *An American Girl in London*, D. Appleton, New York, 1891, p. 53.

19 Upstairs, Downstairs

241 Samuel and Sarah Adams, *The Complete Servant*, Knight & Lacey, London, 1825, p. 18.

242 Frederick Gorst, *Of Carriages and Kings*, Crowell, New York, 1956, pp. 15–16.

242 Harriet Brown's letter to her mother is cited in Frank Dawes, *Not in Front of the Servants*, Wayland Publishers, 1973, pp. 22–3.

244 Isabella Beeton, *The Book of Household Management*, S. O. Beeton, London, 1861.

20 The Brightest of Hues

250 Elizabeth Gaskell, *Cranford*, Penguin Classics, London, 1976 edn, p. 39.

253 William Perkin's efforts are cited in Simon Garfield, *Mauve: How One Man Invented a Colour That Changed the World*, Faber & Faber, London, 2001, p. 37.

255 Alison Matthews David, *Fashion Victims: The Dangers of Dress Past and Present*, Bloomsbury, London, 2017. A brilliant analysis of a whole host of toxic or dangerous dress-related themes.

21 Seaside Retirement

259 Charlotte Brontë, letter to Ellen Nussey, 4 August 1839

259 *The Preston Chronicle*, Saturday 27 July 1872.

266 *The Preston Herald*, Wednesday 17 October 1888.

267 A copy of Anne Sykes's will was obtained from the General Register Office. It was drawn up by Robinson & Sons, Blackburn.

Select Bibliography

Adburgham, Alison, *Shops and Shopping 1800–1914*, HarperCollins, London, 1981

Balsan, Consuelo Vanderbilt, *The Glitter and the Gold*, George Mann Books, Maidstone 1973

Beckert, Sven, *Empire of Cotton: A Global History*, Vintage Books, New York, 2014

Buckley, Charles, *An Anecdotal History of Old Times in Singapore*, Fraser & Neave Ltd, Singapore, 1902

Curl, James Stevens, *The Victorian Celebration of Death*, The History Press, Cheltenham, 2000

Davidoff, Leonore, *The Best Circles: Society, The Season and Etiquette*, Cresset Library, London, 1986

Ehrman, Edwina, *The Wedding Dress: 300 Years of Bridal Fashion*, V&A Publications, London, 2014

Flanders, Judith, *The Victorian House: Domestic Life from Childbirth to Deathbed*, HarperCollins, London, 2004

Garfield, Simon, *Mauve: How One Man Invented a Colour That Changed the World*, Faber & Faber, London, 2001

Hale, R. E., *The Balestiers: The First American Residents of Singapore*, Marshall Cavendish, Singapore, 2016

Helfand, Jessica, *Scrapbooks: An American History*, Yale University Press, New York, 2008

Holcomb, Julie, *Moral Commerce: Quakers and the Transatlantic Boycott of the Slave Labor Economy*, Cornell University Press, New York, 2016

Inder, Pam, *Busks, Basques and Brush-Braid: British Dressmaking in the 18th and 19th Centuries*, Bloomsbury, London, 2020

Johnston, Lucy, *Nineteenth-Century Fashion in Detail*, V&A Publications, London, 2016

Kett, Anna Vaughan, 'Quaker Women and Anti-Slavery Activism: Eleanor Clark and the Free Labour Cotton Depot in Street', in *Quaker Studies*, 2014, pp. 137–56

Kip Lin, Lee, *The Singapore House*, Times Editions, London, 1992

Makepeace, Walter, *One Hundred Years in Singapore*, John Murray, London, 1921

Marshall, Adrian G., *Nemesis: The First Iron Warship and Her World*, NUS Press, Singapore, 2016

Matthews David, Alison, *Fashion Victims: The Dangers of Dress Past and Present*, Bloomsbury, London, 2015

Miller, Amy, *Dressed to Kill*, National Maritime Museum Publications, Greenwich, 2021

Montgomery, Florence, *Printed Textiles: English and American Cottons and Linens 1700–1850*, Penguin, London, 1970

Musson, Jeremy, *Up and Down Stairs: The History of the Country House Servant*, John Murray, London, 2010

Peacock, Molly, *The Paper Garden: An Artist Begins Her Life's Work at 72*, Bloomsbury, London, 2011

Riello, Giorgio, *Cotton: The Fabric That Made the Modern World*, Cambridge University Press, New York, 2013

Rothstein, Natalie (ed.), *A Lady of Fashion: Barbara Johnson's Album of Styles and Fabrics*, Thames & Hudson, London, 1987

Sambrook, Pamela, *Keeping Their Place: Domestic Service in the Country House*, The History Press, Cheltenham, 2005

Siegel, Elizabeth, *Playing with Pictures: The Art of Victorian Photocollage*, Art Institute of Chicago, Chicago, 2009

Staniland, Kay, *In Royal Fashion: The Clothes of Princess Charlotte of Wales and Queen Victoria 1796–1901*, Museum of London, London, 1997

Stevenson, Sara and Bennett, Helen, *Van Dyck in Check Trousers: Fancy Dress in Art and Life 1700–1900*, Scottish National Portrait Gallery, Edinburgh, 1978

Select Bibliography

Stewart, Susan, *On Longing: Narratives of the Miniature, the Gigantic, the Souvenir, the Collection*, Duke University Press, North Carolina, 1992

Sykas, Philip, *The Secret Life of Textiles*, Bolton Museums, Bolton, 2005

Taylor, Lou, *Mourning Dress: A Costume and Social History*, Routledge, London, 1983

Tobin, Shelley, *Marriage à la Mode: Three Centuries of Wedding Dress*, National Trust, London, 2003

Walkley, Christina and Foster, Vanda, *Crinolines and Crimping Irons*, Peter Owen, London, 1985

Wild, Benjamin, *Carnival to Catwalk: Global Reflections on Fancy Dress Costume*, Bloomsbury, London, 2020

Index

Index